Duncan McLean was born in Aberdeenshire and now lives in Orkney. His collection of stories, *Bucket of Tongues*, won a Somerset Maugham Award in 1993. This was followed by two novels, *Blackden* (1994) and *Bunker Man* (1995). He has also written for stage and television.

Lone Star Swing

On the Trail of Bob Wills and his Texas Playboys

Duncan McLean

W.W. Norton & Company
New York • London

© Duncan McLean 1997

Duncan McLean has asserted his right
under the Copyright, Designs and Patents Act 1988
to be identified as the author of this work

First published in the United Kingdom in 1997 by
Jonathan Cape

First published as a Norton paperback 1998 by arrangement
with Jonathan Cape, a division of Random House UK Limited

Printed in the United States of America

ISBN 0-393-31756-0

W.W. Norton & Company, Inc.
500 Fifth Avenue, NY, NY 10110
http://www.wwnorton.com

W.W. Norton & Company Ltd.
10 Coptic Street, London WC1A 1PU

1 2 3 4 5 6 7 8 9 0

For
Kevin Coffey
and in memory of
Arch Montgomery and John Moen

Contents

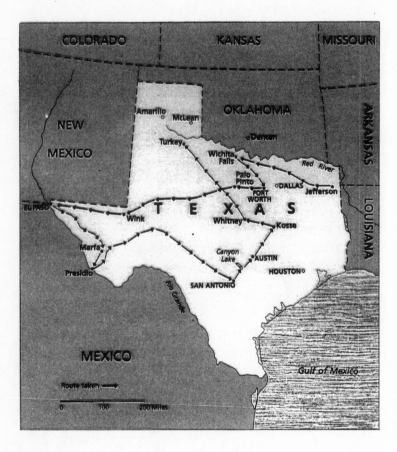

Get With It

The guitar-shaped pool is closed for repairs. I goggle my hands and peer through the meshed-glass door. Corridor light shines off the water and shimmies up the far wall, flichtering across patches and tracks of raw concrete where the tiles have come unstuck. The air is saturated with chlorine. The vapour's so thick that my nostrils fizz and burn when I breathe in. That's good though: it burns out the last traces of my brown box-room's stink. (Sweat-soaked sheets, reconditioned air, stale fag-reek, businessman's beer belch.) There's a plop in the pool: another clump of little tiles scabbing off the ceiling into the deep end. The water ripples, the edges slosh, light-shards shiver up the walls.

I turn and walk away: down the corridor, across the murky, stained lobby, out into the hot Nashville night.

The day's been spent chasing ghosts around the Country

Music Foundation. Their museum has Ira Louvin's mandolin, Little Jimmy Dickens' sequinned stage-suit, Hank Williams' scribbled lyrics. These are holy relics, it's true, but still only relics: husks, shells. Jimmy's suit stands there, the chest puffed out, the arms stiff, the whole get-up full of emptiness. It floats a few inches off the ground as if modelled by some invisible hillbilly. Like I said: a husk. The body's long gone. The spirit too.

Downstairs in the chill vaults of the record library, the spirit feels closer. Listening to ancient crackly 78s through heavy, leather-upholstered headphones, there are times when I think I'm about to catch it. Through a hiss of static, over a frantic background of fiddle, sax, trombone, and tub-thumping two-four bass and drums, two vocalists – one singing swingingly, the other yelping joyously – urge their listeners to *Get With It*:

> *Rhythm here, rhythm there*
> *Rhythm floating everywhere*
> *Get with it, oh get with it*
> *Red hot rhythm now*
>
> *Some like to stomp, some like to hop*
> *But give me the shimmy or the eagle rock*
> *Get with it, oh get with it*
> *Red hot rhythm now*

This is Bob Wills and his Texas Playboys. This is their first recording session, in Dallas, September 1935, the one where the heat was so intense in the makeshift studio that big fans were angled to blow over barrels of ice in the direction of the sweat-lashed band.

This is the hottering chilli-pot of New Orleans jazz, old country fiddling, big-band swing, ragtime, blues, pop, mariachi and conjunto that dominated Texas, Oklahoma, Louisiana, and beyond – all the way to San Francisco in the west, Memphis in the east – from the mid-Thirties till mid-Elvis. *This is western swing.*

It's square dances, reels, and schottisches, stomps, rags and waltzes. It's strings, brass and lap steel guitars, jive-talking, yodelling and scatting. It's the stuff I chanced across in a junk shop in Edinburgh five years ago – one scratchy LP's worth of it – the stuff that has been sending jolts of musical electricity through me ever since. It's the reason I'm three thousand miles from home, six hundred miles from anyone who knows anything more about me than the name on my credit card.

I am not from these parts. I've come a long way in search of real live western swing. I won't find real live Bob Wills, that's for sure: he's been dead twenty years. But his spirit lives on; I know it, I feel it. It lives on . . . somewhere. Not in the battered fiddle in the museum-case upstairs, not even in his three or four hundred vintage recordings down in the cool catalogued vaults. Nowhere in Nashville, probably; Bob always considered himself a jazz man, never thought he had anything in common with corny country music, always said that folk here didn't understand what he was after. (Cause he was always *after* something: he rarely, if ever, found what he was looking for – in life or music. It's this restless searching for new sounds and inflections and ways of twisting old tunes that makes his music so startling, so stimulating, so endlessly fresh and exciting.)

And now I am after something. I don't know exactly what it is, and I don't know exactly where I'm going to find it. But *somewhere* out there, further south and further west – out amongst the country dancehalls, the ranch to market roads, the old musicians hunched over tin-tack pianos and tenor banjos – somewhere in the wide, sun-struck wilds of Texas, that's where I'm going to track down the spirit of Bob Wills. That's where I'm going.

The first eating-place I come to is BK's Country Cafe. Posters in the window announce that this is their songwriters' night. Makes no difference to me: I haven't eaten all day. I walk in.

BK's is a small, dark place with a serving hatch and bar at

one end, a tiny stage at the other, unoccupied. It's easy to find a table: the place is less than half full. At scattered seats across the room, eight youngish men sit tuning and retuning and reretuning guitars. Some of the tuners are sitting with one or two or a whole gang of friends, partners, supporters. In fact, apart from me, everybody seems to be either tuner or supporter: at this amateur level, songwriting is apparently a participatory activity like angling, or knitting, not a spectator sport like baseball or Willie Nelson.

A waitress flits about, bringing long-necked beers, coffee and platters of barbecued meat to the tables; and somebody else, a big guy, goes from tuner to nervous tuner with a pen and clipboard, taking down names, giving out places in the running order. He gets to me before the waitress does.

You not brought your guitar?

Eh . . . no.

He grins, leans on the table to tick his clipboard. No problem. I'll fix you one.

No, listen . . .

You're not going *a capella* are you?

I splutter. Too right I'm not!

Fine, that's settled then. Now, three songs only, that's the limit. You got three?

Well . . .

Sure you have! Every one a hit, eh? He laughs. Right, you're on second. Good luck, buddy!

Thanks, I say, But . . .

Oh, what's your name?

Listen, we're at cross purposes. I didn't come here to sing.

You didn't?

No, I'm just trying to get something to eat.

To *eat*?

Yeah, can I do that? I mean, this is a cafe, isn't it?

Well . . . sure. He laughs again, looks around for the waitress and waves her over.

Yeah? she says. What is it, Grady?

This guy wants to eat, says Grady. *Just* to eat.

Well, not *just*, I put in. I'll listen as well. I look from Grady
to the waitress and back again. I'll eat and listen and watch at
the same time. Is that okay?

Sure, says the waitress.

Sure, says Grady. It's just unusual, that's all.

I shrug. I'm a spectator here, I say. I'm not joining in.

Well, if you change your mind, just let me know . . .

The waitress takes my order, and I sit back and sip on my
beer. Grady is up on stage doing an MC routine, stuff about
arriving in a cab and leaving in a Cadillac. Everybody laughs,
then Grady introduces Billy Ray Pinkerton, all the way from
Elgin, Alabama. A big BK's welcome for Billy Ray . . .

A tall lantern-jawed guy in a T-shirt and waistcoat climbs
on the stage. He has a very expensive Ovation guitar, which
he plugs in, tunes, strums, tunes, then strums again.

This one's called, 'Since You Left I Feel Like Starting
Colonic Irrigation, 'Cause I Miss My Pain In The Ass', he
announces, and strikes a bold chord on the guitar. Actually,
that's a joke, he says.

Somebody laughs loudly at a table down the front.

Thanks Myra. He nods, grins. But seriously, I'd like to start
with this one . . .

And he launches into a song. It's so vague in its imagery,
so twisted in its syntax, so abstract in its language, that even
before the first verse is through I'm completely lost: I haven't
the faintest idea what he's singing about. The chorus doesn't
help much. It goes something like:

Expeditions of immorality in the modern world today
Explorations, navigations, trying to find the way
Seeking to locate the route that leads to what we're
    looking for
You'll know it when you find it, my daddy said of
    yore

Each of the verses describes a different expedition in immorality. I think. Halfway through what must be about the

eighteenth verse, the waitress brings my food, and with relief I turn my attention to pulled pork, onion rings and hot pepper sauce.

The food is fantastic. The songwriters are dire. Every single one of them. By the time I hear the fifth one introduce himself by saying, *I don't want to be just another cowboy singer, I want to be a cowboy singer pushing Jesus*, I'm ready to leap up there, batter him around the skull with his expensive guitar (they all have expensive guitars) and launch into the 'Colonic Irrigation Song'. I've had plenty of dull moments to work out my own version of it . . .

But I don't. Instead I sign for the waitress to bring me the bill, and drag some dollars out of my pocket. When she arrives, the saucer has a thick felt-tip marker on it as well as the little slip of till paper.

Thanks, I say. But I'm paying cash, I don't need a pen.

Hey, she says. The pen's for the wall. Would you sign it for us?

I look at her. Pardon?

Everybody that comes here on a songwriters' night has to sign the wall. In case they get famous, see.

But I haven't sung anything.

She shrugs. It don't matter. Go on! There's a space right there above the sauce bottle.

I look at the wall behind the table. She's right: there are scrawled names and good wishes, and posters and promo pics of nearly famous folk in black hats and big hair-dos all across the wall. But right above my chilli sauce bottle there's a definite space.

I pick up the pen. Are you sure? I say.

Sure I'm sure. Hey, you might end up *anybody*. Then we can cut that piece of the wall out.

And burn it?

Sell it.

I pop the top off the pen. Right, I say. What am I going to write?

Anything you like. She takes the saucer with my dollars

on it and heads off for the bar, sashaying between the tables, the guitar cases, the tapping and twitching toes.

I suck the end of the pen for a second, then reach out, hesitate, reach out again, and rest the tip of the pen on the wall. This is my chance to make my mark on Nashville, to give the country music establishment something to chew on. It doesn't matter a bean who I am. The person I want to bring to their attention is The King Of Western Swing. So I lean over and write, slowly and carefully:

BOB WILLS IS ALIVE AND WELL
AND LIVING IN

I stop. That's not right. What *is* it that folk write up? Oh aye. BIRD LIVES! ELVIS LIVES! That's it: not a bloody address book, HENDRIX IS ALIVE AND WELL AND LIVING IN anywhere, but a bold statement of faith, HENDRIX LIVES! But now I'm committed. I've started so I'll have to finish. Where could Bob be? IN THE HEARTS AND MINDS OF TEXANS EVERYWHERE ... IN HILL-BILLY JAZZ HEAVEN ... IN LYLE LOVETT'S QUIFF ... No no no, none of those would do. Out of the corner of my eye, I see the waitress coming back with my change. Up on stage another expensive-guitar-and-paisley-waistcoat hopeful is singing too many words with too few ideas behind them, too many notes with too little tune. I've got to get out of this place.

I read my sentence so far, then write the first word that comes to mind: SIN.

In the words of swing steel colossus Bob Dunn, at the end of his brief sojourn in Nashville in the late thirties, *I can't handle this shit. I'm going down to Cowtown.*

Deep in the Heart of Texas

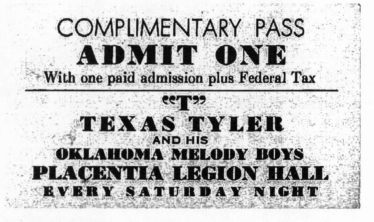

COMPLIMENTARY PASS
ADMIT ONE
With one paid admission plus Federal Tax

"T"
TEXAS TYLER
AND HIS
OKLAHOMA MELODY BOYS
PLACENTIA LEGION HALL
EVERY SATURDAY NIGHT

I came chevying out of the east just as darkness was falling. All the way from Start, Louisiana, I'd been chasing and been chased by three houses on truck-back: big wooden houses, two-storey jobs with chimneys, screen doors, mailboxes with yesterday's issue of the *National Enquirer* jutting out of them. This was moonlight flitting on a grand scale, at a mad speed.

With only half of one lane on the dual carriageway to play with, I'd eased out to overtake, put my foot down till I reached seventy, and found the house pulling away from me. Up to eighty, and the central reservation barriers were blurring by on one side, flowery curtains behind latticed windows cruising along on the other. Up to eighty-five, and I was finally pulling ahead of no. 2197, Interstate 20. Only to find no. 2195 twenty yards further on, the house swaying, a TV aerial whipping back and forth as its lorry bumped over stretches of corrugated pavement. Once past that, there was yet another speeding home ahead. But not 2193! No, leading the convoy was 2199! Somewhere along the way from where these houses had been wrenched from their founds – root systems of drains, mains, cables and phonelines dangling – there'd been a vicious duel for leadership, and no. 2199 had taken the lead.

I passed them all, pulled back into the so-called slow lane, and set cruise-control for seventy-five.

Dense forests of pine trees huddled right up to the edges of the freeway, as they had done most of the day. Every few miles a dead dog would be squelched on the roadway, or ripped open on the hard shoulder. Occasionally there'd be a rash of dead dogs – half a dozen in half a mile. I remembered a guy I'd heard on the radio somewhere back about Tallulah. He was being asked about his addiction to dangerous sports – white-water snorkelling, bungee parachuting, free-fall mountaineering.

I'm not concerned about danger, he'd said. Danger increases my chances of scoring. The interviewer laughed. Seriously, said the guy. Like all the animals that get run over during mating season. They risk running across the road to score. If they didn't dice with death on the freeway, they wouldn't get to pass on their genes. And if I didn't dice with death on the ski slopes, or the race track, hey, maybe I wouldn't get to pass on my genes. And I *love* to pass on my genes . . .

All I'd passed were the three westwardly mobile homes and several dozen flat dogs. Now, skirting round Shreveport, the three houses overtook me again, doing at least eighty-five, taking up about that percentage of the road too. I drove with two Goodyears on the hard shoulder and white knuckles on the steering wheel till they'd passed. Then, just a few miles down the road, the damn things had slowed to under sixty, and I had to dice with death once again and overtake. I had to be in Texas by nightfall.

Well, okay, I didn't *have* to be. But I wanted to be. After five years of loving Texas swing music, after three years of writing to old musicians, record collectors, fan club founders, and friends and relatives of western swing stars like Bob Wills, Milton Brown, and the Light Crust Doughboys, after two years of saving, and half an hour of planning for this trip, I was doggoned if I wasn't going to make it over the border before dark.

And I did make it, though the border itself was no more substantial than the one between Scotland and England: just a couple of signs and a tourist information centre. I suppose I'd imagined myself stopping and setting my camera's automatic timer to capture me staring with eagle eyes into the land of bluebonnets, cowboys, armadillos, nodding donkeys, Lone Star beer and chilli con carne, steel guitar rags and fiddle breakdowns on the old front porch. But I didn't stop. I'd only passed my driving test a month before, (on the other side of the road at that) and was now being pursued by half a town on wheels, smoke belching hellishly from its chrome stacks, horns blaring if ever my speed looked like falling to anywhere near the legal limit. Stopping was out of the question.

So I pressed on till the first junction after the border, at which point I whizzed off the interstate, watching my mirror as I headed up the slip road, praying I wouldn't see the mobile homes harrying me still. But they'd thundered on westwards towards Dallas and the heart of Texas.

Big Pines Lodge was my tip for the night's feed. I'd been given detailed directions on how to find it, but still spent ages following various narrow twisty roads through dark forests and past swampy bayous before chancing across a road narrower and more twisty than all the rest, which also had more traffic on it than all the rest. The pickups and cars were driving fast: hungry people on board. I followed.

Eventually we all turned off the paved road, crunched along a dirt track, and emerged into a large forest clearing, most of it taken up by rows of parked vehicles, the noses of the ones round the edges pushed right up against the trunks of the surrounding trees. At the far end of the clearing was a big log cabin, floodlit, and beyond that

black bayou water with snakes of light skinkling across
it.

Either this is the restaurant, I thought as I walked towards
the door, or it's the local KKK HQ. The vaguely masonic
name had put the idea in my head, I think. I paused on the
front step, listening. The forest was quiet, only insects fizzing
and clicking in the darkness. From inside came the sound
of talk, laughter, music: Sam and Dave singing 'Soul Man'.
Surely not a likely accompaniment to a Klan social? I went in.

In my naive, touristy, first-day-in-Texas way, I'd assumed
that the name Big Pines Lodge referred to the tall trees
surrounding the place. But right by the door, sitting in an
easy chair, with a till perched on a card table in front of him,
was an enormously tall and fat man, with rings on his fingers
and sweat on his brow. This had to be Big Pine. He'd on a
checked shirt and braces stretched so tight over his gigantic
chest and paunch that they'd've twanged a high C if you'd
plucked them.

But I didn't pluck them. I just asked if I could get a
table.

I don't know about a table, he said, But if you wait in line
we'll get you a chair real soon.

I thanked him and looked around for the queue. There
wasn't one really, just a bunch of folk milling about, so I
milled too.

Big Pine's lodge was pretty big itself. The log cabin
frontage concealed two long saloons, with trestle tables set
up the length of both. The lefthand hall was crowded
with diners – groups of big men in baseball caps and tartan shirts, huddles of teenagers, many families. All were
munching away on great chargers of food, talking, laughing, passing empty plates to a team of overalled waitresses
who rushed up and down the aisles with trolleys of fresh
food, dirty dishes, bottles of chilli sauce, jugs of iced tea.
The trestle tables in the righthand hall were covered with
piles of hunting, fishing and ex-military gear: rods, knives,
boxes of bullets, camouflage jackets, boots, walkie-talkies,
ropes, more knives, trenching tools, dehydrated food, books

called *The Green Beret Survival Guide*, and *Hunting For Food And Fun*.

I watched with interest as fathers weighed up handfuls of ammo, then poured them into their kids' cupped palms, and as mothers felt the quality of bullet-proof vests between finger and thumb. Fair enough: if my husband was stocking up on lethal weapons, I'd probably want some body armour too.

After a few minutes I was called over and seated at one end of a big table, with a family group filling the rest of it, engaged in an excited conversation about tanning. To start with I thought they were arguing the relative merits of sunbeds and trips to Florida beaches, but it turned out they were discussing how best to preserve deer skin.

Within seconds of ordering (I'd been told I should try catfish), a tray of goodies and a glass of iced tea were set in front of me. I set to with an appetite: coleslaw, pickled jalapenos, slices of raw onion, chopped red chillies, and big puffy balls of deep-fried dough, that I assumed were the catfish in thick pouches of batter. It was all delicious, and within a couple of minutes I was starting to feel pretty full up; a couple more minutes and another strangely unfishy catfish-ball later, I was thoroughly stuffed. That's when the waitress turned up again, and plonked down a tray of five battered fish-shaped objects by my glass.

Here's your meal, she said. Enjoy!

I looked at the pile of fish, and at the half-empty tray in front of me.

My, said the waitress. You've finished all your hush puppies already! Want some more?

I shook my head, too full to talk, and she departed, leaving me in a quandary: I wasn't in the slightest bit hungry, but I was going to feel a bit daft if, for my first meal in Texas, I didn't even manage to taste the main course. What's more, there was a rope noose hanging on the wall opposite me with a sign pinned beside it: WE CAN DEAL WITH CRIMINALS THE WAY CONGRESS CAN'T. I had the idea that Big Pine might well take a similarly tough stance on anyone who didn't appreciate his food. I loosened my belt a notch, cut off a lump of the top catfish, and chewed.

It dripped grease, was shot through with needle-sharp bones, and tasted like a mouthful of river mud. I considered spitting it out and hiding the mess under a hush puppy. I took a casual glance around: Big Pine was staring straight at me. I swallowed, quickly cut off another slice of fish, and stuck it in my gob. Delicious! I cried, through grease, mud and bones.

After the first fish, I wondered if I could clear any space in my stomach for the other four. On the wall next to the toilet door was one of those full-size paper targets, of a vaguely Asiatic looking soldier with a fixed bayonet and a murderous grimace on his pus. Charge! There were white target rings on his head and chest, perforated with a scatter of, eh, bullet holes. I glanced over my shoulder to see if some kind of William Tell/test-the-tourist's-nerve routine was about to start. Not tonight. But the thought of it did help me clear a considerable space in my digestive system.

When I got back to my seat, I was able to eat another fish and a half. You know, it's amazing what you get to like when you try: after only two and a half catfish I was already able to get a mouthful down without cowking.

I was helped by the music. The jukebox had been pounding out a selection of current honky tonk hits, along with country and soul classics. What came on just as I swilled down my last mouthful of iced tea and chilli pepper? Bob Wills and his Texas Playboys jazzing 'Deep In The Heart of Texas'.

Here was the great man himself, on my first night in his home state, welcoming me with a great big musical howdy! I was maybe only ten miles away from Louisiana, but sitting in the middle of Big Pines Lodge with this wonderful music booming out, it really did feel like deep in the heart of the Lone Star State. It really was too good to be true. In fact, if I hadn't heard it with my own ears, I'd assume I was making it up in order to provide a punchy ending to the first chapter of my travelogue. But I swear, that's the way it was.

Razors in de Air

In the morning I walked around Jefferson, a small town of red
brick streets, shade trees, and 32 State Historical Medallions.
It's a historical place, Jefferson. It's famous for being historical.
In fact, I heard a rumour they were going to set up another
marker at the outskirts of town saying, *Welcome to Jefferson,
State Historical Site: Home to 32 Medallions.* Then one just
beside that saying, *No, 33.* Then another on the other side
saying, *That makes it 34.*

Back in the 1840s and '50s, it was the second largest city
in Texas, known as The Emporium of the South West, with
a population of thirty thousand, the first mains gas supply
in the state (which supplied gas somehow extracted from
pine trees), and a dozen or more steamboats lining the
docks down at Big Cypress Bayou. This was the secret of
Jefferson's success: clear water ran all the way from here to
New Orleans, three hundred miles south, and steamboats

passed downstream laden with iron ore and timber, upstream with all manner of fancy goods and fancy ideas as well as hundreds of westward-bound settlers. The town was so sure of its river-borne prosperity that in 1872 it turned down the chance to have a railroad pass through it. In fact, Jeffersonians insisted that the tracks keep well away from the town. They'd no need of such new-fangled noisy, smoky contraptions!

Oh-oh.

A year later, during operations to clear the bayou of a great raft of logs, the engineers made an important discovery: the logjam had been acting as a giant plug, keeping water levels artificially high. With the plug pulled, the water emptied overnight, and Jefferson was left high and dry, beyond the reach of the steamboats forever. Now the population's two thousand. And that's mostly antique shops. Well, maybe there's not quite that number, but the whole town does have a frozen-in-time feel to it, like a half-eaten tub of ice-cream, forgotten at the bottom of the freezer.

I hadn't seen more than two or three places like it in all my thousand miles driving. It seems that, in the States, progress means obliterating the old. The only place that large chunks of old towns survived was when they were so much of a backwater that nobody wanted to live there, so nobody bothered knocking down the old houses to build new ones.

Now, of course, the historic nature of Jefferson *is* appreciated, though in danger of being suffocated by an excess of pseudo-Victorian frills and flounces: The Gaslight Shop Of Angels, Tootsie's Home Carved Candles and Christmas Store, Yesteryear Nick Nacks, and an antique shop called Granny Had It. What, rickets? Even the local rag, or rather, The Fifth Oldest Newspaper In Texas, is called *The Jefferson Jimplecute*. Now, maybe jimplecute is an old Texan word meaning *incisive and merciless discoverer of government sleaze and business corruption wherever we may find it*. But I doubt it.

In the Jefferson Historical Society Museum, civil war cannonballs, a two hundred-year-old loom, and collections of bottles, dolls and ironstone, vied for attention with minor Old Masters and Annie Oakley's boot last. But even that wasn't enough to detain me from my real search, which finally ended outside a small cafe on West Austin Street. It was there that I came across a plaque commemorating the town's connection with one of my musical heroes, the first national star of country music, perhaps the biggest selling recording artist *ever*. Ladies and gentlemen, hats off to Jefferson native, Marion Try Slaughter II!

What do you mean you've never heard of him? Okay, picture me walking into the Cotton Gin Cafe, ordering Cajun Sausage Plate and Poppers (cheese-stuffed jalapenos) and reading the potted biography on the back of the menu. Then imagine me taking the life-story out of the pot, reheating it, adding a couple dashes of Tabasco, and laying it in front of you now. *Enjoy!*

Marion Slaughter was born on a ranch just outside Jefferson in 1883. Soon the family moved into town, supposedly to make it easier for their son to receive a refined education. Or any education. Unfortunately, Jefferson was already plunging into decline by this stage, and had gained a reputation as a place of desperation, drunkenness and violence. The Slaughters lived on Line Street, an offshoot of which, heading down towards Cypress Bayou River, was known as Murder Alley. One and often two bodies would be found each morning in this alley, says a local history book. It was only a matter of time till the town's proclivities and the family's ill-fated name became entangled. Sure enough, before Marion was even out of short chaps, his father, Robert Slaughter, was stabbed to death in a bar-room brawl with his wife's brother.

Soon after this, the boy started to develop two seemingly contradictory obsessions that would last for the rest of his life. One was to be a tough, untouchable, rough and ready, sharp-shooting cowpuncher. The other was to excel as a singer of light opera. The first ambition was the easier to realise. As a teenager, Marion moved west to the Panhandle of Texas, and worked there as a cowboy: for several years in some accounts, over his summer holidays in others. It was from the names of two farm towns he passed through that he would later conjure up his stage name: Vernon Dalhart.

Marion moved with his mother to Dallas, where he worked as a piano salesman, and then on to New York, where he received some training, and eventually made his mark, in 1913, as the lead in Gilbert and Sullivan's *HMS Pinafore*. From then on he maintained a career in opera grand and light, eventually starting to record in 1917, after an audition in front of Thomas Edison himself. To be exact, the audition was to the side of Edison: being rather deaf, the old inventor had Vernon Dalhart (for so he had become) sing directly into his ear trumpet.

'Can't Yo' Heah Me Callin', Caroline?' was his audition piece, and his first release: Blue Amberol Cylinder 3185. It's a long way from WS Gilbert's tortuously witty librettos, being a heartfelt – histrionic, even – plea in what everyone recognised as southern black dialect: a coon song. Unlike Al Jolson, whose hammy, super-sincere style clearly influenced Dalhart, the southern singer had no need to study and consciously imitate black forms of speech. There's an interesting quote from an interview in the *Edison Amberola Monthly*, December 1918. The interviewer asks him where he learned his style. I never had to learn it, Dalhart replies. When you are brought up in the South your only trouble is to talk any other way. All through my childhood that was almost the only talk I ever heard because the sure 'nough Southerner talks almost like a Negro, even when he's white.

So was Dalhart the first white singer to make records in the style of blacks? The original white man stealing and profiting from the black man's music? A low-down no-good son of the South, happily popularising racial stereotypes even as he made a fortune from the stolen art of the people he was caricaturing? Maybe. But a fairer description would probably be of a man actually less prejudiced than most of his time and place, marvellously open to music whatever its source, whatever its style, whatever its lack of acceptance in polite society of the time. Right from the start of his career, as well as black-dialect pieces, he also recorded dozens of operatic arias, Hawaiian songs (a contemporary craze), comedy numbers, fox-trots, and patriotic ditties to aid the war effort, such as 'When Alexander Takes His Ragtime Band To France'.

It was in November 1924, however, trying out yet another new style, that Dalhart stumbled across the two tunes that would change his life and the listening habits of the whole world. Oh yes. And the style was . . . *country*.

There'd been a few recordings of southern white music before, but none of them – even by charismatic performers such as Fiddlin' John Carson and Henry Whitter (later to feature in a string band with the intriguing name, Fisher Hendley's Aristocratic Pigs) – had been more than minor, regional successes. When Dalhart recorded his own versions of two rather mournful folk tunes. 'The Wreck of the Old '97' and 'The Prisoner's Song', he sparked off something in the hearts of millions of Americans: the start of a chain reaction that would lead directly to Garth Brooks flying about football stadiums on Peter Pan wires. But let's not hold that against him.

It's a bit hard to hear why now – the tunes are lugubrious and sentimental, with stiff instrumental accompaniment – but the record was an enormous hit: it's estimated to have sold as many as thirty-five million copies, all but a few in the ten years following its initial release. Sales were helped by the fact that, in these days before exclusive recording contracts, Dalhart released the songs on probably fifty other labels. He had many other big hits too, including several more million sellers: 'Home on the Range', from 1927, is one that is still widely remembered. He lived in a mansion in upstate New York, drove a Cadillac, toured the USA, Canada and England. More than occasionally he'd still record opera (*Fra Diavolo*), or coon ('Razors In de Air'), or comedy numbers, like 'Eleven More Nights and Ten More Days', the first Vernon Dalhart song I ever heard, back when I was about five:

A bird in another cell asked me,
'How long are you in here for?'
I told him that I'd be here
Eleven months and ten days more

'I'm here until tomorrow,' he said.
'I said, 'You son of a gun!
You're a lucky guy!' He said, 'Am I?
Tomorrow I'm going to be hung!'

But from the mid-twenties onwards, he returned again and again to the rich seam of ballads, folk songs and cowboy tunes (both real and faked-up) that had proved so popular: 'My Blue Ridge Mountain Home', 'A Handful of Dirt From Mother's Grave', 'The Jones and Bloodworth Execution', 'Bury Me Out on the Prairie', 'The Butcher's Boy', even 'The Little Black Mustache'. Some of my favourites are the duets he recorded with his fiddler, Adelyne Hood. Hood specialised in tough-talking, proto-feminist, drink-the-men-under-the-table-and-back-in-their-chairs-again characters, and the interplay between her rasping voice and Vernon's smooth tenor is hilarious in such songs as 'Calamity Jane' and 'Yukon Steve and Alaska Ann'.

By 1925, demand for Dalhart's cowboy style was huge. Rather than let newcomers and imitators cash in, he started releasing records under an astounding flood of *noms de disque*. The full extent of these pseudonymous recordings will probably never be settled (and his total lifetime sales will therefore never be calculated accurately), but historians have rounded up enough names to be getting on with:

The Many Faces of Marion Slaughter

James Ahern : John Albin : Mack Allen : Wolfe Ballard : James Belmont : Harry Blake : Harry Britt : Billy Burton : Jeff Calhoun : Jess Calhoun : Jimmy Cannon : Jimmy Cantrell :

Ed Clifford : Al Cramer : Al Craver : James Cummings :
Frank Dalbert : Frank Dalhart : Vernon Dalhart : Vernon
Dall : Charles Dalton : Vernon Dell : Hugh Donovan :
Joseph Elliot : Frank Evans : Clifford Ford : Jeff Fuller : Jep
Fuller : Albert Gordon : Leslie Gray : David Harris : Harry
Harris : Francis Harrold : Lou Hays : Fern Holmes : Howard
Hull : Frank Hutchinson : Joe Kincaid : Fred King : Louis
Lane : Hugh Latimer : Hugh Lattimore : Tobe Little : The
Lone Star Ranger : Bob Massey : Guy Massey : B. McAfee :
Bob McAfee : Carlos B. McAfee : Warren Mitchell : George
Morbid : Dick Morse : Charles Nelson : Gwyrick O'Hara :
Sam Peters : Joseph Smith : Josephus Smith : Cliff Stewart :
Edward Stone : Howard Stone : Billy Stuart : Will Terry :
The Texas Tenor : Bob Thomas : Al Turner : Allen Turner :
Sid Turner : Bill Vernon : Billy Vernon : Herbert Vernon :
Val Veteran : Vel Veteran : Tom Watson : Bob White :
Bobby White : Robert White : Walter Whitlock : George
Woods : Mister X

George Morbid! (I bet 'A Handful of Dirt From Mother's
Grave' was one of his.) As if the above manic proliferation
of identities wasn't enough, Slaughter also split himself into
duos, trios, and quartets; he became a brother to himself; he
rambled, he panhandled, he blew jugs; he found hometowns
in Arkansas, Alabama, Texas, Virginia, Illinois:

20,000,000 Marion Slaughters
Can't Be Wrong

Allen and Parker : The Archie Ruff Singers : The Arkansas
Travellers : The Arkansas Trio : Ballard and Samuels : The
Barbary Coast Four : The Birmingham Blue Bugles : The
Broadway Quartet : Calhoun and Andrews : The Cramer
Brothers : Dalhart's Big Cypress Boys : Dalhart's Texas
Panhandlers : The Dominio Quartet : Evans and Clark :
Evans and Clarke : Fred Ozark's Jug Blowers : The Harmony
Four : The Jewel Trio : The Jones Brothers : The Kanawha

Singers : Ladd's Black Aces : Mitchell and White : The National Music Lovers Quartet : The Old Southern Sacred Singers : The Oriole Trio : Peters and Jones : The Regal Rascals : Salt and Pepper : The Smoky Mountain Sacred Singers : The Virginians : The Windy City Duo : The Windy City Jazzers

Names and identities split and recombined in a mad programme of cross-fertilisation and interbreeding. But one name is remarkable by its absence: his own. Nobody has been able to trace a solitary record featuring Marion Try Slaughter II; there's not even a single element of it mixed up or misspelt and joined on to something else. It seems to me there must have been some mighty powerful dread operating in the singer's brain, before he could come up with Mister X, Vel Veteran, and Carlos B. McAfee for goodness sake, but *never ever* anything that came anywhere near what he was born with.

By 1930, real competitors had emerged, and, very quickly, vanquished Dalhart and all the clan. His sound had been rendered obsolete by bluesier, less stiff-necked performers like Jimmie Rodgers. The Carter Family favoured similar gloomy folk ballads, but featured striking harmonies and more powerful instrumentation. Gene Autry, also born on a Texan ranch, made a virtue out of his background, stayed in Stetson and saddle, cashed in on the public interest in all things western that the dinner-suited Dalhart had whetted. Sales dropped off as dramatically as a draining bayou, and soon all the trappings of his early incredible popularity were gone. In 1940 he suffered the ignominy of an attempted comeback record, the bizarre 'The Lavender Cowboy', being banned for its supposed obscenity:

> *He was only a lavender cowboy*
> *The hairs on his chest were few*
> *But he wished to follow the heroes*
> *And fight like the he-men do*

But he was inwardly troubled
By a dream that gave him no rest
That he'd go with heroes in action
With only two hairs on his chest

Herbicides and many hair tonics
Were rubbed in on him each night
But still when he looked in the mirror
No new hairs were ever in sight

By 1943, he was forced to find other work, as a night-watchman, and in 1948 he died, almost penniless, and almost entirely forgotten.

So he's remained, more or less. There have been two or three LP reissues of a minute portion of his recordings, and most histories of country music give him at least a nod. That's about it. Oh, and outside the Cotton Gin cafe in his hometown is the plaque recording his debut public performance there nearly a hundred years ago, back when it was Kahn's Saloon. His life from Kahn's was an amazing parabola: from a bitter and violent childhood, through international stardom as big or bigger than Crosby, Sinatra, Jackson, back to his final years as a night baggage handler in the basement of a Connecticut hotel.

The waitress in the Cotton Gin didn't know anything about Vernon Dalhart, but said there was a man by the name of Charlie Johnson (or was it John Charlson, Val Johnson, Charlie Dal, Lentil Dal, Vernon Dali, The Yodelling Dali Brothers?) who'd been trying to start some kind of fan club. I paid for my Cajun sausage, and wandered along North Polk Street to his place of work: The Bazaar, with its snappy slogan: A Collection Of Shops.

Mr Johnson was at the doctor's. I shrugged. What could he tell me anyway? The story is plain: 3,500 recordings! 50,000,000 sales! Look on his works, ye mighty, and despair.

Big Beaver

SHADY GLADE
MARINA • MOTEL • RESTAURANT
RV - FULL HOOKUPS • CADDO LAKE TOURS
SPECIALIZING IN CATFISH & STEAKS

Dallas & Beverly Harris, *Owners*

(903) 789-3295

Cypress Drive
Uncertain, Texas

I was meant to be heading north towards Wichita Falls, but got distracted by a sign for Swanson's Landing, and headed east instead, down to the edge of Caddo Lake. Caddo was enormous – 27,000 acres, my guide book said – but you'd never have known to look at it. Not from where I was standing, anyway. I couldn't see more than about ten metres of clear water in any direction: the whole lake was clogged with crowds of cypress trees, trunks jutting up out of the water on cone-shaped root-stilts, boughs drooping back down into the water under the weight of their own abundant green foliage, and huge burdens of Spanish moss. The moss hung off every tree in great shrouds and streamers; it draped every branch, wrapped every trunk. Sometimes it had grown so thick that its host tree had been suffocated; off to my right was a whole stretch of dead cypresses, ranks of grey-bearded skeletons.

The bony trunks, sparse spindly branches and swathes of hanging moss, all reflected in the still water beneath, gave the lake-forest a strange, hallucinatory appearance. It was like that Borges short story about the actual-size map, as big as the country it represented: here was an actual size Polaroid photo of Caddo Lake, snapped and scraped before the fixer had set, so the whole thing was a great shimmery grey and green smudge.

In places, pond weed and lilies and something like giant cress grew so thick under the trees that they looked like little green islands rising out of the water. Ten metres into the trees was a big untidy pile of kindling-wood: a beaver's lodge. Did Big Pine name his restaurant after one of those? It was built of the same kind of timber, just arranged a bit more neatly. If Bob Wills had had a restaurant in the woods, he could have called it Big Beaver Lodge, after his great swing-band instrumental, recorded in 1940. I hadn't known that beavers lived in Texas, I thought they were a Canadian beast: suddenly Bob's song sounded less exotic, more a reflection on an everyday part of his life.

The surface of the clear channel right in front of me was alive with swimming and skimming insects, fragments of bark, leaf and twig, and the shadowy forms of small fish darting about just below the surface. Somewhere in the distance, muffled by the maze of trees and moss, was the putter of an outboard motor.

I'd originally come across the name Swanson's Landing in the sleeve notes of a Leadbelly LP. Huddie Ledbetter, 'King of the Twelve-String Guitar Players of the World', was born and raised there, before heading off to sing, play, drink and fight his way across Texas and Louisiana, and eventually up to New York City – in and out of jail, in and out of disgrace, in and out of favour with various audiences, from Shreveport brothels to New York coffee houses. But always, always, bellowing out great midnight-hearted songs of love and desire and regret, of prison life, cotton-picking, drink and drugs and murder – songs of real life, and real death: 'Midnight Special', 'Goodnight Irene', 'Take A Whiff On Me', 'Careless Love'.

Other books and record sleeves claim that Leadbelly was born, not at Swanson's Landing, but somewhere else along the shore of Lake Caddo – maybe even on the Louisiana side, near Mooringsport. But why let quibbles over mere facts get in the way of a good connection? (Only connect! as T. Texas Tyler said.) And here is the connection: Swanson is an Orkney name.

Okay, to be exact, it's probably a Scandinavian name – son of Sweyn – which got established in Orkney during the long Norse rule up to the mid-fifteenth century, and dropped off here and there around the world, wherever other Scandinavians settled. Let's see: there's a Svenson in Oregon, and a Swenson in north-west Texas. (I drove through it later on my way up to Turkey: Swenson, Stonewall Country, pop. 185 – halfway between Peacock and Old Glory. Points of interest: its name.) Back in the heyday of western swing, there was even a dancehall called Barry Swenson's Pavilion, near Meridian. But the vowels of these other names all retain the original Norse value: none of them has the Orcadian *a*. No, I've quite convinced myself: Swanson's Landing was founded by an Orcadian émigré some time in the middle of the last century. And certainly before 1869, the earliest reference to the place I've found. That year the steamboat *Mittie Stevens* burned and sunk just off it, with the loss of sixty lives, the tragedy being made all the more poignant by the fact that the lake was only three feet deep at that point, and the passengers could have waded to safety if only they'd tried. More, the founder was probably a relation of mine, for my wife's granny's father's name was Swanson. Captain Swanson, to be exact, of the steamer *St Ola*, which plied the wild waters of the Pentland Firth between Orkney and Scotland! It all ties in.

There's a story told about Captain Swanson, and a particularly stormy equinoctial crossing seventy years ago. The boat was lurching and rolling so violently that the passengers were becoming worried for their safety. Scrabster pier had long since disappeared in the spume behind them, and the safety of Scapa Flow and Stromness harbour was still a long way off. One particular southerner, a gentleman, was deputised to go to the wheel (not even a wheelhouse – its only shelter from the gales and green water was a canvas awning) and find out how much longer the passengers would have to suffer this hell of seasickness, stinging salt spray, and terror.

I say, my good man, said the southerner, tapping the captain on the shoulder. I say, we're all getting rather anxious back there – well, the ladies are, you know – and we were wondering, well, how much longer?

Captain Swanson smoothed brine out of his walrus moustache. As long as it takes, he said. Can't do it any quicker than that. And he turned back to the helmsman, to shout instructions over the roar of the wind. Then he was being tapped on the shoulder again.

Now look here, said the southerner, Just tell me, I only want to know, where's the nearest land?

Captain Swanson whirled around, glowering, biting the ends of his mouser to stop from bursting out with a curse. He put an arm round the southerner's shoulders, and convoyed him three or four steps across the pitching, slopping deck, and leant him over the brass rail there. The furious green water spat in the southerner's face.

The nearest land, said Captain Swanson, Is STRAIGHT DOWN! And he returned to the wheel, to make sure the *St Ola* didn't take that particular route.

There were a lot of distinguished sailors and voyagers amongst the Swansons. I'd never heard of any of them coming to Texas in particular, but seeing the name of this place on the LP sleeve in Nashville had got me thinking. What could be more likely than that some nineteenth-century Orcadian should tire of battling across the Firth, or round the Cape, or out to the far haafs and back, and settle instead for the easy life, skippering steamboats up and down the warm and sluggish waters of the east Texas bayous? I felt certain that, somewhere amongst these forests of cypress, pine and moss, would be a little stone croft, oddly out of place amongst its clapboard neighbours, called something un-Texan like Windybreck or Hoymansquoy. And outside would be an

old, old man, with a beard like Spanish moss, who'd take
me in to meet his father, an even older old man, blind with
age – but not *completely* deaf, so that when he heard my
accent his ears would prick and he'd sit up in bed – so old that
his children and grandchildren and great grandchildren and
great great grandchildren thought he was going senile when
he told them tales from his bairnhood of fishing for gulls off
clifftops, of seals coming out of the sea and walking amongst
men, of fiddlers disappearing inside greeny grass knowes and
reappearing ninety-nine years later, aged not even a day. And
I would assure them, No no, such a place really exists, such
things really happen – though auk-swaaping's not as popular
as once it was – and here in my pooch I have a lump of peat
from Brinkie's Brae, a swallow of whisky from Highland Park,
a breath of air from the Yesnaby cliffs . . .

But I couldn't find Swanson's Landing. All I had seen
were trees, roads leading back on themselves, grey moss
everywhere like some vile infestation from an H.P. Lovecraft
story. I looked at my map. I definitely hadn't imagined that
sign, but there was no trace of the place on the page, and
the road I'd thought the sign indicated had just petered
out at the waterside. There was, I now saw on the map,
a cemetery called Swanson, in Latex parish about twenty
miles south. That's where the old, old, even older man
would be. Enough romantic notions: any direct Orkney
connections would have gone six foot under decades ago.
Now that my eye had got accustomed to the smallest print in
the road atlas, I also spotted an Aberdeen cemetery, a Boggy
cemetery, the Elysian Gas Fields, and another burial ground
called Pope City – I wonder what denomination of church
folk are buried there? And just south of Swanson cemy was a
hamlet called Lotta – a cousin of the Orkney island of Flotta?
It'd be nice to think so.

Off to my left, the sound of the outboard motor was
getting louder, and I could see a small craft threading past
the cypress roots, catch glimpses of an old man in a baseball
cap sitting upright at the rudder as he flitted between the
trunks and curtains of moss. Then the outboard cut, and the

boat coasted across the stretch of still clear water towards the shore just the other side of a dense stand of pines.

I locked the car and walked through the woods, coming almost immediately to a small sunlit clearing with a caravan, a battered pick-up and an Alsatian chained to a stake in the ground. Down at the water's edge was a rickety landing stage with two ripped car seats and a beer cooler at the end, and the old man climbing on to it out of his boat. He looked up, waved me over.

Would you hold this? he said as I approached, and handed up a fishing rod and a string bag with two big fish in it. He clambered up himself, and started making fast the boat.

Been fishing? I said, the Sherlock Holmes of the bayous.

Yup. Caught enough for lunch. I'll go out this afternoon and catch enough for supper. That's living!

I examined the ugly, whiskery fish. Are these catfish, by any chance?

Sure are.

They look as good as they taste, I said.

He squinted at me, rubbed his white-grizzled chin. You're not from round here, are you? He started to walk back up the clearing.

No, I said. I'm from Orkney. Where the Swansons come from. He kept walking. I clunked my heel on the planks of the landing stage. *This* isn't Swanson's Landing, is it?

No sir, he said. This here's Shady Glade.

Oh. I started to follow the guy: I was still holding his rod and bag.

He stopped and looked back at me, lifted his cap to scratch his head. Where did you say you were from? England?

Well . . .

Do you want a cup of tea?

Eh . . . aye, that would be great. If it's not too much trouble to you.

No trouble to me, I'll get my wife to make it. He laughed, kicked the Alsatian affectionately, and stepped up into the caravan. Come in, come in!

I stepped past the dog, didn't kick it. It stopped wagging

its tail and growled: heh, a masochistic German Shepherd. I followed him up the metal steps into the sweltering heat of the tiny caravan.

Howdy! said a small bespectacled woman with a pot of boiling water in her hand. Oscar's told me all about you. Come in, sit down. Oscar, move that cat, and move that knitting, and put them fish in the sink before I get to yelling.

Oscar and I shuffled about each other. He took the bag and rod off me, and I sat down.

Oscar says you'd like a cup of tea, being from England and all, she said. *We'll* have coffee if you don't mind. It's a wonder we have tea in the house, we never drink it.

Tea, coffee, anything, I said. It's hot out there and I'm lost! Maybe you can help – I'm looking for Swanson's Landing.

As in Gloria Swanson? said Oscar from over by the sink.

Oh! I never thought of her!

Listen, we've no lemon. Do you want lemon?

Me? No. A drop of milk. Thanks.

She handed me a mug of steaming grey stuff, with a label on a piece of thread wrapped round the handle: Dr Wilbury's Camomile Tea.

Swanson's Landing, I said. I was wondering how it got its name. Do you know?

Names! she said. I'm Maryann Plott, and this is my husband Oscar Plott. Did he tell you we were married? I bet he didn't! He hasn't got into the habit of it yet, you see – it's only been six months.

Congratulations! I said, and took a sip of tea. Speaking of marriages, I went on quickly to hide the ripples of shock my tastebuds were spreading out across my face, My wife's granny was a Swanson, and I was wondering if somebody of that family ever came here and gave their name to the place.

Uncertain, said Oscar from the far end of the caravan, eight feet away.

Yeah, me too, I said. Maybe I'll never find out for sure.

No, said Maryann. The name of this place is Uncertain.

I frowned, almost took another sip of tea, then remembered not to. You mean *no one* knows what it's called?

Now Oscar laughed. No! We all know for *certain*, it's called *Uncertain*!

I looked at him, and he laughed more, and so did Maryann.

How did it get such a weird name? I asked.

I'm not sure, said Maryann.

Now I was laughing.

But I think, she went on, It was back a hundred years. And there were two villages in these parts, tiny places. With a name each, of course. But the tiny villages were getting bigger, and closer together, till finally the houses joined up – one big village! But which name to use?

And one of the names was Uncertain? What was the other? Doubtful?

No, no – they were called something like Smithsville and Jonesburg, said Maryann. But when they had the vote – cause all the people got to vote . . .

All the *white* people, put in Oscar.

All the white *men*, said Maryann. They had two boxes, one for each of the names, and then another box, for them that couldn't make up their minds. And more folk voted for Uncertain than anything else!

We all laughed. Oscar came forward with some digestivey biscuits on a plate, then asked if I wanted more to eat. He could go out and catch another fish and I could stay for dinner if I liked. I told them thanks but no. Though I admired his skill in being able to pluck the fish out of the water to order, as easy as lifting them out of the supermarket deep freeze.

The lake's a lot cheaper, said Maryann. And it keeps him happy, she added, holding her mug to the side of her mouth to shield the words from her husband.

It's a good life, Oscar was saying. An American life. Some folks say it's just Texas, but I was raised in Michigan, and it's the same there. If you don't shoot or catch what God provides, you have to pay for what Wal-Mart provides.

Back where I live a lot of folk are into it too, I said. Especially fishing. I've tried it: trout out of the lochs, beautiful big things. But you know my problem? I can't bear to kill the blighters!

Oscar frowned.

You've got this big fish flapping about in the bottom of the boat, I went on, And you pick it up to get a good grip on it and bash it dead, when – yah! – the blooming thing catches your eye! This beautiful beastie's looking up at you, pleading with you, Don't kill me! Don't eat me! Put me back in the water with my mates! I mean to say: it's heartbreaking!

No, said Oscar, You've got it all wrong. It's kill or be killed, that's what it is.

Not many people get killed by trout, said Maryann.

That's what you'd think, said Oscar. But appearances can be deceptive. What about squirrels? Nice fluffy, cuddly animals, that's the propaganda. Garbage! They're vicious brutes! Try cuddling a rabid squirrel and you'll soon know all about fluffy. *You have to get them before they get you.*

I took a bite out of a biscuit. So do you go out shooting squirrels?

Whenever I can.

What else do you shoot?

Oh, buzzards, crows. Coots.

Coots?

Egrets.

Do they spread rabies?

You never can tell.

I thought it was just mammals.

That's what they tell you. He tapped the side of his nose. But do you really trust what they tell you?

Well . . . who?

And what about rattlers? You have to know how to deal with one of them babes! It's just speed – ha! – whack! – ha! – you catch them over the back of the head with your stick as soon as you see them. Don't wait for them to see you. Same goes for water moccasins – whoee, they're even worse. I shoot the bastards whenever I spot them. Wriggling across the lake like it was dry land – it's not natural! If one of them bites you, you have to get your knife and dig! Scoop that bite mark right out. You've got ten seconds to do it, boy, or you're dead meat!

I swallowed my last piece of biscuit. Is there anything you wouldn't shoot? I asked.

Sure, said Oscar.

What's that?

A turtle.

A turtle. Why not?

Goddam bullets bounce off their shells and come straight back at you!

He hooted with laughter, and I kind of joined in, thinking all the while that I'd have to get myself a knife. And a stick.

Oscar wiped tears of laughter from his eyes. It's the American way of life, he said. Look after yourself, and *never trust anyone.*

That's right, said Maryann. Would you like another cookie?

Shanty Town

It was Saturday morning when I drove north out of Jefferson.
I headed straight up till I got to Paris, at which point I turned
left. There was an enormous soup factory on the outskirts,
but apart from that it looked like any other industrial town.
Motherwell, for instance. Like Motherwell with sunshine.
And industry. And six million tins of Campbell's cream of
armadillo.

So much for romantic Paris, Texas from the film of the
same name, I thought to myself as I zoomed round the
bypass. Typical of a movie-maker to come up with such
bewitching images of such an average could-be-anywhere
place. But then I thought, Hold on a minute, wasn't the
town purposely average, if not actually downright ugly, in
the film? Wasn't it contrasted to the stark, elemental beauty
of the desert that what's-his-name with the beard walks out
of at the start? But that's the problem with driving across a

strange land on your tod in a hired car, with nothing for
company but sixteen western swing tapes, one road atlas,
one *Texas Off The Beaten Path*, and the *New Grove Dictionary
of Jazz* for bedtime reading. You can't stick in the video and
check the plot. You can't look up *Halliwell's*. You can't even
ring up Tanya the film buff in Get Taped Videos and ask for
a quick summary, cast list, cinematographer, awards received,
etc. etc. You have to rely on your memory. And make up the
bits you've forgotten.

Then, six months later, when you're sitting at home with
your videos, your *Halliwell's*, your Get Taped down the road,
you don't want them. (Harry Dean Stanton.) You need
something else entirely. Because you're trying to recall what
cruising through Texas on a Saturday morning in April is like,
and what you really need now is a virtual reality recreation of
driving west on US Highway 82. But all you can do is rely
on your memory. And make up the bits you've forgotten.

West of Paris, I passed a gas station with a jet fighter parked
in the forecourt. (No, I'm not making that up.) A bit further
on, I drove by a vast field of vintage three-wheeled tractors
in neat rows; bulbous, brightly painted bonnets stretched to
the horizon. (That's true too.) An hour later, I stopped in
a town called Muenster for something to eat, and found
nothing but German bakeries, German sausage-makers, German street-names. The girls serving in the roadside drugstore
were tall, blonde and blue-eyed, the spit of those javelin
throwers you always see in clips from the 1936 Olympics.
(True true true.)

I drove on again and hit Wichita Falls at six o'clock. Bad
idea: rush hour. Rush hour at this hour, on a weekend? Hell,
maybe the damn place was *always* this busy. Whatever, I was
shaken at being suddenly plunged into a tumult of traffic.
All the way across the States, I'd been driving relatively
open highways, taking detours along deserted back roads,
crawling about quiet streets in sleepy country towns. That's
what I'd been doing till 5.59 p.m. today, too. Then, as
Highway 82 changed into Interstate 44, as I crossed the

Wichita Falls city limits, all vehicular hell broke loose. I was suddenly being swept along in a cataract of semi-trucks, station-wagons, pick-ups, yuppie jeeps, cars full of kids, cars with nonagenarians trembling at the wheel. And the lower the numbers on the speed-limit signs got, the faster the traffic roared along. Somebody was right up my exhaust, somebody else was wobbling about in the outside lane, trying to squeeze their stretch limo in front of me any time I allowed a gap of more than three feet to build up between my bumper and the petrol tanker ahead. There were two lanes of traffic zooming along to my right, another one to my left, and beyond these on each side was a concrete crash barrier: I felt like I was sitting in a giant Chevy marble being hurled around the curves of a city-sized pinball machine.

Every half-mile or so, an exit would appear on one side or another of the road – 14th, 13th, 12th Street – and I'd try and edge over and take it. But by the time I'd ducked and dodged across to the proper lane, the slip road would've flashed past, signs would be coming up for the next exit, on the far side – 11th, 10th, 9th Street – and I'd have to start edging over that way. The whole city was in the grip of an insane one-way system, and the whole population gripped by an equally insane need for speed. A distinctly uncold sweat was breaking out all over me, making my hands slip on the steering wheel.

Still the streets went flashing past – 8th, 7th, 6th – and still I was being hurled along. At last, after arriving in the far right lane just as the exit to 5th Street flashed past, I decided to change my tactics and stay where I was: let the exits come to me! I'd stop shuttling back and forth, and just sit here till 4th Street came up. Or, if that ramped off the other side, 3rd Street.

I drove on. No 4th Street on this side. I drove further. No 4th Street on the other side either. I drove. Still no fucking 4th! I whizzed along, craning my neck to look to the sides, and away ahead, but it was true: there was no exit to 4th Street, let alone 3rd, 2nd or 1st! But up ahead there *was* a slip road! It led . . . somewhere! Off this Road of Sudden

Death! (Something an Environmental Christian said to me once flashed into my mind: In the midst of traffic we are in death. They're not a big group, the ECs; their main tenet of faith is that Christ's cross was made of wood from a managed, sustainable forest.)

I dived off the Interstate at the exit, keeping my foot to the floor till I was well clear of the torrent. Then I slowed, looked around, tried to work out where the hell I was, what the road signs said, why there was an enormous razor-wire fence and men with machine guns up ahead.

Ah-ha! I was about to penetrate a high-security area, that's why. Sheppard Air Force Base, 'Headquarters, Euro-Nato Joint Jet-Pilot Training'.

I pulled into the side of the road, wiped the sweat off my hands and forehead, and consulted the city-map up the back of my road atlas. I cross-referenced to my list of cheap hotels, then set off back down Sheppard Access Road.

Wichita Falls would probably not be near the top of anybody's list in the Must-Visit-In-Texas stakes. Including the folk who actually live there. Back in the Forties and Fifties it had been home to a great western swing outfit called the Miller Brothers Orchestra – one of whose members, Sam Gibbs, became Bob Wills' manager in his declining years. But they're long gone. Apart from that, there's the Air Force base, a few oil company offices, a restored nineteenth-century mansionette called The Kell House ('seven fire-places!'). There's a small university, the usual malls and McDonald's, a couple of streets of big houses, and a hundred streets of small, nondescript houses, slowly baking to pieces in the hot, dry climate (which is better, admittedly, than being instantaneously flattened by a tornado such as the one that hit the city in April 1979, killing 53 people.) And Interstate 44 runs right through the middle of it.

I avoided the mad highway this time, and took side streets and residential roads instead, going under 44's flyovers once or twice, tracking down the town's hotels.

The first place I tried, the Econo Lodge, was full up. So was the second, The Hampton Inn. Just up the road was the Ramada: full. Then La Quinta: no vacancies. Further down Central Freeway was the Traveller's Inn, and the Days Inn: both jam packed, no room at the inns. I was amazed. Every night of my trip so far I'd just rolled up, strolled into reception, and got a choice of rooms: ground floor or first, facing out or in, smoking or non. What was so special about Wichita Falls that all 1,154 of its hotel beds were occupied? Nothing visible to the naked eye.

I tried the last name on my list, the Trade Winds Hotel on Broad Street. Full up. The clerk said I could always try the Sheraton. It sounded expensive, but I was getting desperate. Night had fallen. In the time it had taken for 'Can I have a room/sorry we're full/oh shit/you could always try the Sheraton,' the blazing sun had disappeared and black night swept in across the parking lot. And the rest of the city. So not only had I nowhere to lay my head for the night, I couldn't even see where it was that I wasn't able to lay it.

I walked into the plush reception of the Sheraton. Hello, I said, I was wondering if you had . . .

Sorry, we're full, said the clerk.

Oh shit, I muttered.

You could always try . . .

It's no use, I've tried them all!

I'm sorry. Let me check. She looked at her computer screen. Oh, yes!

Yes?

We have vacancies for tomorrow night.

Tomorrow?

Yes sir!

Well . . . if I did book a room for tomorrow, how early could I check in?

How early were you thinking of, sir?

About twenty-four hours early.

She frowned. Like, *now?* I'm afraid that wouldn't work.

I sighed, was about to turn away and head off in search of a shady lay-by, when I thought I'd have one more try. Spreading my list of hotels out on the counter in front of her, I said, Maybe you can give me some information. Is there really nowhere else but these places in the whole city?

She glanced down at the list, then away again, shifting uneasily. I'm not really supposed to help John Does, she said. Unless they're guests. In which case they're not John Does.

How *can* I be a guest? I cried. You're full up!

She shrugged.

Alright, alright, I said. What if I were to say I'd like to book a room, right now, for tomorrow night?

She looked at me. *Are* you saying that?

I sighed. Yes, I am saying that.

Very good sir! Would you like smoking or non-smoking? North or south facing? How would you like to pay? Breakfast is not included, but a full choice is available from . . .

Listen, I said, We'll do that in a minute. But let's sort something out for tonight first, eh?

Certainly, sir! I'd be delighted! Let me see your list. She frowned over it, then shook her head. I'm afraid if they're all full, you'll have to go up to Lawton.

Lawton, where's that?

Oklahoma. About seventy-five miles north of here.

But listen, it's pitch dark out there, everybody's driving like maniacs. I'm likely to end up at the bottom of the Grand Canyon if I get into that traffic!

No sir: that's in Arizona, not Oklahoma.

Plus, I'm meant to be meeting somebody here for breakfast. An old friend I've never met before.

Oh dear. She frowned. Well, there is always . . . *no.*

No, what?

Oh, nothing.

You were going to say something there, a name, a place I could stay.

I don't think you'd like it.

As long as it's got a bed I'll like it fine! I can't drive seventy-five miles now and then all the way back in the morning for cinnamon rolls and coffee. It's mad!

Well, she said, then hesitated, a pained look crossing her face.

Well?

There is the . . . River Oaks Motel. She whipped her head round to see if either of the other clerks had heard her suggestion and were coming after her with pitchforks. They weren't, so she looked back to me, leant forward on the counter. I wouldn't recommend it, she whispered. In fact I'm absolutely *not* recommending it. But you might get a room there.

Great! I said. Can I phone from here? Have you the number? No, better still, you phone for me.

Ehm, alright. If you're sure.

I nodded, and she stepped to one side, spoke into a phone for twenty seconds, holding the receiver all the time between thumb and first finger, as if it were contaminated with something or other. Then she hung up and turned back towards me, a smile of sorts across her face.

There was some kind of argument going on in the lobby of the River Oaks Motel. The fat stubble-faced man behind the desk didn't want to give a room to the thick-necked skinhead and the young girl in party clothes.

I don't want none of that trouble like we had last night, the clerk shouted.

I wasn't here last night, the youth shouted back.

Fighting in the courtyard! Cops all over the place! How'd you like that?

Come *on*, Rocky, said the girl.

Sir, said the youth, I am with the US Air Force – I am not interested in violence.

The girl laughed.

The clerk glared at her, then wiped the back of his hand across his mouth. Cash, he said.

After they'd cleared off I stepped up to the desk. The fat clerk glanced over from the war film he'd turned back to. We're full, he said loudly. He had to speak loudly, because the telly was turned up high and he was six inches away from it.

I booked, I said.

No you didn't.

Well, somebody booked for me. From the, eh, Sheraton. He looked me up and down. On the phone, five minutes ago.

He heaved up from his TV chair, came over to the counter. Twenty-six bucks, he said.

I gave him my credit card, he ran it through his machine and punched a few numbers in. The machine beeped. He frowned. Well well well . . .

What is it?

Rejected. Over your limit, boy.

It can't be!

He tossed the card across the counter at me. Got another one you'd like to try?

No. But, eh, I should have some money . . .

You better have, boy.

I emptied my pockets and came up with enough crumpled notes and chicken-shit coins to pay him. He fished a key out from under the counter, slammed it down. Have a nice night, he said, heading back to John Wayne v. The Japs.

The motel was two prefab stories high, arranged round a car park. I drove in, swerving to avoid a couple of speeding pick-ups racing out, and found my room, on the ground floor near the end of the block nearest the Interstate. I lugged my bag inside, looked around.

Everything in the room was thin. The carpet was threadbare; the bed had one sheet on it and one blanket no thicker than the sheet; the only furniture was a wire-legged kitchen chair and a Formica television; the curtains were gauzy and orange, and the courtyard security lights glared through them. Worst of all, the walls and the door were like matchwood. From the room next door came television noises, a man talking in a low urgent voice, and a woman protesting shrilly; I couldn't tell if the argument was on the telly or actually going on in there. From outside came the noise of a car over-revving, somebody laughing, a snatch of blasting heavy rock; the sounds echoed around the court, booming and screeching.

I unpacked my bag and took my toothbrush through to the shower-room. There was a strange smell in there, a burnt, meaty smell, like somebody had been barbecuing roadkill in the sink. The towel was made of a thin, bandage-like material, and treated with some kind of water-repellent that made it quite impossible to dry my dripping hands after I'd washed them.

Back in the bedroom, I lay across the bed and tried to write a few notes on the day's drive. I found myself scribbling derogatory things about towns I hadn't even stopped in. How could I possibly say that Paris was an ugly, depressing place when all I'd done was zoom on a loop road through its industrial outskirts? Terrible. But if I didn't write that, then what the hell could I write about it? 'Dear Reader, As I was unable to settle in Paris, Texas, and live there for a couple years, getting to know its quiet backstreets, its hidden charms, its friendly inhabitants, its cultural highspots, its lively nightlife, I feel I have no right to say anything about it whatsoever. Goodnight.'

Jesus, I was getting myself in knots. It was hard to concentrate, there was that much noise going on. Outside tyres were birling, engines throbbing, brakes screeching. Upstairs somebody was pacing the floor in cowboy boots. Doors were banging somewhere, hard enough to make my walls shake. The argument in the next room reached a crescendo; then there was a sudden silence, a slamming door, and almost immediately a gurgling roar: the pick-up parked next to my car speeding off.

I thought I heard the woman next door crying. But I might've been wrong, it might've been the telly. No, it wasn't the telly.

I gave up on writing (as so many times before – usually for worse reasons) and grabbed over the phone. I called the free number on my card to try and find out why I hadn't been allowed to charge a measly $26. The line clicked and fizzed, then contact was made. I should've known that I'd get through to the credit card HQ in Milton Keynes or somewhere, but still it was a shock to hear the telephonist's strident English voice – the first British accent I'd heard for weeks. I gave all the details and asked if there was some problem with my account.

No, said the voice of England.

So why was I not allowed twenty-six dollars on it?

I have no record of such a transaction being denied, she said.

But it was only ten minutes ago!

Ah . . . We did have a call from a River Oaks outlet in, eh, Wichita Falls. In TX. But that was a request for $20,364. And that's above your credit limit.

Too right!

So that was that. I lay back on the bed, wondering if the fat clerk had made a mistake, if his fingers had been too thick or clumsy to hit the right keys, or if he'd deliberately tried to charge me 783 times the proper rate for the room . . . The worrying thing was, he could probably have charged 7 or even 83 times the proper amount, and I'd never have known. Until I tried to buy some fuel or food next day, and found myself busted: washed up in Wichita Falls.

I looked at my watch. Only nine o'clock. I didn't fancy going out and playing marbles with the traffic again, though. What was I going to eat? I rummaged amongst my clothes, found a bag of marshmallow cookies Maryann Plott had thrust upon me, and pulled it open. Mixed in with the clothes was my Walkman and a couple cassettes. I stuck the headphones on, and listened to my jaws working noisily for half a minute till I found the tape I wanted: the town's finest, the Miller Brothers Orchestra.

First up was 'Marcheta', a Spanish tinged love song set to a swaying swingbeat, with mariachi-style horns backing the singer and breaking out in swaggering brassy solos between verses. Next came 'Miller's Boogie', a driving twelve-bar instrumental, with a riff-based arrangement featuring sophisticated sax and piano interplay. Count Basie might have come up with something very similar and seen that it was good.

Were the Miller Brothers influenced by Basie? I could guess
yes – after all, what swinging band of the Forties and Fifties
wasn't? – but in truth I just don't know. In fact, I don't know
much about them at all, despite the fact that, in 1955, *Cashbox*
magazine rated them the third most successful western group
in the USA. I know that the core of the band really was a
bunch of brothers, and that their name was not really Miller,
but Gibbs. I know they started up shortly after the war, and
disbanded in the mid-Sixties. (But even this last statement is
muddied by fact, the band didn't actually split up, as such.
They just sold their name – to a fiddler called Bobby Rhodes,
from San Jon, New Mexico. What he did with the name I
have no idea.) I know that they owned a night-club called the
MB Corral, and played there regularly, as well as broadcasting
six days a week in classic Texas territory band style. When
they were away on tours, other big name acts would be
booked in to play their night-club; from this grew a booking
agency, Sam Gibbs' Orchestra Service, and, ultimately, Sam's
managership of Bob Wills.

They recorded a handful of great swinging songs for Delta
Records in 1947, then went on to back vocalist Tommy
Duncan in the studio after he left the Texas Playboys. In
the late Fifties they laid down total of about fifty songs for
4-Star Records, though I've never heard any of them. My
favourite of the early sessions is 'Shanty Town', a jazzed-up
version of the old tin pan alley hit, 'A Shanty in Old Shanty
Town'. Its hep lyrics had gained a whole new depth since I'd
been driving around the band's home town, and I decided I
should try and get them all down on paper. I got my notebook
and pen, and played the song over and over on the Walkman,
marvelling each time at Lee Cochran's rip-it-up trumpet solo,
stumbling each time on certain tricky phrases.

It's only a shanty on a little plot of ground
With the green grass growing all around, all around
Something old roofs are bending way down
                                    [Slanty? Plenty?]
On most of the shacks they are touching the ground

Just a little old shack and it's built way back
About twenty-five feet from the railroad track
Something something *and my old black flivver*
                              [With my old rocking chair?]
I'll head right back to the Mississippi River

If I were as sassy as Haile Selassie
And I were a king, it wouldn't mean a thing
But the boots in the hall read the writing on the
   wall   [?]
Now it don't mean a thing, not a doggone thing

There's a queen waiting there in a rocking chair
Just blowing her top on 'gator's beer   [what's that?]
Looking all around and trucking on down
Now I gotta get back to my shanty town

That's as close as I could get. Words never look as good
written down as when you're listening to them being belted
out by some top-notch tonsils over a swinging backbeat. I still
like the line about Haile Selassie, though I'm not sure what it
means. Maybe it don't mean a thing, not a doggone thing.

Even through the music, noises kept seeping in from
outside, and the state I was in they were making me nervous. I kept thinking I heard thumping on the door, or
somebody scratching at the window. But when I whipped
the headphones off there was nothing there. Well, there was
plenty there, but it was nothing personal. Just the same, I gave
up on transcribing the lyrics and put the Walkman back in
my bag.

Engine noise, sharp braking, a clinking of bottles, a wall-
shivering door-slam. My nextdoor neighbour was home. A
few seconds later I heard his voice, a low but hard-edged
murmur. Then the woman said something, then he replied,
louder this time. I lay back, pulled the pillow over my
head. I suddenly had the feeling that I'd walked into a
Charles Bukowski short story: the fleapit motel, the bottles

of cheap wine, the broken-nosed old drunk, pissed on his winnings from the dogtrack, alternating between slapping and fucking the even drunker young woman he'd picked up in some last-chance saloon. Any minute I expected to hear the sound of classical music coming through the wall – who'd've thought a desperate smashed-up drunk like that would listen to Beethoven! – and somebody beating hell out of a battered old manual typewriter, declaiming the lines of poetry as he bashed them out:

Stuck in River Oaks
the leg-man and the broad
with the legs
drank themselves stupid.

If they weren't
stupid enough
before.

But who gives a damn?
Drink tonight, for tomorrow we
die!
(And I'm not talking
about my reading
at Midwestern State University.)

'Why must you smoke those Goddam cigars in bed?'
she said.
'I always smoke after sex,'
I replied.
'But we haven't had sex, you bastard,'
she cried.
'*You* haven't,'
I said, and laughed myself sick.

'And one more thing,'
I said as I wiped my mouth on my old stained shirt,
'If that Goddam limey next door

doesn't stop writing down
what I'm saying
RIGHT NOW,
I'm going to break through this wall
And rip off his balls.'

And there's not many poets
who can say that
and mean
it.

In short, I felt that things could not get much worse.

I turned on my telly. An ancient episode of *Are You Being Served?* was on. Jesus, things had just got worse.

Right, this was it. Levels of boredom, anxiety and depression were high enough that I was officially declaring a State of Personal Emergency. That meant emergency solutions were called for. I went out to the car, recalling some lines from a novel (*Beer In The Snooker Club* by Waguih Ghali) that I read about ten years ago, and that have always stuck in my mind:

What do people who do not drink do on such occasions?
Face the facts perhaps. But facing a fact is one thing,
and overcoming it is another. Cognac was going to
overcome the facts.

I opened the boot of the car. Stashed up the back was a duty free bag. I'd been carrying it around for three weeks untouched, but at last its moment had come. I pulled it out, closed the boot-lid, and stood there looking all around. There were lights on in most of the rooms around the courtyard, and quite a few doors were standing open, despite the evening chill. Different telly programmes and different varieties of music were blasting out of more than a few rooms. Up on the access balcony of the block opposite, a bunch of teenagers were running in and out of each others' rooms. Half a dozen shirtless guys sprayed each other with shook-up beer cans, then charged through an open door. There were yells and screams, and they ran out again, laughing, and disappeared into the next room. Then a bunch of girls in shorts and cut-off vests came out of the first room, looked around, and dived in after the boys, skirling. More laughter and screams from inside, then the music turned up, then the door slammed shut.

I went back inside, got into bed, and started slugging the bottle of Glenlivet, trying to conjure up some happier images: the Miller Brothers' final grab at glory, their only appearance on film. It is 1972, and the band has been resurrected to play for a dance in a high-school gym. The movie is Peter Bogdanovich's *The Last Picture Show*.

Not enough hours later I was jolted awake. It was dark, my head was splitting, the phone was ringing. I grabbed the receiver, scrabbling for my watch on the bedside chair, before I remembered that I'd never taken it off.

I got the phone up to my ear. Yeah? Hello?

Tell Bobbi to get home, said a man.

What? It's the middle of . . .

Get her ass *up* here!

There's no Bobbi here, I said. You've got the wrong number.

What did you say? said the voice, slowing and slurring.

I said . . .

Fucking *Bobbi*, man, tell her to get up here.

I hung up, went through to the shower-room for a drink. The smell of burnt meat made me feel sick when I dipped my head to the tap. Through the vent on the window I could hear trucks thundering past on the Interstate twenty-five feet away. I tried to dry my hands, failed, went back to the bedroom. My heart was racing. I held my wrist up to the light coming through the orange curtains: three-thirty. God's sake.

The phone rang again. I jumped, looked at it. It kept on ringing. Somebody started muttering through the wall. I picked up the receiver, didn't say anything.

Tell Bobbi to get home, said the same voice.

Listen, I said, There's nobody called Bobbi here. There's just me, and *I'm* not Bobbi. Am I?

If she don't get up here I'm coming down and whip her ass. Yours too.

Here, don't start . . .

Bobbi Bobbi Bobbi, WHY?

My eardrum buzzed. Look, I said, I promise you . . .

I paused, waiting for the interruption. It didn't come. There was just silence down the line, then a swish of static. Or was it distant laboured breathing?

I promise you, I went on, There's no one called . . .

Tell her she's not getting in. She can come back now and BEG and I wouldn't . . . I wouldn't . . . I'll fucking KILL her man, I'll . . .

Listen, I said. Forget her: she's out of your life. Quite right too! You don't deserve her, man. Now sod off and leave me alone.

I hung up, then reached over and pulled the cable out of its socket by the floor.

A Good Man is Hard to Find

RADIO STATION K. W. B. G.   HUTCHINSON, KANSAS

Jack Moser

AND HIS OKLAHOMA PLAY BOYS

PHONE 125   ARTIST_____

I left the River Oaks an hour before I'd arranged to meet John Moen. I didn't want to be late: John was the reason I'd come to Wichita Falls. In fact, if it hadn't been for John, I'd probably never have come to Texas at all.

The previous night's nightmare driving had prepared me for the worst, and I'd allowed plenty of time to navigate just a few blocks. It seemed that John hadn't after all been joking when he'd warned me that, 'as the old settlers used to say, Wichita Falls was originally laid out by a drunken Indian riding a blind mule'.

But everything seemed so much easier on a sunny Sunday morning; the streets were quiet, almost empty, and I found his home in about five minutes. Shit: now I was far too early. I cruised on another block or so, and pulled up in the enormous car park of Luby's Cafeteria. I strolled over to the door, thinking I'd get a cup of something to pass the time. It was locked. Seemed the place opened at 11.45 on Sundays. What was the time? 11.43. I leant against the wall by the door, and gazed out across the crowded car park.

Jesus! Every car had a middle-aged couple in it, and they were all staring right at me, mentally undressing me. They were looking for the mark of Satan burned into my skin . . .

There was a clank behind me, and I jumped again. A lady in a pinnie was unlocking the door. Immediately the doors of every car in the lot swung open, and several hundred men, women and children climbed out, straightened and patted flat their Sunday best, and marched towards me. Or, to be exact, towards the door right behind me. Okay, they'd all been waiting first, but, what the hell, all I wanted was a coffee: I didn't fancy standing in line for six hours to get it. So I jumped the queue, nipped in in front of the lot of them.

I found a seat in the gymnasium-sized dining area, and sat sipping and watching families, couples, gangs of teenagers, posses of old folk, all tucking in to vast platefuls of grub: roast beef, mashed tatties, gravy, green beans boiled grey, fried mushrooms, buttered squash, eggplant stew, pinto beans, garlic bread, side salad, hot sauce. Plus soup and rolls to start, and peach cobbler and ice cream to finish. And beakers of iced tea all round. What was it with these folk? Had they not eaten since *last* Sunday? Then I noticed that just about every single goddarned one of them had a thick black, leather-bound book by their sideplate: bibles. Of course, they'd all been in church since dawn, hadn't had time for breakfast. Hey, maybe they didn't believe in making breakfast on a Sunday, cause it was working on the Sabbath! I stayed in a B&B in Torridon once where the landlady took that approach: she'd shovel endless porridge and scrambled eggs in front of you Monday to Saturday, but on Sunday you had to help yourself to cornflakes. Yup, that was it, these folk had been dreaming about lunch all through the sermon . . .

I'd been corresponding with John Moen for about three years. It happened this way. Once I got bitten by the western swing bug, I scavenged Scotland for secondhand records, bootleg tapes, and reissue CDs. They were thin on the ground. Sure, C&W was big there, and most keen country fans (but not even the most fanatical of jazz fans, unfortunately) had heard of Bob Wills. They could even reel off a few of his hits: 'Faded Love', 'San Antonio Rose', 'Roly Poly'. But nobody I met had much more than the same old greatest hits collections. Soon I came up against a dead end: I had all the western swing that Scotland could offer.

Then, on the back of a Presto Transcriptions LP I'd bought from a stall at the Glasgow Barras, I found an address in Oklahoma City: the HQ of the Bob Wills Roundup Association. I wrote, only to find from Glenn White, head honcho, that the Association had been wound up; as he put it, 'support has declined in the last few years, especially since so many of the old Texas Playboys are now deceased'. Glenn was able to give me, though, the address of a radio announcer in Wichita Falls, who he said had an extensive collection of Wills tapes available. I wrote, tentatively, to John Moen c/o KWFT, and received the first of many long, wry letters in return, and the offer of thirty-two ninety-minute cassettes: the Complete Recorded Works of Bob Wills and his Texas Playboys. I accepted. Imagine it: up till then I'd had maybe ten LPs, and thought I was doing well. Suddenly I had the equivalent of about sixty albums to explore.

Since then, John and I had continued to correspond, me with questions about the history of western swing, him with fulsome replies and more tapes. Tapes of newly discovered Wills transcriptions. Tapes of early influences on Wills, like the remarkable blackface yodeller Emmett Miller. Tapes of just about any recording artist between the years 1910 and 1960, that I happened to mention. Like Bob Crosby; I mentioned to John that someone had compared Crosby's band of the late Thirties to the Texas Playboys. The only similarity between the two groups, replied John, was that they both had leaders called Bob. Oh, and both bands played musical instruments. Still, he enclosed a great compilation tape of the Bobcats.

John's recent letters, all full of good advice on my trip to Texas – where to visit, who to talk to, which side of the

road to drive on – had been threaded with gloom, because
of the poor state of his health. He was, he said in one note,
suffering from:

1. Ear infection.
2. Psoriasis of the private parts.
3. Prostate problems.
4. Kidney infection.
5. Gall stones.
6. Diabetes.
7. Insomnia.
8. Boils on the posterior.

He mentioned all this, not to evoke sympathy, but to explain
the deterioration in his handwriting, and to make me understand that he wouldn't be an active native guide to Wichita
Falls. But still he was keen to visit with me.

John's address was 2913, but he didn't live in the house with
that number. Nor did he live in the granny flat out the back
of 2913. His home was a little wooden shack out the back of
the granny flat out the back of 2913.

I knocked. Come in! called a bass voice, and I stepped
inside. It was very dark, very hot, and very smoky – and
there was John, struggling to get up from an old settee under
the tightly blinded window. He grunted, made it, stumbled
over to me. We looked each other up and down, laughed,
and shook hands. For the first ten minutes we kept talking
over each other, but then we began to get accustomed to each
other's rhythms, and were able to really talk, and start getting
to know each other in a way you can't by letter, no matter
how long you correspond. The tone of voice. The draws on
the cigarettes that punctuate the jokes. The times you catch
somebody's eye, and the times you don't.

John was tall, balding, with a cropped grey beard and thick
glasses. The lenses of his specs were smeared with gluey
fingerprints. I was surprised he could see anything at all.

I'm so darn clumsy these days, said John. It's this diabetes,

it's made my feet and my hands go numb. I can't feel a thing!
So I trip up. I break my glasses. And when I try to fix them,
my fingers get fuddled and I mess them up. He shook his head,
inhaled. Who cares! I could find my way around here even in
the dark!

It was noon, but the door was shut, and the windows were
covered with slat-blinds. The walls, ceiling and floor were all
made of pitch pine, and every surface was stained with years of
cigarette smoke. Only a single low-watt lamp burned on the
coffee table, by John's ashtray. It *is* dark, I said.

John looked around, as if surprised, then chuckled. I don't
like to let the heat out, he said.

It *is* hot, too, I said.

Is it? No air conditioning, see. He shrugged. I don't notice
it. I feel cold. I'm an old man. Sixty-five!

I laughed, and he did too. That's not old, I said.

What's that? he said. What d'you say, young un?

You should get new glasses though.

I can't get to the opticians, he said. Can't see to drive.

Don't be daft. I'll drive you.

No no no. He shook his head. I don't want new glasses.
These'll see me out. Ha ha! See me out!

He shuffled over to the fridge – there was a kitchenette at
one side of the room – and got me a can of coke. I can't
drink these no more, he said. Too much sugar. I'll give you
the whole lot when you go.

What about all your illnesses, John? How are you feeling
these days?

He shook his head. Let's not talk about that, he said. Here, I
want to show you my photo album. It's not often I get a visitor
to tell my life-story to!

We sat on the settee and leafed through the album. All the
pictures were captioned with jokey identifications of who,
when and where. John expanded on everything we looked at,
till I wished I'd had a tape-machine handy to record his stories.
They blazed with life, and humour, and strong emotion: pride,
anger, loneliness, love.

John's father had come over from Norway in 1906, while

still a teenager. The boat journey, including all meals, had cost twenty-five dollars. (I laughed: even the River Oaks cost more than that now – for one night!) Old man Moen had worked at various jobs – there were pictures of him on a cattle ranch, in chaps and spurs – before settling in Duncan, Oklahoma, about sixty miles north-east of Wichita Falls. Oklahoma had become a state as recently as 1907, and was still wide open for all sorts of enterprise. But Moen had met a girl from Arkansas, they were fixing to get married, so he started up in a small way as a boot and saddle maker. There was a photo of him in a long apron, standing in front of a small shop with his name on it. Then another picture, some years later, of a bigger shop, and four staff in their aprons standing beside him.

John Moen was born in 1928, grew up both sporty and bookish. He studied journalism, played college football, then went on to a long career in radio and TV, in both Oklahoma and Texas. Eventually he ended up in Wichita Falls, where he lived at the YMCA for no less than seven years after his arrival. I'd be there still, he said, But they needed the bed. So he found this hut – I suppose it had been the maid's quarters originally, though 2913 didn't look big enough to have required a maid – and had been here ever since.

He read avidly, was a keen bowler (trophies lined the top of the bookcase), smoked non-stop. He never married, didn't travel, rarely drank. It's not that I *don't* drink, he said, It's just that it never occurs to me to buy the stuff. Judging by films of England I've seen, you can't walk into somebody's house without having a glass of liquor thrust into your hand. Well, it's not like that here.

I rolled my eyes. So I've noticed.

He laughed.

His interest in the music of his childhood gradually crystallised around Bob Wills, and he determined to build up a complete collection of all the music Bob ever recorded. He wasn't interested in the records, you understand – he borrowed most of them from disparate sources, and sold the few he had acquired with little regret when his medical bills started mounting – it was just the *music*. It took him ten years, three thousand dollars, and a lot of late night taping at the studios. And I was one of just five folk he'd copied his collection for. (One of the others was Glenn White, and another was a retired musician and pro ball player down in Del Rio. Who were the other two, I wondered, who were lucky enough to share in the bumper results of John's labours?)

His own copy of the collection, and his scores of classic film videos, were arranged neatly, with meticulous labelling, on the homemade wooden shelves that flanked his hi-fi. In fact, everything in the house was neat and ordered; the only things that looked at all out of place were the model planes that John had carved out of scrap wood, and painted in bright dayglo colours. Half a dozen of these hung from the ceiling on thread, swaying gently in the updraft from the heaters.

For the past few years he'd been DJing a weekly request show on KWFT, playing nostalgic stuff, mostly: Gene Austin, Paul Whiteman, the Coon-Sanders Nighthawks. And, of course, Bob Wills. He'd loved doing that show, and it had been real popular, with requests and letters coming in from all over north Texas and south-west Oklahoma. He got corresponding with a lot of people all over through that radio show. Including a real nice couple, the Montgomerys, up in Turkey, Texas. He'd have to give me their address, seeing as I was planning on going there for the Bob Wills Memorial Weekend.

And remember, I said, *I* wrote a request to you once: for an Emmett Miller tune, wasn't it?

He smiled. Yeah, that was the second most distant request I ever got.

I raised my eyebrows. Only second?

Yeah, one time somebody I'd heard had died the week before requested 'La Marseillaise'. I don't know where *exactly* he was writing from, but I'm sure it was further away than Orkney, even!

Then he'd been struck down with illness. He'd been unable to keep up his show, and, having never had enough spare money to invest in medical insurance, was relying now on Social Security. Medicare was paying for the treatment of his

kidney problem and his diabetes, but the other problems . . .
they were being left to their own devices.

That sounds bad, I said.

He shrugged, fumbled to light another cigarette. Let's not
talk about it. He inhaled, leant back in the settee. Did I ever tell
you that my dad and my grandfather are both in the Country
Music Foundation? he said. They were no great shakes as
singers, but they made a tape for me of songs no one else in
the family remembered. Ha! Turned out no one else in the
world remembered them! So that tape's in the museum now.
He looked at me, grinning. It makes me laugh. They couldn't
sing for peanuts, and they're in a musical museum! It just goes
to show . . .

He didn't complete the sentence. It goes to show what? I
asked, at last.

He stubbed out his cigarette, sat back, then leant forward,
lit another cigarette, and said, Anything you do, you should
do it cause you love it. Makes no difference if somebody else
tells you you're good at it, or bad at it. What do they know?
Forget them. *Do it for the love of it.*

After a while, John's girlfriend, Pat Watson – somebody else
he'd got to know through his radio show – came round.
A short, serious woman in electric-blue slacks, Pat told me
how much she loved John, how much everyone loved him,
and how he drove her crazy too: he just *refused* to look after
himself. He'd do anything for anybody else, but nothing for
himself.

Then John came out of the bathroom and we left the house.
I was amazed to see that he left his door unlocked. Where did
he think he was? Orkney? He just laughed. I've nothing worth
stealing, he said.

We ate a late lunch, not at Luby's, but at another cafeteria,
Piccadilly's, in a mall on the far side of town. John couldn't
take meat, nor anything sweet, as he was trying to control his
diabetes through diet.

He can't afford insulin, said Pat.

It's not that, said John. I just don't like needles.

After a long meal – with John apologising all the time for being so clumsy with his cutlery, this was why he never ate in public any more – they took me on a tour of the mall, and insisted on buying me a cowboy hat in Wal-Mart. Wal-Mart was Texas's answer to Scotmid, and the first ten hats I tried on made me look like a reject from the Beverly Hillbillies. The eleventh, though, a wide-brimmed black felt number, was a perfect fit, and pretty darn cool. John chose it for me, plonked it down on my skull, then stood back and laughed. That's what I call cool.

We sat in a moulded plastic seat in the lobby of the mall, so John could have his cigarette. Pat was having a look around a shoe shop.

Well, John said after a minute, I guess you better be getting along.

You fed up with me already?

Ha, no! But Texas is a big place, and it sounds like you've a lot to see.

Definitely Fort Worth, definitely Austin; probably San Antonio, maybe El Paso . . .

All in four weeks?

A bit less than that now.

Don't forget Turkey!

You ever been there, John?

Nope. Never got round to it. Funny, eh? It's only a hundred miles away and I've never been. And here's you, come all the way from Scotland to go to it!

Do you want to come with me? I could pick you up in a couple weeks, and . . .

No no no. He shook his head, took a long drag on his Marlboro. I'm too old and sick for that now. You go, tell me all about it. Okay?

Okay. I nodded. It's a deal.

Dog House Blues

I drove down Central Freeway, skirted the trees and flower-beds of beautiful Lucy Park, and pulled into the luxurious car park of the stately Sheraton Hotel. At the reception, I explained that I hadn't slept well the night before, and needed a nice quiet room. And block all calls, I said. Though seeing as nobody but John knew where I was, and he didn't have a phone, I don't know why I bothered. They put me on the top floor, my picture window facing south over the park. Well away from thundering traffic, rampaging teenagers, drunken wifebeaters. Lovely. And a trouser press all to myself! I could crimp my hair in that later on. I dumped my bags and lay down. A couple hours sleep would do me the whirl of good.

I couldn't get to sleep. I kept thinking of John lying in his stifling shack, and me here in the damn Sheraton. It didn't seem fair. But hey, that's the American way, I thought to myself. It was no consolation.

Somewhere along the road I'd picked up a newspaper called
the *Weekly World News*, a hard-hitting, highly informative
tabloid which (in tandem with another similar journal, the
National Enquirer) seemed to provide most folk I met with
their insights into the world's current affairs. I fished it out
of my bag, and propped myself up on some of the pillows
to read.

The lead story in this particular issue was headlined:

SATAN'S BURIAL GROUND FOUND!

Graveyard full of horned skulls
proves Devil's army walked the Earth,
says scientist!

A report from Phoenix, Arizona – squeezed on to page 8 by
the size of the front page headline – revealed that:

> The discovery of thousands of horned skulls in a mass
> grave west of here proves that a satanic army of demons
> has walked the earth throughout history, bringing untold
> pain and misery to mankind.

There was some scientific stuff detailing where the grave
was, and what the skulls were like, and the archaeological
techniques that had been used to uncover them – all a bit
technical for me. But the ending really struck home:

> Bible scholars and clergymen are particularly interested
> in the find. Dr Margaret Terrell, author of the book,
> *Demons Among Us*, said: As far as I am concerned, the
> discovery of this demon burial ground is just another in
> a series of modern miracles that proves the end of the
> world is near.

I hoped the world wouldn't end before I got back to Orkney,

or, at the very least, before the Bob Wills weekend in Turkey at the end of the month. I didn't want to have come all the way here, just for the planet to explode before I got to meet the Texas Playboys.

The next story I came to really cranked up my worries, though. For in it the *WWN* uncovered more proof that the end is nigh. (The paper obviously takes a strong editorial stance on the end of the world.) **NASA uncovers new sign of the End Times**, it said:

Earth moving through space at 66,666 m.p.h. – THE SPEED OF SATAN!

Earth orbited the sun at a speed of 65,992 m.p.h. for billions of years, but all that changed on February 23, when the planet mysteriously sped up and started orbiting at 66,666 m.p.h. – the Speed of the Satan!

'Everybody knows that 666 is the Bible's Mark of the Beast. Well, 66,666 is the "Speed of the Beast" – and yet another sign that the end of the world is at hand,' Dr Catherine Renard, the famed Bible scholar, told reporters.

'It is my belief that God has changed the speed of orbit as a sign to men who have eyes to see and ears to hear.

'Unfortunately, the United States government has chosen to keep this information secret, which makes our officials pawns of Satan in the most dangerous "game" the world has ever known.'

Dr Renard's claims were proven by the fact that White House officials would neither confirm nor deny the story.

On a more cheering note, *WWN* was also able to report an alternative scenario, wherein the world might survive for several centuries more, at least long enough for the United States' cultural dominance over the rest of us to be made even more comprehensive. Next to a photo of Price Charles with a speech bubble saying **Howdy y'all!** superimposed, and the caption, **Future English monarchs will probably learn to**

speak English as good as the rest of us, was an incisive
report by Ed Anger:

> I'm madder than Dumbo the Elephant with earache
> over a comment made recently by that idiot Prince
> Charles of England.
>
> This prissy, polo-playing potentate says that Brits
> speak the only proper English and that Americans are
> ignorant bumpkins who have trashed the language.
>
> 'We must act now to ensure that English – and that, to
> my way of thinking, means English English – maintains
> its position as the world language well into the next
> century,' sniffed the prince. 'The illiterate Americans
> are well on their way to destroying our noble language
> by creating bogus words and phrases and misusing those
> that already exist.'
>
> Well, excuuuuuuuse me, you flap-eared, horse-faced
> imbecile.
>
> The truth is, the only Brit I've ever been able to
> understand was the late, great funnyman Benny Hill.
> In plain English, folks, the people of England talk
> gibberish.
>
> If the Brits can talk so damn good, why the hell don't
> they tell each other to take a bath once in a while?

So far – with the minor quibble that I never thought Benny
Hill was all that funny – so good. I could imagine reading
the same report in a similar quality Scottish newspaper – the
Sunday Post for example – with the word 'Scots' replacing
'Americans'. That would accurately reflect the opinions of
the ruling classes of Britain, no doubt about it. Then the
warmth of Ed Anger's argument led him a bit off course:

> And if you can understand ANYTHING anybody from
> Scotland says, you're a goldurned genius. Whatever the
> Scots paid for English lessons way back when, they
> oughta get their money back, if you ask me. They

talk like they've got their mouth full of crumpets, for Pete's sake.

Now I know why the Scots invented Scotch tape – so they could put it over each other's lips and not have to listen to the way they're butchering the language.

Well, excuuuuuuuse me, Mr Anger! I don't think we did invent Scotch tape – tarmacaddam, steam engines, postage stamps, telephones, television and golf maybe, but not that stuff. Get your facts right!

He made up for his errors, though, in his closing paragraphs:

> But what makes me so pig-biting mad is this sissy Prince Charles accusing us of making up words. Sounds to me like he's ticked off because the Brits aren't smart enough to add a little bit to the language now and then.
>
> And I'll bet you a dollar to doughnuts that when the King of England greets somebody a few hundred years from now, he'll stick out his hand and say, Howdy, y'all.

I'm sure he was right on this last point. And on the previous one too, except that he should have said the *English* aren't smart enough and so on. Because of course Scottish folk (including a fair number of writers) have become extremely good at making up words recently.

About this time, forfauchlet, I dovered ower into a sloom.

I woke to find the sun had shifted and was blazing straight in on me as I lay on the bed. I jumped up, and looked out the window; it was nearly six, but still very hot and bright. Time for a walk in the park.

I went downstairs and through the lobby, dodging two policemen and a Doberman rushing across its great expanse as I headed for the door. Aye aye, I thought, what's going on here? Outside in the car park was a big van with WICHITA FALLS DRUG ENFORCEMENT AGENCY on the side, and bars on the back windows. That's a bit ironic, I thought. Last night I was in a low-down dive in fear of my life, but it's the high-class pricey place the cavalry come charging into. Probably some rich kid in the penthouse suite tipped the porter with a gram of coke, gave the game away. I grinned to myself, and walked on through the rows of parked cars towards Lucy Park.

Paths wound through trees, lawns and flowerbeds, wandering up and down the steep banks of the Wichita River. Rollerbladers whooshed past me going downhill, and I strolled past them as they laboured at the next up slope. Meanwhile, the river flowed past, the colour of caramel. Exactly the colour of the caramel layer in a Mars bar. If you bit the chocolate off the top of a million Mars bars, and laid them all out on the river bed, then somehow melted the top layer so the brown sticky stuff melted and flowed, swirling round rocks, eddying about tree roots, then that would look pretty much how the Wichita River looked.

And here, as tanned tourists in khaki shorts gazed in wonder, the brown water was tumbling over brown rocks in four big leaps: the falls that gave the town its name. Ah, not quite. A study of the sign by the viewing benches revealed that the waterfall was in fact artificial, and only nine years old. Apparently the original falls washed away in the nineteenth century.

I turned and retraced my steps towards the hotel. I'd been out of my room for about thirty minutes, which I reckoned was at least two dollars-worth. An end to this reckless wastage. I'd go back to my room and have a couple baths, or something.

Imagine being so in thrall to the name of your town, that when your waterfall wore out you had to build a new one. What were folk worried about? That the Place-name Police would come galloping in shouting, Okay, so-called Wichita Falls, where's your goldurned *falls*? Eh? Eh? What do you mean they washed away? Not good enough! It's demolition for this town: sit back and Watch-it-all Fall! Haw haw haw!

On the other hand, it probably pulls in tourists. In this

parched part of the States, where the rainfall's been a quarter what it should've been over the past few years, a fifty-foot cascade of water probably ranks as a wonder of the world, no matter how brown it is. And I dare say that tourist authorities at home would build up grandiose artificial Edinburghs, Glasgows and Aberdeens – if only they knew what an Edinburgh looked like. What shape *is* a Glasgow? What colour *is* an Aberdeen? That was the thing about names here: they were so literal. Like, if you were building a town on the Wichita River, close to a waterfall, you called it Wichita Falls. If you lived in the middle of somewhere (or the middle of nowhere) you called your settlement Center. If a green spiky plant was sprouting up right where you wanted to stick your Main Street, you called the village Cactus. What opaque names there were, seemed to be either Indian in origin – Tahoka, Quitaque, Wichita itself – or else imported by European settlers – Edinburg, Abernathy, Strawn. (They weren't very good at spelling, these settlers, were they? The last name, applied to a small village a little west of Fort Worth, is surely nothing but a miswritten version of the Deeside hamlet of exactly that pronunciation. Of course, the *correct* spelling, the *Aberdeenshire* spelling, is Strachan.)

Thoughts of Aberdeenshire place-names prompted a minor revelation. The literalness of so many names in the USA is down to the fact that they haven't been around long enough for the language to change sufficiently to render them opaque. The name Three Rivers still indicates that three rivers meet nearby. But, as Ed Anger pointed out so forcefully, language is constantly changing. In a couple hundred years Three Rivers might be as non-referential as Torphins, (from the Gaelic *torr fionn*, white or light-coloured knoll), where I grew up, or Stromness, (from the Old Norse *straum nes*, point of land protruding into racing waters), where I live now. Aye, that's it exactly: if I'd been a bairn in Texas it would have been in Light-Coloured Knoll, and if I bade here now it would be in Protruding Point (pop. 32).

It was a new and strange experience for me to walk and drive through a landscape named so referentially. As

if everybody you met had a name that described their
appearance or character. But come to think of that, many
western swing musicians were known by just such names:
Tubby, Judge, Tiny, Sleepy, Rusty, Spike and Smokey
were not Another Seven Dwarfs, but all members of the
Texas Playboys.

Bob, like many a charismatic, patriarchal figure – Hemingway,
for instance – had a habit of bestowing nicknames on friends
and acquaintances, whether they wanted them or not. What
lies behind this, I wonder? A refusal, perhaps, to accept that
these folk were around with their own identities before Papa
ever noticed them? A desire to make them into kids again,
'Play*boys*' – babies even, so young that they haven't been
named yet – so they can be gathered more reasonably and
completely under the protective wing of the Old Man? I'm
sure that's partly the case, though no doubt it was good radio
to establish memorable, lovable characters with descriptive
nicknames.

I turned on to the narrow footbridge that led across the
river to the hotel, my head swirling in a mist of names and
places, signposts at the city-limits and certificates of baptism.
Suddenly there were shouts:

Look out!

Stop him!

STOP!

Charging towards me across the bridge came a big brown
flop-eared goat, with a little girl on a lead being dragged along
behind, racing to keep up and keep her feet. A middle-aged
woman, a prick-eared boxer and two teenage kids were
running after it from the far bank, shouting and waving
their arms:

Trudy, stop!

STOP HIM!

Don't let him get away!

The dog barked.

The whole lot of them were careering straight for me,
the narrow rope-hung bridge swaying under their weight,

tipping the narrow surface of it at an angle to the rushing brown water below. I hesitated, froze.

That was exactly the thing to do, it seemed. The goat looked up, saw me standing there, and froze too. The attached girl grabbed on to the bridge's handrail for support and anchor, and the whole family surrounded her and the goat half a second later.

Trudy, are you okay?

I'm fine Mommy, fine – he ran, I couldn't hold him, I couldn't . . .

Don't worry, hon, don't worry. She looked up at me, smiled. Thanks, she said. I was getting scared: Porsena is so headstrong! He just saw the grass over this side and *went* for it!

The older girl and boy, thirteen or fourteen, were climbing up on the ropes of the bridge, making it shudder violently, and causing the boxer to shiver and whimper.

Jane, Zack, get down from there! said their mother. Here, hold this rope. And DON'T LET GO!

Trudy didn't let go, said Zack, And look what happened to her: she was dragged to her death.

The young girl started to cry. I'm not dead! I'm not!

Quiet! shouted their mother. The boxer rolled over on its back. Thank you, she said, turning to me again. Thank you so much.

I shrugged. I really didn't do anything, I said. I just stood here and . . .

Oh! The woman threw up her hands. That accent!

Sorry, I said, I'll speak slower.

No! she cried. I love it! What is it? English?

No, Scottish actually.

She tilted her head on one side, looked sorrowful. You must be so sad.

It's not that bad really. The weather's not too hot, but . . .

No, she said, putting a hand out to pat my shoulder in sympathy. I'm talking about James Herriot. Didn't you hear? He died yesterday.

Oh . . . oh. Oh dear. That's a shame.

I cried all day. I was *so* upset. We *all* were, weren't we?

Yeah, muttered the kids, without much conviction.

We just love his books. We've read them all, every single one. There won't be any more! What'll we read now, eh kids?

There are other books though, I said.

There are? Scottish books?

Hundreds! There's Lewis Grassic Gibbon, Janice Galloway, James Kelman . . .

James Kelman, he sounds good. Is he like James Herriot?

Well, they're both called James.

Great! Thank you! She smiled broadly. Gee, I'm so glad we met you here.

Come *on*, Mom, said Jane.

All rightee, said Mom. Let's go. Trudy, hold my hand. Zack, Jane, go ahead. Tyson, *heel*. And Porsena, you just behave yourself, you naughty old goat you. Bye!

The car park of the Sheraton was packed with police cars, armoured vans, and even a couple big motor bikes with flashing lights and gleaming chrome. The cars had silver stars on their sides, and badges of a dozen different police departments: Fort Worth, Amarillo, Lawton, Oklahoma City, Little Rock, Abilene. Men and women in uniform milled about the vehicles, many of them straining to hold big muzzled dogs in check. Urgent conversation, walkie-talkie static and muffled barking filled the air. Jeez, I thought, This must be the biggest bust in Texas history. The management'll be mortified to have this going on in their posh hotel!

I walked through the lobby, and into the lift. A burly woman with a Labrador on a choke chain got in after me, and we zoomed up. Somewhere about the fifth floor the dog thumped its tail on the floor, caught my eye, and tried to give my hand a lick. The woman yarked it away from me, impassive.

We both got out on the top floor, and both turned right down the same long corridor. The corridor wasn't the restful, silent, air-conditioned avenue of plush it had been when I'd last seen it. Now dozens of men and women were standing drinking beer from bottles and laughing. Loud music played from a couple of competing ghetto-blasters. A man in a uniform grabbed hold of a woman in a red dress and tried to wrestle her to the floor – except it wasn't a woman, it was another man, in tarty drag. Behind the closed door of room 817 at least three dogs snarled and growled ferociously. Three policemen were playing a game that involved tossing their peaked caps down the corridor, trying to get them landed on top of the wall-mounted fire-extinguisher. The burly woman who'd chummed me up in the elevator followed me all the way down the corridor. Then, as I stopped and turned to unlock my door, she stopped too, kicked open the door of the room next to mine and shouted PARTY! before diving inside, the dog leaping after her.

I slammed the door behind me, and just stood there for a second. What the hell was going on? Outside in the corridor, something or somebody crashed on to the floor with a tremendous thump. There was laughter, and cheering, and the sound of beer cans popping and spraying. In the next room, an under-rehearsed choir started singing the theme from *Scooby Doo*. It was the River Oaks all over again! Maybe I'd been being unfair to the place, maybe *every* hotel in Wichita Falls was the Texan equivalent of last night at Club Med.

I rang down to reception. Look, I said, I don't want to stop anybody having any fun . . .

I beg your pardon? said the receptionist. It's a bad line.

It's not, I said. It's all the noise in the corridor here.

I can't hear you, she said.

Can I get another room? I shouted. I'll get no rest here!

I can't hear . . .

A trio of dogs howled right outside my door, drowning out her words. I hung up, grabbed my bag, and started stuffing into it the few things I'd unpacked earlier. Then I rolled up my *Weekly World News*, and walked out into the mad, birling corridor, hefting the bag, wielding the newspaper baton to fight off any attacks, canine or human.

He's got a body in there! shouted a policeman. Stop him!

He made a lunge for my bag, tried to grab it off my shoulder. His friends pulled him back, laughing.

A body! he yelled after me. He's getting away!

Various folk shouted and laughed at me as I dodged up the corridor. Somebody offered me a bottle of Becks. Somebody else barked at me. A man in a dress said, Hiya sweetie, you got a light? Eventually I reached the lift doors, which were just opening to let out more dogs, more police, and a giant inflatable banana. I ducked in past them, pressed the button for ground floor fifteen times, and threw the *Weekly World News* out the door just as the two halves of it slid shutwards. A delaying tactic, in case I was being followed.

Down in the lobby I told them I'd have to have a new room, the one I was in was impossibly noisy.

But it's on the top floor, the girl said. It's the quietest floor in the building!

Not today, it's not, I said. I don't know what it is, a raid or a rave, but it's one hell of a racket. Please, anything, anywhere, but just not there.

She pursed her lips, frowned, and gave me the key to room 214.

Waiting with my bag by the lift doors, I gazed around the lobby. A pinboard set up on an easel by the sitting area had big letters across the top of it – **SHERATON WICHITA FALLS WELCOMES** – and then smaller writing stuck on, slightly squint, underneath. I went a couple steps closer. Who was the Sheraton welcoming today? Of course: **The NATIONAL NARCOTIC DETECTOR DOG ASSOCIATION Annual Convention**.

Ping!

Eagle Riding Papas

HILLSIDE 8311

THE FRONTIERSMEN

PERSONAL BAND MANAGER
EDDIE LAWRENCE

6365 SELMA AVENUE
HOLLYWOOD 28, CALIFORNIA

I drove south out of Wichita Falls. The traffic seemed a lot lighter in this direction, or maybe I was just getting used to the madness of it. What am I saying? That I was going crazy? Quite possibly. I hadn't done a lot of travelling before I came to Texas. I'd only left Scotland a handful of times, and never travelled very far even then. And I'd never gone anywhere by myself. I remember reading a quote from Samuel Beckett once. My only ambition, he'd said, Is to sit on my arse and think about Dante. I could sympathise with that. My only ambition had been to sit on my arse and think about Bob Wills. But then I wrote a book of stories which won a prize, and the prize-money had to be spent on foreign travel. It wasn't in me to hand the cheque back, I just couldn't do it. I took the money, and found myself committed to going abroad till I'd spent the lot. For weeks I'd been depressed at the prospect. I wondered if I could buy a wee boat and sail a mile or so out into the Atlantic every day, then go home; would that count as leaving the country? Or would I have to leave British Territorial Waters, whatever they were? Then something occurred to me. If all I wanted to do was listen to Bob Wills, why not use the dosh to go to Texas, and listen to him on his home ground? Well, not Bob himself, cause he'd died in 1975. But I could visit the places he used to live, I could meet other western swing musicians who were still on the go, I could try and track down folk who used to know him, or play with him, if any of them were left. Aye, and most of the time I could be sitting on my arse – in the car, cruising across the prairies – with the good old Texas Playboys blasting out on the stereo.

And so it came to pass. Except I didn't have western swing playing as I headed down US Highway 281 – I had Icelandic indie pop. One of the few non-Texan tapes I'd taken with me was Bjork's first album, and one of the songs in particular had come to have great resonance for me since I'd been careering about the wide open spaces of the prairie interstates:

> *i live by the ocean*
> *and during the night*
> *i dive into it*
> *down to the bottom*
> *underneath all currents*
> *and drop my anchor*
>
> *this is where i'm staying*
>
> *this is my home*

Aye, it was strange to be cut off so completely from all the moorings I normally took for granted. I couldn't say that I liked or disliked this solitary wandering: liking didn't come into it. I could think back to places I'd travelled in Britain, and say, *I like Westray*, or, *I don't like Preston*, because they seemed small enough (in my memory, at least) to be spoken of as a whole, as a single entity. But Texas was far too big for such comments. And travelling through it was far too big an undertaking for such a brief summing-up to have any meaning. I was launched on this course, and had to follow it through to the end. It would be like me trying to decide whether I liked or disliked life. Some parts of it were enjoyable, some were exciting, and some were scary or depressing or tedious.

Okay, I'd only been in Texas a few days, and only had a few weeks till I'd have to leave again, but both of those boundaries seemed very remote to me as I passed through Scotland (pop. 440), Windthorst and Agnes – so far off as to be unimaginable. Back home, I couldn't drive for twenty *minutes* in any direction without meeting the edge of the island, the sea, and having to stop. To worry about the end of a journey that would last more than twenty days into the future was impossible for me. I was aware that there were a lot of places I wanted to go, a lot of folk I wanted to meet, a lot of music to hear and a lot of miles to cover, but that was just the way things were. I couldn't worry about the inevitable end of my trip any more than I could worry about my equally inevitable but even more distant (I hope) death.

I was the Existential Traveller, concerned only for the choices of the moment, defined by nothing more than what tape I chose to stick into the sound system next. Aye, music was the only sure thing in my little portable world. Everything else was relative and flexible: music was the one fixed point. And I had the *New Grove Dictionary of Jazz* in the boot (or should I say trunk) to prove it.

Territory Band. A term applied to dance bands of the 1920s and early 1930s that worked in a very large area bordered roughly by St Louis on the east and Denver on the west, and extending from Texas to Nebraska. It is normally used of bands that were based in small regional capitals and made extended tours of the outlying area, playing in local dancehalls. From the mid-1920s there were more than 100 active territory bands, among the most important being those of Alphonso Trent (Dallas),

Doc Ross (El Paso and Oklahoma City), Troy Floyd
(San Antonio), Walter Page (Oklahoma City), and Jesse
Stone (Missouri and Kansas).

Had the Grove editors allowed Stetsons and steel guitars
between their hallowed pages, they might have added such
names to this list as Bob Wills and his Texas Playboys (Tulsa,
Oklahoma); Milton Brown and his Musical Brownies, The
Crystal Spring Ramblers, The Light Crust Doughboys (all
Fort Worth); Tommy Hancock and his Roadside Playboys
(Lubbock); Billy Briggs's XIT Boys, The Pioneer Playboys
(both Amarillo); Hoyle Nix and his West Texas Cow-
boys (Big Spring); Adolph Hofner and his Texans, The
Tune Wranglers (both San Antonio); Roy Newman and
his Boys, Bill Boyd's Cowboy Ramblers (both Dallas); Doug
Bine's Dixie Ramblers (Waco); The Village Boys, Shelly
Lee Alley and his Alley Cats, Leon Selph and the Bar-X
Cowboys (all Houston); Cliff Bruner and his Texas Wan-
derers (Beaumont); The Miller Brothers Orchestra (Wichita
Falls). And many more.

For back in the Thirties and Forties, Texas – too enormous
to be dominated by any one band – was informally divvied
up between a score or so first-rate dance outfits. Top leaders
like Bob Wills, Milton Brown, and Adolph Hofner tended to
attract the finest musicians, the best-paying sponsorship, and
the recording contracts, all based on their rock-solid foundation in one well-defined geographical area. The definition
came largely from radio broadcasts.

All musicians active at this time have similar tales: of
broadcasting daily – for thirty minutes at noon, say – playing
requests, advertising sponsors' products, reading out listeners'
dedications, plugging forthcoming dances, before jumping
into the band bus and driving ten or fifty or two hundred
miles to set up for that night's dance. How far away they
travelled was determined by the distance they could drive and
still get back in time for the next day's show. Also relevant
was how far their radio station could broadcast: minor-league
outfits like KTUL in Tulsa might have 250-watt transmitters

that only reached a score or so miles, but its Goliath rival KVOO was a hundred times more powerful: when Bob Wills first played there, a free eight by ten photo was offered to the furthest flung listener; a man from Oakland, California, 1,800 miles west, claimed the prize.

After playing till midnight – or however late the audience demanded – the band would stagger back on to the bus hoping they'd get home in time for a few hours' sleep in their own beds before it was time to rendezvous at the studio for the next day's broadcast. Walt Kleypas, pianist and leader of the San Antonio band The Texas Top Hands, told me later how his band would be driving back from their relatively small-time gig in some town like Corpus Christi on the gulf coast, or Brownsville, way down on the Mexican border. They'd have the radio on in their bus, and hear Bob Wills and his Texas Playboys' late night broadcast on KVOO:

There they were, with their wonderful music, beaming all the way down from Oklahoma. Those beautiful horns! And there we were bumping along in our bus, fresh from some old honky-tonk . . .

Of course, this lifestyle was extremely exhausting and stressful. Musicians' health suffered, and so did their marriages. It would all have been a lot easier if the radio stations could've done without live broadcasts. But all the way through the Thirties, the record companies wouldn't allow their discs to be broadcast. They'd got the idea into their heads that broadcasting would reduce sales: why buy when you can listen free?

Later on, after the war, bands such as Bob Wills' would bypass this ban by laying down huge numbers of tracks in mammoth sessions specifically for radio play. Some of this excellent stuff has recently been reissued under the names of the promoting companies: the Presto Transcriptions, the Tiffany Transcriptions. Up in Turkey, I was to get the chance to talk to Johnny 'Texas Drummer Boy' Cuviello, who drummed with the Texas Playboys in 1946 and '47. He told me about his memories of recording non-stop, all day long: a hundred songs a day, he claimed.

We never rehearsed a number, he said. Bob would just recall a tune we knew, next second he'd be up on the bandstand: *Ready, set, go!* One number after another. In the can!

Selections of these tunes were then put on to sixteen-inch discs and sold to local radio stations across the land, where Bob's huge popularity would attract listeners and advertisers. Tiffany's sales pitch for their transcriptions called them:

A Sure-Fire Audience Builder for Your Station.
A Powerful Selling-Vehicle for Your Sponsors.

Another Tiffany ad lists 'a few of the selling successes' won by KLX, a Californian station using the recordings:

Pocket-type adding machines . . . . . 10,086 in 10 months
Candid cameras . . . . 5,000 in 4 months
Plastic Easter bunnies . . . . 4,000 in 2 months
Bob Wills picture give-aways . . . . . . 11,265 in 18 days

And, it adds, Bob Wills transcriptions are a sure cure for that dangerous listener malady – **dial fidgets**.

Radio stations would usually fake up their own programmes, making on that all twelve or so of the Texas Playboys were crammed into the tiny studio in Slapout, Oklahoma, or wherever. Announcers would come up with effortfully casual links along the lines of, Well folks, I hear Eldon Shamblin a-banging on the studio door, so let's have Bob and all the boys play 'Keep Knockin' But You Can't Come In' – and right after that we'll have a message from our friends down at the Slapout feed store.

The Playboys knew which side their tortillas were buttered on: they wouldn't do much to break the illusion of their presence *in a studio near you*. The words of their signature tune, made available for all buyers of the transcription to top and tail their programmes, reveal the kind of relationship they had with their audience. At the beginning of each show, vocalist Tommy Duncan sang:

Now listen everybody from near and far, if you want
*   to know who we are*
We're the Texas Playboys from the Lone Star State

If you like the way we play, listen while we try to
*   say*
We're the Texas Playboys from the Lone Star State

*   And all day long*
*   We're going to sing this song*
*   If you get this song*
*   You can't go wrong – and how!*

We wear a smile, make things bright, make you happy
*   from morn to night*
We're the Texas Playboys from the Lone Star State

And at the end of each show, there'd be this envoy:

Now we never do brag, we never do boast, we sing
*   our songs from coast to coast*
We're the Texas Playboys from the Lone Star State

If you like our song, you think it's fine, sit right down
*   and drop a line*
To the Texas Playboys from the Lone Star State

*   And I'll declare*
*   We'll get it there*
*   And if we have*
*   Some time to spare, somewhere*

Sometime we're down your way we'll drop in and
*   spend the day*
We're the Texas Playboys from the Lone Star State

The theme tune has an interesting pedigree. For its jaunty

tune is not a Wills original, nor were the words more than modified by him. It was first made famous by a western swing band – The Light Crust Doughboys – in the very early Thirties. But this was not just any band, this was *the* band, the *Ur*-band. Its vocalist was Milton Brown, its fiddler Bob Wills, and its plectrists – Herman Arnspiger, Derwood Brown, Sleepy Johnson – the first big names of western swing guitar. The original line-up only lasted a couple years, and only recorded a couple sides, but all the members went on to have important musical careers. Anyway, this swinging string band needed a theme tune for its radio broadcasts (sponsored by Light Crust Flour), so someone, probably Milton Brown, dusted off a song released a couple of years earlier by The Famous Hokum Boys, a Chicago-based group featuring Big Bill Broonzy and Frank Brasswell on guitars, Georgia Tom on piano, and all three on vocals. Their 'Eagle Riding Papa' bumps along in a rough and ready but very affecting stumbly-swing, with Georgia Tom's vocal boasting of the band's fame and friendliness in more or less identical words to those noted above. (And in essence only differentiated from the boosterism and bragging of modern rap groups by their relative gentility of expression.) Some of the differences *are* significant, though. Instead of the Playboys' anodyne 'We wear a smile, make things bright, make you happy from morn to night', the original words go, 'We'll make you loose, make you tight, make you shake it till broad daylight', which gets to the heart of the matter much more directly. And their final verse – 'We never have one girl at a time, we always have seven, eight or nine' – had to go completely, of course.

Things are never as simple as they seem to be, however, even in the bible-belt, and that exact risqué couplet *was* sung by Bob Wills – and recorded, several times – but in an entirely different song: 'Sittin' on Top of the World'.

But all this is a detour from a detour. What has to be remembered about all the above is that it relates to the late Forties and early Fifties: transcription services didn't really get going till then. And there were no records on the air either, back in the early days of western swing.

The upshot was one of those occasions when technology and economics conspire to squeeze an unexpectedly happy result from a difficult situation.

More and more young folk were leaving the farms to live in towns and cities; they became known as 'the nervous generation' because of the traumas of getting accustomed to urban ways. Amongst them, inevitably, were a fair number of country fiddlers and guitarists, greatly enamoured of the citified ragtime and New Orleans-style jazz sounds. The radio stations needed music – live music – to fill in the gaps between plugs. It didn't particularly matter what the music was, as long as it was popular; that's what the advertisers said. So the raw young musicians streaming in from the backwoods and prairies got to play long programmes of music, which required them to build up a large repertoire of tunes, which in turn encouraged them to mine various disparate musical seams.

There was no time for daft ideas of musical purity; they had to pick up good tunes wherever they could find them, whether blues, ragtime, jazz, breakdowns, ballads, cowboy songs, waltzes, hymns. So Milton Brown and Bob Wills listened to rent-party blues records, and adapted the songs to their own purposes. And sometimes they didn't adapt, but did more or less straight covers, as in the Fort Worth Doughboys' recording of 'Nancy Jane', another Famous Hokum Boys song. The Fort Worth Doughboys was a pseudonym for Light Crust Doughboys, apparently adopted for this one recording session because their sponsor disapproved of them recording – especially off-colour material.

Brown and Wills, and all the other musicians, would learn material from piano rolls, from rival radio shows, from other bands' dances, from records (though not, in these early years, from recorded western swing, for such a thing didn't really exist); they would set to music lyrics or poems sent in by fans, or penned by sponsors or sponsors' offspring; they would dredge from their memories half-remembered tunes and resurrect them, or recreate them, usually claiming a copyright for themselves in the process. Sometimes they'd work up an original tune from scratch. They'd rehearse the new song – in somebody's kitchen, on the bus, at the dance, or, briefly, in the studio – then they'd go on the air.

Over the weeks and months, the early western swing bands built up their repertoire this way, and the challenge of having to master such a wide range of material stood them in good stead for a long time to come. In the mid-Thirties, Milton Brown and his Musical Brownies had a repertoire of at least 150 regularly performed songs. A few years later, Bob Wills could dig into this treasure chest and pull out 220 numbers for the Tiffany Transcriptions, and then 100 more (with far from complete overlap) for the Presto discs. So if the 4,000 plus lyrics Tommy Duncan claimed to know seems incredible, it probably wasn't wildly exaggerated.

The variety of sources plundered by these Texas musicians is amazing. Consider, for instance, the eighteen tracks laid down by Milton Brown and his Musical Brownies at their first sessions, recorded at the Texas Hotel in San Antonio in 1934. As well as several of their own compositions such as 'Brownie's Stomp' and 'Joe Turner Blues', designed to show off individual instrumentalists' prowess, they recorded such tracks as 'Do the Hula Lou', a Sophie Tucker show-stopper; 'Garbage Man Blues', a comic blues number adapted from a Washboard Rhythm Kings song called 'Call of the Freaks'; and 'Four, Five or Six Times', originally recorded by Jimmy Noone's Apex Club Orchestra, featuring Earl 'Fatha' Hines on piano. (It wasn't only songs the Brownies adopted. Their pianist was so besotted with the great Hines that Milton came up with a version of the same nickname for him, and he became known as Fred 'Papa' Calhoun.) 'Where You Been So Long, Corrine' was probably learned either from Cab Calloway – a favourite of many Texas musicians, for both his swing and his humour – or from one of the numerous country blues versions in circulation. 'Just Sitting on Top of the World' came from the records of a black string band, The Mississippi Sheiks. Bob Wills was to record this song no fewer than six times; over the years it has been covered by many other blues and western swing acts.

Interestingly, the Mississippi Sheiks chose to play almost

exclusively for white audiences, and seem to have been as much influenced by white roots music as by the blues. Often it seems these categories were invented by record companies to divide their catalogues neatly and help target perceived audiences: the musical differences between many 'Race' and 'Old Time' or 'Novelty Hot Dance' discs were minimal. For crossovers were working in all directions, even in the strictly segregated Twenties. Boundaries were so flexible – at least when the colour of the musicians couldn't be seen – that one of the Sheiks' records, 'That's It', was released on their label's white country series. A contemporaneous white duo, on the other hand, The Allen Brothers, found their jazzy 'Chattanooga Blues' had been issued in Columbia's race series – normally the preserve of black artists. They so feared the damage this would do to their career, that they sued the record company. Percolate, mama, percolate! urges Austin, during his brother Lee's guitar solo.

'Get Along, Cindy' is a traditional folk song and fiddle breakdown; the Brownie's version sounds very similar to an arrangement worked out by one of the greatest white string bands, The Skillet Lickers, in the late Twenties. 'Trinity Waltz is another, gentler traditional Texas fiddle tune, recorded by just about everybody, under various names: Bob Wills called it 'Dreamy Eyes Waltz'. 'Loveland And You' was written in 1910 by an English music hall singer, W.R. Williams; its full title was originally 'I'd Like To Live In Loveland (With A Girl Like You)'. God knows where Milton picked that up; a west Texas band called Bob Skyles and the Skyrockets recorded it too, four years later, but they probably learnt it from the Brownies' version.

Necessity required the Brownies to acquire such a wide range of material; their own eclectic musical tastes made the task exciting rather than onerous. The result was a body of tunes and songs drawn from virtually every type of music in existence at the time. Milton Brown died following a car crash in April 1936, and the Brownies split up soon afterwards, all of the members going on to have important careers in Texas music, either as leaders or influential sidemen. Their legacy was the establishment of a hundred or so tunes as the core repertoire of western swing, added to and drawn from by every band that came in their wake.

Zooming into Fort Worth from the north-west, I was getting severely jittered by the speed and the density of the traffic: the way it was building up was beginning to make even Wichita Falls look like Twatt on a wet Tuesday in March. Especially as I became aware that the road I was driving on had turned into Jacksboro Highway – the very road on which Milton Brown had had his fatal car crash in 1936. I shivered, drove on. Carefully. I crossed the west fork of the Trinity River, then took Robert's Cut Off south to White Settlement Road, and turned right. White Settlement was the site of another landmark in the history of western swing, and the Musical Brownies in particular, for it was four miles out of town down this road that Papa Sam Cunningham had his Crystal Springs dancehall – plus swimming pool and fishing pond. (Sam kept an especially huge catfish in the pond with '50' painted on its side. The deal was that whichever customer caught the monster got $50 too.) It was here that the Brownies established themselves as the biggest draw in Fort Worth, and here that they had the regular, long gigs that enabled them to experiment with the mix of styles that would eventually meld and (even more eventually) become known as western swing.

But the dancehall was long gone. A home-painted sign nailed to a telephone pole claimed that this was Crystal Springs Mobile Home Park – **No Dumpin' Fishin' Parkin'** – but even that facility had disappeared. The birthplace of western swing was nothing but a weed-infested, rubbish-strewn vacant lot.

You're Bound to Look Like a Monkey When You Grow Old

APPLICATION FOR MEMBERSHIP

Name_____

Street or Rt._____

City_____ State____ Zip_____

Date of Birth: Month   Day   Year

___Fiddler..........................$17.50 per Year

___Accompanist....................$17.50 per Year

___Out of State Fiddler......$17.50 per Year

___Associate.......................$10.00 per Year

Print name and address clearly, check proper
category (See description above), clip card, and
mail dues to:

TEXAS OLD TIME FIDDLERS ASSOCIATION
10124 Stoneleigh Dr.
Benbrook, Texas 76126

Newsletter is included with membership. Make checks
payable to Texas Old Time Fiddlers Association.

Okay, I was getting desperate. Nearly a week in Texas already, and no sign of any real live western swing. Don't believe what you read: the guide books I'd swallowed in a gulp back home had given the impression that great Texas music was to be heard bopping out of every bar room, every crossroads honky tonk. It hadn't turned out to be quite like that. You have to really look for good music, even in Texas. You have to be prepared to travel to unexpected, out of the way places. Like the West Side Care Center.

Lunch was finished, and there was still one hour, three minutes and twenty-two seconds — according to the iron-clad schedules that rule such places — before afternoon coffee could be served. Meanwhile, the television had been turned down (not off, don't be daft) and there was to be ENTERTAINMENT.

In one corner a silver-haired lady and three distinguished elderly gents were tuning their instruments: the band. Porters had cleared the last of the dishes from the tables, and the partition between the dining room and the chapel had been pushed back, so the lady-pianist could play the Sunday piano. A limp Stars and Stripes hung on the wall between her and the little wooden pulpit, and an exuberant arrangement of dried flowers – looking very like the trail of debris left by the exploding space shuttle a few years ago – crowned her instrument. She struck a resonant D chord, and the others continued tuning up.

About two dozen old folk were scattered across the room – a group of three men around a table here, a couple together there, but everybody else sitting alone. One or two people were talking to themselves; one ancient man was staring fixedly at a copy of *National Geographic* opened in front of him; a lady with pink hair and a pink cardigan twitched in her wheelchair just in front of me.

Howdy folks! The fiddler had leant forward to speak into his mic. We'll be playing a few tunes for you real soon, just as quick as we can get tuned up. If you don't mind waiting . . .

Nobody looked like they were going to rush off anywhere. Nobody looked like they *could* rush off anywhere. Except for the staff: nylon-uniformed nurses flitted about at great speed, talking to the old folk, handing out pills and polystyrene cups of water, wiping up drools, handing each other sheaves of paper, darting in and out of a glass-walled office in the far corner of the room. And overalled porters wheeled huge old ladies about with huge energy, hefted piles of chairs from one side of the room to the other, shifted tables, picked up magazines and cutlery from the floor, all the time addressing the residents with pally insults and loud endearments.

Maybe old folks' homes wouldn't be so depressing, I thought as I shifted my seat slightly to get a better view of the band (still tuning), if *everyone* sat around and stared into the middle distance. What is really sad is seeing half of the folk in the place – the residents, the inmates –

sitting slumped over jigsaws or tottering very very slowly towards the toilets, while all the staff skite about like hyperactive bluebottles. They're just so goddarned *full of life*, the staff.

I shook my head, looked about. It was the way they were all sitting alone that was the most depressing thing. A neat, bespectacled lady, somewhat younger than the average, was sitting along the table from me.

Hello, I said. You been in here long?

Oh, about twenty minutes.

I nodded sympathetically. Just arrived, eh?

Sure have.

There's worse places to be, eh? I mean . . . you can get anything you want here. I suppose.

I suppose you can, she said.

Can I get you . . . a glass of water or anything?

No, I'm just fine, thank you. She turned to face me. You're not from round here, are you?

Me? No.

I could tell. Your accent. I like it!

I'm from Scotland.

Scotland! Wow! Did you drive here?

I looked at her. Well. Not all the way.

She nodded. That would take too long, I suppose.

Eh . . . yes. I'm here for the music, actually. I'm a big western swing fan, you see, and I heard there were some fine musicians doing a show here today, so . . .

All the way from Scotland!

Well, not *all* the way today. I came down from Wichita Falls today.

Let me tell you, honey, she said, You speak English *real* good. Well done!

Eh . . . thanks.

There was a shriek of feedback from an amplifier, and the pianist did a little exploratory rake of the keyboard. My companion faced back to the front again. I'm here for the music too, she said.

Really?

Yes. I'm Ellen, married to Roy Lee, on the guitar. I drove out with him today.

Oh, I . . .

The band started. They were so out of tune that it took me a couple choruses to recognise the song: 'Alabama Jubilee'.

Ellen Brown looked over at me, smiled. I smiled back, gritting my teeth against the discords.

The song ended, there was scattered applause, and the band immediately started tuning up.

The fiddler leant forward to speak into his mic again. (He must've thought it was everybody else that was out of tune, not him; I'm not sure I agreed.)

Well, hello, folks, he said, Thanks for that. You're a great audience, we love you. You know, we've all played on a lot of back porches around here over the years, playing the kind of stuff we've been listening to since the Thirties. So we're going to play some more of it for you today, to try and preserve it for future generations, or something like that.

Apart from me – and the staff, who weren't paying much attention – there weren't any members of the future generations present.

Milton Brown led one of the most famous string bands of the 1930s, he went on. The Musical Brownies. So we're awfully glad we've got his younger brother with us today. So here's Roy Lee Brown singing 'El Rancho Grande'.

And they launched into the Tex-Mex classic, Roy Lee flashing a big white smile around – looking amazingly like Milton in all those old photos – as he grinned and strummed and crooned the cod-Spanish lyrics of the thing in a warm, slightly nasal baritone.

Ellen leaned over towards me. He's no idea what he's singing about, she said. I hope it's nothing bad. She laughed.

I laughed too. The music was atrocious. Well, the individual musicianship was okay, but they were just so terribly out of tune it was hilarious. I began to envy the deaf members of the audience. And I began to feel sorry for Roy Lee, because he was actually a really fine singer, recognisably a Brown, with a warm, flexible intonation very similar to his famous elder brother's. Six years younger than Derwood, eighteen younger than Milton, he'd been just a boy at the time of the Musical Brownies greatest successes. But he'd done duty changing strings on Derwood's guitar, and obviously soaked up a whole lot of style.

The song ended, and they all started tuning up again.

It's like a symphony orchestra fixing to play, said the bass player, a big man in a plaid shirt, white hat, and tinted glasses.

When you play with just a fiddle and a guitar you can get in tune just fine, said the fiddler. But when you get a big band like this you start getting big problems!

Okay, the fiddler said at last, Let's try a Jimmie Rodgers number.

Give me an A, said the bassist, but it was too late, for the fiddler was already singing:

> Way out on the windswept desert
> Where nature favours no man
> A buffalo found his brother
> At rest on the sun-baked sand
> He said, Brother, what ails you?
> Has sickness got you this way?
> But his brother never said, cause his brother was dead
> Been dead since way last May

The instruments were very nearly in tune now. To counter the increased harmoniousness, however, the intercom – with speakers concealed all around the room – gave out a burst of static, then broadcast a matronly voice during the yodelling break urging, Porter to room four-eighteen, please, porter to four-eighteen. Undaunted, the fiddler continued:

> Big Chief Buffalo Nickel
> A mighty man in his day
> Never once used a sickle
> To clear the bushes away

He would go round from tent to tent
Eating everything in his sight
He loved the squaws, every one he saw
He loved a new one every night

With one final yodel, the song ended, leaving me still wondering what the Chief *did* use to clear the bushes away if it wasn't a sickle.

These guys were unstoppable: they were tuning up again. Practice makes perfect, though, and from now on they were so remarkably in tune that I could only sit back, marvel, and enjoy their set, as varied as any western swing aficionado could desire:

Waltz Across Texas. Originally a hit for Ernest Tubb, 'The Texas Troubadour', and former Jimmie Rodgers imitator: the operation that ended that phase of his career was commemorated in a song about his surgeon called 'He Took 50 Dollars and My Yodel, When He Took My Tonsils Out'.

Johnson's Rag. An instrumental, performed in a kind of shuffle arrangement. Made famous in the Forties by Glenn Miller. Did anyone ever dance to that? asked Roy Lee. I did, said Ellen.

She's Gone Gone Gone. A honky tonk number that mixed mournfulness with weird exultation. Written by Corsicana, TX, native Lefty Frizzell – the thinking man's Hank Williams.

Four Or Five Times. An excellent vocal by Roy Lee on this old jazz standard, with Cab Calloway-ish shouted responses from the others. The Musical Brownies recorded it with a similar arrangement at their first session, in 1934.

Walking The Floor Over You. The hit that established Ernest Tubb, and has been covered countless times since. Roy Lee later told me that he used to sit opposite Tubb every morning in Rockefeller's hamburger place, Fort Worth: he would be having something to eat after his night shift working in a bakery, and Tubb would be having coffee on his way to work as a breakfast-time singer ('The Gold Chain Troubadour') on KGKO radio. I'm sure they could have had a lot of interesting conversations. Unfortunately, they never spoke.

Wabash Cannonball. One of the great country train songs of all time, originally recorded by the Carter Family, I think. It was also one of the first country songs I heard, initially in a skiffle version by the great Lonnie Donnegan, Glasgow's answer to Riley Puckett.

When My Blue Moon Turns To Gold Again. A sentimental ballad, recorded by Elvis, amongst other movers and shakers. A brief discussion took place between various band members before this number started:

Roy Lee: You going to sing it?
Pianist: He ain't going to sing it.
Bassist: I'll sing it.
Fiddler: You are?
Bassist: You want to?
Fiddler: Me? No.
But he did.

Faded Love/New San Antonio Rose. A Bob Wills medley, sung with real warmth of feeling by Roy Lee Brown.

Bonaparte's Retreat. A classic traditional fiddle tune, with lyrics added late in life, which have the song refer to itself in the third person, as it were:

Oh the stars shone bright as I held her on that night
And I heard her say, Please don't ever go away
Then I held her in my arms and told her of her many
*   charms and*
Kissed her while the fiddles played Bonaparte's Retreat

12th Street Rag. There have been many fine jazz and western swing recordings of this tune (composed by a Fort Worth pianist, drunk and sometime junk dealer called Euday L. Bowman), but the West Side Care Center band wasn't playing jazz. This afternoon it was straight melody right down the line. The audience were content with that, clapping along enthusiastically. Well, some of them were definitely clapping. Others may just have been twitching. JOHN HATCHET LINE 3, blared the intercom. HATCHET LINE 3.

Chinese Honeymoon. Another old Milton Brown favourite, given a jaunty treatment, and followed by the fiddler introducing the members of the band: he was Joe Grady Thomas, the pianist was his wife for life Lenna Thomas, C.A. Dacus was on bass. (Any relation to Smokey Dacus, Bob Will's first drummer, I wondered? No.) And of course Roy Lee Brown was on guitar and vocals.

Well, said Joe, Our time is about up. We've enjoyed playing for you so much, and we sure appreciate your applause. We'd like to close our programme with a little tune made famous by Mr James Robert Wills. Its called 'Goodnight Little Sweetheart', and that's what y'all are to us, our sweethearts. We love you, and we hope to see all of you again soon. Goodnight.

> Goodnight little sweetheart, goodnight
> I've enjoyed every moment with you
> I know that the stars up in heaven
> Are all getting jealous of me too
>
> Goodnight little sweetheart, goodnight
> The parting will make me so blue
> Though after you're gone memories linger on
> Goodnight little sweetheart goodnight

At the end of the song, with Roy Lee and Joe harmonising sweetly, there was scattered applause, and a murmur of conversation and monologue restarted. In fact, it had probably been going all afternoon, but had just been drowned out till now by the music.

I yawned. I'd been well and truly lullabied. What time of night was it? Three twenty-five.

Hey! Excuse me! It was Ellen Brown, tapping me on the shoulder. Don't rush off. Come and meet Roy Lee. He'll be thrilled to think you came all this way to see him.

Well . . . Great, I'd love to.

She guided me over towards the band, who were busy packing up their gear, and introduced me. A big fan of Texas music, all the way from Scotland. I shook everybody's hand, told them how much I'd enjoyed listening to them.

It's especially great to hear you sing, Roy Lee, I said, Cause you recorded one of my favourite western swing tracks of all time.

Me? He paused in putting his Stratocaster back in its furry case. I did? He frowned. What the heck was that?

'The Ice Man Song', I said. I love it! So funny! I can sing it, listen:

> *Any ice today lady? It's nice today lady*
> *How about a little piece today?*
> *It's only a quarter, so don't you think you oughter*
> *Have a little 'fore it melts away?*

Roy Lee looked worried, glanced around me, checking for Ellen. She was talking to Lenna. I sung on:

> *There's a lady lives down our street*
> *Her name is Mrs Brown*
> *She got a great big lump today*
> *She's got the biggest box in town*

Shh! said Roy Lee. That's just a piece of old nonsense.

I was going to put in a request for it while you were playing, I said. But then I thought, maybe everyone wouldn't get the joke.

That blue stuff . . . said Roy Lee, and sucked in his cheeks. That's the only track I ever recorded like that, and . . . Ellen don't like it *at all*.

I looked over my shoulder: she was still deep in conversation. What *is* an ice man, exactly? I asked. I must've read that Eugene O'Neill play *The Ice Man Cometh*, but I don't remember much about it. I didn't like it nearly as much as I like your song.

He chuckled. Back in the days before refrigerators, folks bought big blocks of ice to keep their food cool – or to keep

whatever they liked cool. He snapped the case shut, stood up.
I did that job myself for a while.

Really? *You* were the ice man?

I delivered ice all over this town!

I laughed. Brilliant. So is the song autobiographical?

Roy Lee looked me straight in the eye. No, he said.

Good, I said. That's what I always say too.

What Makes Bob Holler?

★ *Burbank's Family Billiard Center* ★

BUDDY RAY'S BILLIARD ROOM

POOL AND SNOOKER
1313 NO. SAN FERNANDO RD.
BURBANK, CALIFORNIA
843-9769

THE FINEST BRUNSWICK TABLES AND EQUIPMENT

I had a few Buddy Ray tracks on compilation tapes in the car. The one that stuck in my mind was 'Tulsa Twist', recorded in 1941 by Dickie McBride and his Village Boys. It's a twin fiddle instrumental, memorable because it's all in a minor key, without a tinge of the usual country-whine: it's more manic depressive than mournful. The fiddles of Ray and Dickie Jones whirl wraith-like up and down the G minor scale, intertwining like wrestling spooks.

Ray was somebody I knew very little about. He didn't get a mention in any of the reference books I'd checked, and there was no reissue album devoted to him (perhaps because he'd mostly been a sideman rather than a name bandleader). But even my fairly casual acquaintance with his unique, bluesy, thick and throaty tone on the likes of 'Tulsa Twist' and 'Rakin' It Back' was enough to convince me that he was well worth seeking out.

Somebody at the nursing home had mentioned that, at the age of seventy-five, and less than a year after major heart surgery, Ray had taken on a new lease of life and was tearing up the small jazz venues of Fort Worth again, just like he had – here, in Houston, in Shreveport, and all over California – forty or more years before. In fact, he was meant to be playing that very night in the Noble Bean Coffee Shop on Camp Bowie Boulevard. I say 'meant to be', because I'd also been told he was intending giving up music for Lent and so might not show.

I ate at Angelo's BBQ on White Settlement Road: barbe-cued brisket sandwiches in rolls the size of a baseball mitt, smoky beer, and smoky air. The whole place swam in a reek of hickory smoke: the walls were smoked brown, so was the ceiling, the tables, the window. The stuffed moosehead by the door was smoky, so was the stuffed bear; the servers behind the counter looked half-kippered too. The words of a Gram Parsons song eddied around my mind:

> *Now when I'm lonesome I always pretend*
> *That I'm getting the feel of hickory wind*

I'd never really known what Gram was singing about, but now I did: he was describing sitting downwind of Angelo's barbecue ovens.

Big black clouds rolled in from the west and blaffs of wind spun mini duststorms out of the gutters as I drove down Camp Bowie and parked outside the Noble Bean. There was a photocopied poster on the door – **Tonite: Bruton/Price Swingmasters Revue featuring Buddy Ray** – but I didn't need subtitles: on the other side of the cafe's front window was the combo, playing so loud that the plate-glass shuddered sympathetically in four-four time.

I bought a big glass of something that looked like coffee with whipped cream on top. The cream tasted of shaving foam and the coffee tasted of, eh, nothing at all. But I wasn't caring: the band was double espresso strength. Drums up front, string bass and keyboards at the back, and an amazing goateed guitarist who was up front, round the back,

and, during 'T-Bone Shuffle', right out the door and down
the sidewalk, still playing. The keyboard-player was dressed
like he'd just walked off the golf-course, including a floppy
sky-blue bunnet; he introduced the numbers: from 'Shopping
Mall Blues' to 'I Want A Bow-Legged Woman'.

The oldest guy on the stand was also the hottest musician: a
shortish, barrel-shaped guy, with a close-cropped white beard
and an electrified fiddle tucked under it. I found my mind drifting
a bit, my eye caught by the rain starting to smash down outside;
but whenever the fiddle burst in, I came to with a start: this was
jazz of great intensity and imagination. The tone of the fiddle
was beautiful and unmistakable: sandpaper spread with honey.

The Swingmasters took a break, and I approached Buddy Ray.

Mr Ray, I said. I've come from Scotland to hear some
western swing.

Sorry to hear that, he replied.

Pardon?

Well you're not hearing much swing tonight!

Eh, no, no. I suppose it's more boppy.

You could call it that.

It doesn't matter! I mean it's great just to hear you, you
know!

He laughed. You mean it's great to find me alive!

Eh . . . what I mean is, I've got you on records at home.
With Dickie McBride's Village Boys, and The Modern
Mountaineers. And I know you played with a lot of great
musicians.

They're all dead now. Hell, not surprising the way we lived:
drink and pills and women! But I gave it all up. For my health:
my lungs, you know. Heh, if I'd known I was going to live so
long . . .

You'd've looked after yourself better?

Well, I'd've *paced* myself.

We sat down at a small table next to the stand. There were
only about a dozen folk in the Noble Bean, but they all seemed
to know Buddy, and to want to say hello to him.

Your fiddle style there, I said, It reminded me of Stephane
Grappelli.

I didn't hear much Grappelli until late on. During the war, I think, was when I first heard him and the Hot Club. He was European, you see.

So who were you listening to, then? I mean, fiddle isn't usually thought of as a jazz instrument these days.

Well back in the Thirties you had people like Stuff Smith, Eddie South, Joe Venuti – have you heard them?

I've heard some Venuti – duets with Eddie Lang on guitar.

Yeah, yeah. But check out Stuff. He was my big hero. He could *really* play.

How about the more western swing folk? I mean, how about Bob Wills?

Ha! Bob? He grinned. Bob really couldn't play. Not jazz, anyway. Breakdowns, maybe, but not jazz. Bob Wills was a two-fingered fiddler.

I'm going up to Turkey in a few weeks time, I said, For the Memorial Weekend – a lot of the old Texas Playboys are going to be there. It's amazing to think I'll actually be meeting actual Texas Playboys.

Heh, you're meeting one now!

I leant forward. Pardon?

I played with Bob Wills out in California – '44 I guess it was.

Wow! I mean . . . you played with the great Bob?

Sure. Now, talk about drinkers . . .

What was he like? I mean musically? Was he into the same folk as you, Stuff Smith and all?

Bob was into everything: jazz, blues . . . He hired me because I was a jazz player. That's what he liked, that's what he wanted in his band, though he couldn't play it himself. I'd never heard Bob much before I joined the Playboys. Well, I'd *heard* him, but I'd never *listened* to him. I was a jazz fan, period. So, my first gig with them, I was singing 'Outskirts of Town' – Bob'd heard I liked the blues, you see – when I heard this holler right at my elbow. It was Bob doing his famous Ah-ha! But I'd never heard him do that jive-talking shit before, see, and I got such a shock that I jumped in the air, stopped singing. And Bob got such a shock at me stopping singing, that he stopped hollering!

I laughed. He recorded that song later on, 'What Makes Bob Holler'.

You knew you were doing something right if Bob started yelling!

It was time for the Swingmasters to play their second set. I got another glass of froth and brown water. The band was joined by a guest vocalist, a guy about a third Buddy's age, who sang 'Don't Roll Your Bloodshot Eyes At Me', which I knew from an album by Asleep At The Wheel, and always suspected to be ripped off from Shakespeare. If I ever get to fulfil my ambition of directing a western swing version of *Macbeth* – not as unlikely as it sounds, there was a rock'n'roll version of *Othello* in the Sixties called *Catch My Soul*, starring Jerry Lee Lewis as Iago – I'll be sure to have the guilty king sing a stomping 'Never Shake Thy Gory Locks At Me'. Another stand-out number was a jumping version of 'Pipeliner's Blues', originally recorded by The Modern Mountaineers in 1940, with Moon Mullican on vocals and piano. And who played fiddle on the Mountaineers' session? Buddy Ray! It was incredible to sit there and listen to one of the all-time western swing classics, being played by the fiddler who'd help make it a classic, fifty-five years before.

And the music was great. Buddy'd been right, there was little swing evident, western or otherwise; the drummer was dominating the sound with his explosive 4/4 be-bop rhythms. But it didn't matter. They were all playing from the heart, and playing well, and making it new with every note. The coffee was crap, the cafe was cramped, and the only lightshow was courtesy of the sheet lightning that was starting to slash down on the other side of the plate-glass window. At one point, a siren started wailing out in the street: not a police siren, but a loud, insistent air-raid-warning type siren.

Hey, said the keyboard player. Sounds like a tornado warning! Better go out with a song. 'Big Stars Falling', that'd be appropriate.

The band all laughed, then tore into the number with all the power of an F5 twister.

At the end of the set, Buddy came up to me. Well, I was

hanging about the door and he went past me. You say you're
from Scotland? he said, pausing. Heh, I was in a film about
Scotland!

Playing fiddle?

No, I was a villager.

What was the film?

It was called *Brigadoon*. Ever heard of it?

I laughed. Of course! It's a classic!

Brigadoon, you'll remember, is about a couple of Americans
strolling through a Technicolor-tartan Highlands and discov-
ering a picturesque, character-filled village full of long-limbed
dancers in mini-kilts. It turns out that the village only bursts
into life every hundred years, and is a wasteland the rest
of the time. (In a couple weeks, when I got to Bob Wills
home-town for his Memorial Weekend, I was to be struck
by a feeling that I'd driven into a similar setup: *Turkeydoon*.
But that comes later.)

I was in a lot of shit like that: *A Star Is Born, Jailhouse Rock,
Giant* . . .

Garland, Presley, Dean – some co-stars!

I was never the star – I've never been the starring kind,
really. Never wanted to be. I just wanted to play my music.
But all my life I've been cursed with having to make a *living* out
of music. That's different: playing what somebody else wants
isn't the same as playing what you want.

Bob Wills always wanted his musicians to play just the way
they felt it, didn't he, whether it was technically right or not.
With *soul*.

Buddy chuckled. Well . . . I didn't stay with Bob too long.
I guess he didn't like my soul.

Who else did you play with, Buddy? I'm embarrassed that
I have to ask.

Oh, you name them . . . Merle Travis, Jimmy Wakely . . .
Spent a few years with T. Texas Tyler in the late Forties – he
had a good outfit: Jimmie Widener on guitar, Danny Alguire
on trumpet, Don Decker. Don was a temperamental kind of
guy, but he played *real* good hot viola.

There's not many folk you can say that about! The night

was close and humid, and I was breaking into a sweat just watching the other band members carry amps and drums and mike stands out of the Noble Bean and into their cars.

One of the best gigs I had was leading a quartet out at Sun Valley Rancho in 1956. Joaquin Murphy was on steel, do you know him?

I know the records he made with Spade Cooley. I always liked his name: kind of half Spanish, half Irish, an interesting combination.

Stuff Smith used to come and sit in with us for twenty bucks a night. Think of that: the greatest jazz violinist ever, playing all night for twenty dollars!

I was wondering about The Modern Mountaineers, I said. Was that the same Modern Mountaineers that Smokey Wood was in?

Well . . . there were a couple different Modern Mountaineers. The first lot I was in were the same band Smokey had started – with J.R. Chatwell on fiddle. But then we used the name again to record in 1940; really we were The Texas Wanderers, but we were contracted to a different label, see, so we had to come up with a new name – moonlighting!

Smokey Wood was some character, eh? I *love* his stuff – kind of Fats Waller with a steel guitar.

Buddy laughed, shaking his head. Smokey was crazy: he'd light up his reefers right there on stage, radio Mars on the PA in the middle of a song . . . He was a wild cat.

I'd listened to that song 'Everybody's Truckin' a hundred times before I noticed that half the time he wasn't actually singing *trucking*!

By this time the band's gear was all loaded away, and the other musicians were saying goodnight and heading off. Buddy stretched, picked up his fiddle case.

I shook his hand. It's been great talking to you, I said. And great hearing you play. I've been in Texas a while now, and to be honest I've been getting worried – till tonight I hadn't heard any good music. But you were *great*.

Buddy shrugged. I don't know if it's great, but it sure is fun: I just get up there and do whatever the hell I want to.

I like the sound of that.

Shake Up Your Gourd Seeds

Bob Skyles and his Skyrockets

FOR YOUR REQUEST

NAME OF SONG_____

DEDICATED TO_____

Thank You

SEAL AND GIVE TO WAITRESS

In an era notable for its love of musical novelty, in a state renowned for its love of weird cross-cultural effusions, Bob Skyles and his Skyrockets were perhaps the most novel, the weirdest, the most cross-eyed of all. They couldn't settle to a single image – photos of the time show them in white dinner-jackets and bow-ties one moment, huge lopsided straw sombreros the next – let alone to a single musical style. Look at the titles of some of their recordings: 'The Arkansas Bazooka Swing', 'Sweet As Sugar Blues', 'Swat The Love Bug,' 'The Fox Trot You Saved For Me', 'The Hill Billy Fiddler', 'Jive And Smile', 'Eskimo Nell', 'One More Drink And I'll Tell It All'. (The last track remains, tragically, unreleased.)

They couldn't even settle on what instruments to play. Leader Bob Skyles (real name Bob Kendrick) recorded on maybe a dozen instruments, from tenor sax to electric mandolin to musical saw; brother Sanford ranged from trumpet to string bass to trombone; the youngest brother, Clifford, was on drums. And also temple blocks, tuned cowbells, washboard and sizzle cymbals.

It was Cliff that I was going to meet today, at his home in Palo Pinto in the rolling wooded hills west of Fort Worth. I'd been given the address by Kevin Coffey, singer with the Price/Bruton Swingmasters, and been told he had a fund of colourful stories. I got in the mood as I drove by listening to the Skyrockets' own song about the man – half tribute, half threat – recorded back in 1938: 'Swing It Drummer Man'.

> *Listen to me mister drummer man, I've got a few*
> *   words on my mind*
> *You've been fooling around the band, playing out of*
> *   your time*
> *I'm going to give you a great big chance to take your*
> *   place and show*
> *Are you ready, on your marks, steady – let her go!*
>
> > *Now's your move*
> > *Get in the groove*
> > *Play it smooth*
> > *Swing it drummer man!*
> > *Rippling rhythms*
> > *Cowbells with them*
> > *Jungle rhythm*
> > *Swing it drummer man!*
>
> *Now every beat turns on the heat, so let's all cut the*
> *   rug*
> *Swinging, trucking, shagging – I feel the bite of the*
> *   jitterbug*
> *Oh go to town, round and round, hit it sound*
> *Swing it drummer man!*
>
> > *Now's your move*
> > *Get in the groove*
> > *Play it smooth*

Swing it drummer man!
Rippling rhythms   (woodblocks pop)
Cowbells with them   (bells jangle)
Jungle rhythm   (tom-toms pound)
Swing it drummer man!

But not even the wild and exuberant antics of that song could have prepared me for meeting the man himself.

Hi! Hi! Come in, have a beer, have a seat – no! – I'll give you a tour. Would you like a tour? Built the place myself you know, fifteen years it took, fifteen years – weekends only, but *every* weekend; every weekend I'd come out from Fort Worth where I worked – tuning pianos! I'm not even blind – I'd come out and build a little more, a little more, a little more, till *finally*, after fifteen years, I got it fixed just about right. And my wife died. Well not right away, but later, later – Judy – so I've got the whole place to myself now, what do you think of it, do you like it? Eh, do you like it?

I did like it. Or at least, I could see that it matched exactly the personality of its owner – just as perfectly as John Moen's modest home had suited him. Cliff was not a big man, physically, but he had a Mount Rushmore-sized presence. Mischievous good humour radiated from him, as did a constant stream of jokes and banter. He looked a lot younger than his seventy-six years, despite a white Tolstoyan beard that streamed down over his chest. Of course, Tolstoy never worse a white Stetson. Not in the house, at least.

Cliff gave me a guided tour, pressing cold beer into my hands in the kitchen when I asked for coffee. (Coffee? he said, No, I can't give you that: never drink the stuff. I guess I've been lucky: I never did start drinking coffee, I never had to pick cotton, and I never was raped.) He whisked me through his painting studio, barely slowing to let me glance at his latest work on the easel – a meticulously detailed grizzly bear in a landscape of even more meticulously detailed snowy mountains – before hurrying down a hallway lined with shelves of books, fossils, bullwhips and other curiosities of a Dickensian variousness, and darting into the bedroom, where we paused a while. We paused because I asked a daft question:

Cliff, you see that calendar on the wall, with all the writing on it? Different coloured asterisks and so on? What does all that mean?

He laughed. That's every time I've had sex with my girlfriend, he said. All the different stars tell you just what we did. See, a *blue* star means . . .

It's okay, I said. I can imagine.

Got to keep fit at my age, he said, taking a deep breath, slapping his chest. Thought I'd keep a record, check I wasn't getting past it.

Well, there's a lot of stars there! And that's just April!

Eighty-three times so far this year, he said, grinning. What do you think?

I'm jealous!

Ha! The older the fiddle the better the tune!

We moved on. In the bathroom was another of Cliff's pictures.

My brother Bob got sick of me painting all the time, thinking I was good, see. So he said to me, Man, if you're so good, go paint me a picture of . . . of . . . of a *coathanger*. He thought I couldn't do it, see, but I did, I did. And just to make it more interesting, I painted a woman's brassière dangling from the hanger. Ha!

So you did. Was he impressed?

Of course! But he's in a rest home now – and the nurses weren't impressed. Wouldn't let him put it up. So I've got it.

We went through the living room and up to a kind of mezzanine, which was done up like . . . nothing I'd ever seen before. Two dozen lights hung from the ceiling: crystal chandeliers, strip lights, glass-shaded lamps out of a bar advertising Coors, Busch and Lone Star; another shade was made out of punched copper, there was a trio of red-bulbed globes, a blue neon light behind a grille, flashing red traffic-intersection lights, and – to cap it all – plastic snake lights, drooping all around the room, hanging in great loops from the ceiling beams. There were racks and racks of cassettes, a dozen or so Cliff original oil-paintings, a rocking chair, a model stagecoach with windows that lit up from inside, a table with a hi-fi on it, other tables covered with knick-knacks and executive toys and LPs and statuettes and mini one-armed bandits and at least two pairs of maracas. But pride of place was taken by a gleaming red drum kit – bass drum, floor tom, two side toms, snare, hi hat, and four crash cymbals. The snake lights twined in and out all through the kit.

Them lights pulse on and off in time to the drumming, said Cliff. Pretty spectacular! I'll show you later. But first, first, *first* I want to show you my photo album. Cause I know it's the old music you're interested in, so I'll tell you all about that first. Sit down! Sit down! Bob Wills, you said? Couldn't play to save himself. A showman, is all he was. But that's what it's all about, I guess. Sit down!

I sat down, sipped on my Budweiser, and looked at the first photo. It showed four rows of benches arranged in front of a makeshift stage. On the left, a truck; on the right, a wagon with a canvas awning shading some kind of serving hatch. On the front of the stage, in big letters, **FREE SHOW**, and underneath, smaller, **F.G. Gassaway Co., Ft. Worth, Tex**. There was a drum kit set up on the stage, and stands holding several other instruments. A skinny figure in white lounged off to one side.

That's me, said Cliff. And this is where it all started: my old man's medicine show. Him and my mother toured all over west central Texas selling wonder cures. Mostly vegetable oil, plus a little bit of whiskey: that's where the wonder came from. And we were the band, me and my two brothers. Our old man – Doc he called himself, though he weren't a doctor no more than you or me – he sung and played guitar a little, and pitched the medicine to them. He'd been doing that since he was a kid: medicine shows, nigger minstrel routines . . .

What, he actually blacked up his face?

Yeah, we all did at one time or another. That's what was

expected in those days. We'd all get blacked up and play that jazz and sell those wonder cures!

Ah! Jazz! Is that what you and your brothers played?

Well, we tried. Started off as more of a string band, I suppose, but we loved the sound of the saxophone, you know, and everybody was getting into pop songs then – this is the early Thirties I'm talking about – so that's the direction we went in. The old man hated it at first, but he soon came round when he saw how the audience lapped it up. That's what it was all about.

We looked at more photos. The Skyrockets – for that's the name they'd come up with – in front of a car dealership: Sanford raising his trumpet high, Bob honking on a sax, a very young Cliff on drums, and Doc hamming it up like Charles-Hawtry-meets-Sammy-Hagar on a metal resonator guitar. The band looked smart in matching blazers, white slacks, and polka-dotted ties, the snazzy effect being only slightly spoiled by the fact that Doc's breeks were far too long for him, and were scuffing the dirt – despite three-inch turn-ups.

Your dad looks like a real character, I said.

He frowned, for the first and last time. That's one way of putting it.

I love that song he sings – there's only one, isn't there? – 'The Laughing Song', from the April '38 session. It's like something from another age.

Well, it was another age, it was 1938.

No, but I mean another age before that, even. It's like some old British music hall act – that amazing crotchety voice he had, and the daft lyrics: 'I got a croup from eating soup' and all that. Mad! The only thing I ever heard like it is some of the comedy routines Emmett Miller does over the intros to his songs. And you did record his 'Anytime', didn't you? Was he an influence?

I don't recall ever hearing of him. Everybody was doing that nigger minstrel shit in those days, though.

I suppose, even Bob Wills.

Cliff tapped the photo. That picture was after we wound

up the medicine show, though. We'd been playing parties and clubs during the winter while we were off the road, see, and we found that we could make more money by doing that all year round. Bob got to be the leader more and more after that: he got us our bookings, the record deals and so on. But Doc acted like he was still the boss. For years he wouldn't even pay us nothing at all. We had to go on strike. Striking against our own father! But it worked: me and Sanford started getting five bucks a week – between us! In the end, the old man just got drunk all the time, couldn't get his act together, lost us work. So we split from the old bastard. It was tough, but we had to do it.

More photos: those two taken five minutes apart, one with the Skyrockets as a sophisticated dance orchestra, one with them as cornball cowboys.

That was out in Hobbs, New Mexico, in 1938, said Cliff. We were there a good long time after we split from the old man. And I mean a *good* time! He'd never let us drink or nothing, so you can imagine, there we were in these wild night-clubs with all these wild women – showgirls! – we sure made up for lost time.

I love all the records from that period, I said. 'Turn Loose And Go To Town', 'What-Cha Gonna Do When Your Wife Comes Home', 'Rubber Dolly' . . . The two-four beat on that's so accentuated, it sounds almost like reggae.

Ho! I remember recording that down in some hotel in San Antonio. Dave Hughs was playing the trumpet so darn loud, they couldn't get it recorded right. The needle was jumping all over the place. He had to stick his trumpet out the window in the end, that was the only way to get it to sit in the wax.

It's a great record, I said. It's pure joy, the noise you made: swinging, but with so much humour. Even your titles – 'Shake Up Your Gourd Seeds' – brilliant!

We thought all that stuff was terrible. Corny as hell. The record company, they wanted a comedy band, see, like Bluebird's answer to the Hoosier Hotshots. We hated it. But we went along with it – fooled around, played that stupid whoopee-whistle. Bob came up with all those dumb songs – we never played them in the clubs, you know; we played straight dance stuff, and jazz, then. But hell, who were we to complain? Those records sold well, earned us a bit of money. And that's what it was all about.

I suppose you never imagined anyone would be listening to them sixty years later.

Hell, I wouldn't've imagined anyone listening to them sixty *days* later. We sure never did.

So what went wrong with the Skyrockets? I asked, draining the last of my Bud. You played all across west Texas and New Mexico . . .

And California.

And your records sold well.

Real well.

But you stopped recording in '41. Did you split up entirely then?

More or less. The war came along, you know. We'd shifted record labels, to Decca, and that didn't work out. And . . . He shrugged. We just went our separate ways. Brothers, you know. You can't play forever. You got to grow up sometime.

I looked around his den. Do you?

Cliff threw his head back, hooted with laughter. The hell you do! Come on, let's hit the skins!

Fifty Miles of Elbow Room

Cactus Inn

Gordon and Jane Sheplor

Rt. 66 - West
P.O. Box 107
McLean, TX. 79057

(806)
779-2346

Iris DeMent's two albums provided the soundtrack for my drive through the small towns of west central Texas: Gunsight, Breckenridge, Albany, Funston. It was small town music: 'These Hills', 'Childhood Memories', 'Our Town'. I reckoned that was a good thing for music to be. She didn't write her songs, or sing them, like anybody in Nashville or New York had told her to do it that way. She just wrote and sung exactly how she wanted to: focused in closely on the details of everyday life, full of thwarted ambitions, great dreams being slowly whittled away, small but valuable consolations fiercely held on to:

> My life, it's half way travelled
> And still I have not found my way out of this night
> My life, it's tangled in wishes
> And so many things that just never turned out right

But I gave joy to my mother
I made my lover smile
And I can give comfort to my friends when they're
　　hurting
I can make it seem better for a while

She was so nakedly emotional that the songs were almost painful to listen to: there was raw hurt in her lyrics, and her voice.

One tune was a bit different – I could sing along to it without tears coming to my eyes – and it seemed particularly suited to the wide open spaces *between* the small towns: 'Fifty Miles Of Elbow Room'. At first I assumed it was a description of the type of prairie landscape I was passing through, with its widely spaced farmsteads, ranch-roads that disappeared over the horizon, fields that stretched for unbroken miles. Then I listened more closely, and found the song was actually describing heaven:

When the gates swing wide on the other side
Just beyond the sunset sea
There'll be room to spare as we enter there
There'll be room for you and room for me
For the gates are wide on the other side
Where the fairest flowers bloom
On the right hand and on the left hand
Fifty miles of elbow room

Ah well. Texas? Heaven? Same difference.

The next town I passed through was Anson, famous for its annual Cowboy Christmas Ball. Held annually since 1885, this event was more noteworthy here than it would have been in most places, for a local law prohibited public dancing, with this once-a-year exception. Hence the well known Texas tag, No dancin' in Anson.

Over the decades, many bands of good local repute have

played their mix of swing, honky tonk and traditional fiddle music under the Anson mistletoe: Arch Jefferies and his Blue Flame Boys, Bob Burks and the West Texas Wranglers, Leon Rausch and the Texas Panthers, L.C. Agnew and the Dixie Playboys, and, most recently, Vernon Willingham and the Texas Rhythm Boys. Unsung heroes, on the whole – though Rausch gained fame as vocalist for Bob Wills in the Sixties, and is still going strong – but the type of rock-solid western swing that keeps folk two-stepping all night long. And that's what it's all about.

A few miles further on, I passed through a village called Noodle. Hey, that reminded me, I was hungry! So I pulled off the main drag at Sweetwater, and drove round in circles till I found a good looking diner: Allen's Family Style Meals.

The waitress sat me down at a big table with a bunch of folk *I didn't know*, for God's sake, then immediately started sliding dishes of food in front of us: fried chicken, red beans, potato salad, turnip greens, more fried chicken, black-eyed peas, macaroni cheese, honeyed squash, steaming cornbread and, oh yeah, more fried chicken.

By the end of the meal I knew the folk around me a lot better. I knew who liked beans, who liked greens, who liked whipped margarine(s). Everybody liked fried chicken.

On again, through Loraine, Westbrook, Coahoma, Sand Springs. I stopped for a few minutes in the northern suburbs of Big Spring to take a look at The Stampede, an unprepossessing block-built shed to the untrained eye, a western swing mecca to the aficionado.

A local fiddler and Bob Wills fanatic, Hoyle Nix, built the dancehall for his band, The West Texas Cowboys, in 1954. The Cowboys were hot all through the Fifties and Sixties, retaining great popularity despite the encroachment of rock 'n' roll, which was making life hard for other swing musicians. The Cowboys had some great line-ups, featuring talented ex-Texas Playboys like guitarist Eldon Shamblin, fiddler and saxophonist Louis Tierney, and pianist Mancel

Tierney. In 1960, Hoyle's eight-year-old son Jody joined the band, first as drummer, and later – after his father's death – as a fiddler.

One of the all-time classics of western swing was recorded by Hoyle Nix, in 1949. It captures something of the wild, joyous release of Friday night dances in these parts:

> *Working on the railroad, sleeping on the ground*
> *Eating saltine crackers, ten cents a pound*

> *Big ball's in cow town, we'll all go down*
> *Big ball's in cow town, we'll dance around*

> *Put on your new shoes, put on your gown*
> *Kick off your sad blues, the big ball's in town*

> *Big ball's in cow town, we'll dance around*
> *The girls are all happy cause the big ball's in town*

There wasn't any ball, big or otherwise, tonight, so I drove on. I drove till the city of Midland rose out of the prairie in front of me like a mirage. After miles and miles of flat, scrubby land, much of it virtually desert, it was bizarre to suddenly come across a cluster of elegant steel and glass skyscrapers, the setting sun turning their thousand-foot mirrored windows into blazing towers of red and yellow. There was nothing but empty land for hours all around: why on earth did the buildings have to be squeezed into such a small area, and forced up so high?

I stayed the night with Nancy, a friend of a friend of a friend. It seemed she commuted to university in Fort Worth several days a week – by plane.

I went to bed early and read Cary Ginell's new biography of Milton Brown, which provided a healthy antidote to Charles Townsend's long-revered biography of Bob Wills. While Townsend made out that Wills invented western swing more or less single-handed, Ginell claimed that it was all the work of Brown and his band. Both writers weakened their case by exaggerating the claims of their particular hero. (As Jelly Roll Morton did when he claimed that he alone invented jazz.)

Although it was Wills' records that had first got me interested in the music, I'd also liked Milton Brown for years. And one of the best things about coming to Texas was that I was beginning to come across the names and records of other great bands – dozens of them – which gave the lie to the notion of western swing being invented by *any* one individual. Western swing was a name given retrospectively to a music that was played over a huge geographical area by hundreds of musicians, all of whom put their pinch of spice into the great chilli pot. Focusing on the (remarkable, but not definitive) talents of individuals missed the crucial, exciting point of this great music: it is as diverse, as varied, as ever-changing, and as rich in contradictions and surprising juxtapositions, as the country that spawned it.

Next morning I drove west out of Midland having another listen to Roy Lee Brown's 'Ice Man Song'. For another thing I'd learnt from Ginell's book was that Cliff Kendrick had played the drums on that session.

> *Any ice today lady?*
> *It's nice today lady*
> *How about a little piece today?*

> *We wouldn't try to fool you*
> *Or try to be coarse*
> *But if you want a bigger piece*
> *Well I'll go stop my horse*

It was obvious now: the crispy and snappy snare-work, the exuberant thrash around the cymbals, the mad yelps and shouts of encouragement in the background. Hell, I wouldn't be surprised if someone told me that Cliff'd *written* that song.

West, west, west. Through Odessa, Penwell (good home

town for a writer), Imperial, Grandfalls (with a roadside food stall called SPUNKY BURRITO), Royalty (with a sign advertising AFRICAN PYGMY HEDGEHOGS FOR SALE), Monahans, and Kermit.

Milton Brown died following a car crash, caused by his falling asleep at the wheel while out 'catting around with some sixteen-year-old', as an acquaintance of his put it. I'd learned that from a record sleeve years ago. What I hadn't known till last night was that, as he lay in hospital, critically injured and feverish, he was heard to call out long strings of names of country dancehalls, cross-roads honky-tonks, and back-of-beyond towns his Musical Brownies had played in or passed through. I was beginning to think I knew how he felt.

So I stopped for a while in Wink, planning to visit the museum of the town's most famous (okay, *only* famous) son: Roy Orbison. But it was closed, and the lady at the town hall who had the key was on her lunch break. So I cupped my hands to the window, peered into the gloomy interior of the place, then gave up. Hell, I didn't really like Roy Orbison much anyway, even if he had started out in a Wills-inspired band called the Wink Westerners.

One thing *was* nagging at me though. The painted cut-out of Roy in trademark shades and black jumpsuit I could understand; but why the mural of the Pink Panther on the other side of the museum door? Why the pink 100lb weight at his feet? Why the pink three of clubs?

There was a strange smell in the air in Wink. In fact, I'd been getting whiffs of it on and off since leaving Midland. The whole place smelled like a petrol station. All day I'd been passing nodding donkeys – little, car-sized oil pumps – in fields, on verges, in folks' back gardens; occasionally clumps of big derricks would sprout up out of the flatness. I suppose each of those little wells was producing just a few barrels a day; but there were thousands of them. And one of them was leaking.

I left town, passing a series of signs spaced out over a couple hundred yards of verge:

I RAISE COWS

THEY EAT HAY

DON'T THROW TRASH

ON THE RIGHT OF WAY

I buzzed down my window, sniffed. Nope, no cows: just oil.

Five minutes out of Wink, I was bored again. It wasn't that the landscape was featureless, it was just that there was so much of it. I put on the radio. A preacher was quoting approvingly from Leviticus. Something about wizards, who he equated with spirit mediums, the kind of folk whose adverts crowded the back-pages of Texas newspapers, offering contact with passed-over loved ones, financial and personal advice based on insights from the other side, tips on how to win the lottery. The preacher declared that we should all go along with the bible and stone these mediums to death. Even people who *consult* mediums should be stoned to death.

I stuck in a tape: Miles Davis' 'Round Midnight'. Cool, sparse, leisurely. The perfect soundtrack for desert driving. I cruised on towards noon, chilled out by Miles, and the air conditioning.

Driving in east Texas hadn't been too different from driving in Orkney. Well, there were traffic lights, which I wasn't used to. And traffic, that was new to me too. But at least the roads were on a recognisably human scale. The further west I went, the bigger and wider the landscape got, and the straighter and emptier the roads. Now, skirting the New Mexico border, highway 652 ran completely straight and completely flat in front of me, for as far as I could see.

On the distant horizon was a range of jagged, snow-streaked mountains. I drove for an hour: they were no closer.

It was like only being allowed to speak in the present tense. It was hard to remember where I was before I got on the road, and it was hard to imagine ever reaching a destination, and stopping. All I had was *now*, the moment, the driving. No past, no future, just present continuous.

Cheesy Breeze

I was lying in a sweltering motel room directly under the flightpath into the airport. My head hurt, I'd been throwing up, my bed was doing the panhandle shuffle. For the first and last time I'd eaten Gulf Coast Prawns in the Bombay Bicycle Club, El Paso. It had been daft, come to think of it, even to try seafood here – hundreds of miles from the nearest bit of salt water. The thought of salt water made me think of boats, which made me think of Captain Swanson's roly poly *Ola*, which made my stomach heave again. I needed distraction.

The bedside radio was playing classical music – 'Liebestraum', very soothing. Bob Wills recorded a great big-band version of that in 1941, which wasn't soothing at all, but really punchy, with some great trumpet and sax solos. As a music scholar friend, said, Wow! I'd never have thought *anyone* could make Liszt swing!

The music was interrupted by a high-pitched whine,

simultaneously grating and piercing, followed by a calm but terrifying voice – terrifying because it was so *obviously* making an effort to appear calm. The announcer sounded like Orson Welles in *The War of the Worlds*:

> This is the El Paso emergency broadcast system. The broadcasters in your area, in voluntary co-operation with the federal, state, and local authorities, have developed this system to keep you informed in case of emergency. This is a test. If it had been an actual emergency, the signal you just heard would have been followed by official information, news, or instruction. It is in the interests of everyone in the El Paso area to listen when the signal is given. This concludes today's test of the emergency broadcast system.

A false alarm. It could've been a Cuban missile attack, a swarm of killer bees, or maybe an earthquake. Wink, seemingly the most somnambulant town in the South-West, had been hit by a serious tremor a few weeks before, and I'd bought the bumper sticker to prove it:

WE SURVIVED THE GREAT EARTHQUAKE!
Wink, Texas – April 13, 1995
Robertson's Grocery, Wink

I'd asked the man behind the counter in Robertson's if much damage had been done. Not exactly damage, he said, But our beer got all shook up.
Hey, I said, That wasn't Roy Orbison, that was Elvis!
What in hell you talking about boy?
Nothing, nothing . . .
More likely, though, the emergency broadcasts would be for severe weather warnings. Back home, the weather was something you moaned about; in Texas, the weather was something you ran from. As I'd watched Buddy Ray and the others in Fort Worth, lightning had flashed, thunder

had crashed, and warning sirens had wailed in the streets. Nobody took much notice, so neither did I. Next morning it was reported that 160 people had been hurt, in Oakcliff, over towards Dallas. Tornadoes had smashed an apartment block, torrential rain had flooded the sidewalks. One woman died after being sucked down a drain. John Moen told me he'd witnessed the terrible Wichita Falls twister of April 1979, the one that killed 53 folk. Cars were flattened, trees uprooted, houses smashed to kindling, he said. What should I do if I see one coming? I asked. Put your head between your knees, and kiss your ass goodbye, he replied, and laughed.

Back home in Orkney you might get snowed in for a day or two each winter, or have your flowerbeds flattened by equinoctial gales. Here you were more likely to be knocked unconscious, have your windscreen smashed, your roof tiles cracked, by hailstones the size of baseballs. That's what Texans were always saying: hailstones the size of baseballs. I actually didn't know how big a baseball was, but Nancy had had some stored in her freezer. (Hailstones, not baseballs.) She'd collected them the last time there was a storm in Midland, and planned to bring them out next time a visitor asked for scotch on the rocks.

Me, I didn't fancy living in a meteorologically challenged area. I was quite happy getting my ice cubes from a wee tray in the top compartment of the fridge.

After sleeping for a while, I woke again, lashing with sweat.

I switched on the radio. If you don't mind cooking with Satan, said a cheery voice, Leave out the vanilla and substitute a little Jack Daniels.

I don't know if the chef at the Bombay Bicycle Club was in league with the devil, but I was certainly feeling hellish.

Cliff had told me a story about appearing at a club here. As well as the band, there was an MC, and he fancied himself as a bit of a singer. He'd get out and rove about the tables, Cliff said. He *was* pretty good. But he had this one song that didn't go over too good. He'd take a dollar bill out, and he'd wave it around the tables as he walked about, and he'd sing an old song he called 'Tessie'. It went something like:

> *Tessie, pull down your dressie*
> *Cause I was only teasing you*
> *Just because I waved a dollar bill in my hand*
> *That's no need for you to misunderstand*
> *Oh Tessie, pull down your dressie*
> *For I was only teasing you*

This one night, one guy was there with his wife and grown daughter – maybe one of them was called Tessie, maybe *both* of them were, I don't know – anyway, the guy raised up a coke bottle and BLAM he knocked that singer cold. Then the whole family took off. He he he! The MC never sang that song again. I guess it gave him a sore head just to think about it. But hell, I don't know what the guy who hit him was getting so insulted at: a dollar was a good price! Why, over in old Mexico a woman cost twenty-five cents! And if you can't get five, take two, as the song goes . . .

El Paso Maso-chist. How about that for an album title?

Later still, I picked up the Milton Brown biography again. Was it just my semi-delirious state, or was the author really president of the National No Sense Of Humour Society? His very interesting Song Analysis, for instance, included details on the origin and arrangement of all 119 tracks the Brownies recorded under Milton and Derwood, including 'Cheesy Breeze', a novelty track that the Musical Brownies recorded in 1935. It consisted of a series of tongue-in-cheek solos, followed by Milton crooning:

> *Cheesy breeze*
> *Cheesy breeze, cheesy cheesy breeze*
> *Just my girl and me*
> *Sitting in that cheesy breeze*

That's it. None of the Brownies revealed what the cheesy breeze was, reports Ginell. But they all snickered when questioned about it.

I read that sentence over and over, imagined Ginell earnestly questioning the old musicians about the deep significance of the stupid song they'd laid down more than fifty years before, and I couldn't help laughing. I laughed and laughed, read the sentence again, pictured the scene again – If you wouldn't mind me pressing you on this point, Fred, what *exactly* did Milton mean when he said the breeze was cheesy? Speak into the mic, now – and laughed again.

I laughed until I was sick.

It's Bad to Be A Good Girl
(When You're Nine Miles Out of Town)

Through the scorching summer of 1940, El Paso jitterbugged, trucked and shagged to the bumptious beat of Bob Skyles and his Skyrockets. Moon Mullican, later to be famed as the King of the Hillbilly Piano Players, prime inspiration for the likes of Jerry Lee Lewis, joined the band for the season. Strangely, he received no special billing, despite his recent success pounding the keys with the likes of Cliff Bruner's Texas Wanderers. What's more, the piano stool already being occupied by Max Bennet, Moon was restricted – though that's hardly the word – to bass, accordion, vibes, and homemade electric organ. He sure beat the hell out of them vibes, Cliff had said. Unfortunately, Moon never made it into the studio with the Kendricks, though, at their last good recording session, in Houston in 1940, they did prevail on their accordionist, Frank Wilhelm, to play vibes. The results were bizarre, but great fun.

The owner of the city's Castle Club, an ex-con named Bob Davis, had fitted the place out with stucco turrets and mock fortifications – this is *inside* the hall. The Skyrockets played under an arched alcove, their spare instruments and stylish deco music stands (each one with a different 78 Bluebird release nailed to the front under the band logo) spilling out on to the dance floor. Couples had to dodge the mic leads and jutting trombone-slide as they swayed and sweated past.

Aubrey Mullican had gained the much more jazzy nickname 'Moon' because of his liking for moonshine whiskey: he could drink it all night. Such stamina was essential for musicians playing at clubs like the Castle, and rougher taxi-dance joints like the Tokio Club (another Bob Davis venue) in Hobbs, New Mexico. Taxi-dancers were women paid to jitterbug or truck around the floor with relaxing roughnecks (shagging wasn't entirely ruled out either) with a set charge for each dance. The band was encouraged to play songs as short as they could get away with – ideally only two choruses long – in order for the taxis to rack up the maximum number of fares. Solos were strictly rationed. So were breaks between tunes: four beats, then on to the next little stomper, the next dime dance, the next ride around the block.

And these ninety-second epics had to keep coming all night long! At the Tokio Club, the band members got paid an extra dollar each if they were still playing when the sun came up.

Bob Skyles and the Skyrockets lasted over a year in El Paso, even after Moon abruptly quit the band following the sudden and mysterious death of his girlfriend. I, on the other hand, had only lasted two days. The blistering heat was too much for me. So were the boots: every road I took across town seemed to end at a Tony Llama discount boot store. Ostrich, shark, lizard, rattlesnake, rodeo bull, bison, bat, cat, cockatoo, cockatrice, coot: whichever exotic beasts' hide went into making them, boots is boots is boring when they march out before you in their tens of thousands of pairs.

I had failed to find any trace at all of the Castle Club, or of anyone who looked like they might remember the Skyrockets (or any kind of rockets, apart from the ones being tested at

Fort Bliss, the massive army missile base at the edge of town, 'Home of the Desert Stormers'.) So I decided to head back east, for San Antonio, 558 miles away along Interstate 10.

558 miles? Nothing to the likes of me! The great thing about these interstates was that they were wide and smooth and free-flowing. The traffic just bowled along them. You got out of the city limits, set your seat to maximum recline, and that was you – 65 m.p.h. non stop till you got to your destination. So I left El Paso, confidently expecting to arrive in San Antonio in precisely eight hours and thirty-eight minutes.

Nine miles out of town, just past the turning to Clint, the free-flowing mid-morning traffic started to clog and slow as cones narrowed then completely closed the freeway. We braked, stopped, crawled forward again, siphoning off the interstate and up a narrow slip-ramp. At first I reckoned there must be a roadworks up ahead, or a pile-up, but I soon saw there weren't just one or two traffic cops directing the cars, there was a whole bunch of them, and they were waving us one by one into a vast wall-less Dutch-barn type building that straddled the slip-road. I couldn't see what was happening up ahead, but buzzed down my window, stuck my elbow out, and inched forward whenever the queue moved. A couple miles to my right, the jaggy mountains of northern Chihuahua shimmered and shook in the desert heat haze.

Another car-length forward, towards whatever was happening in the shade of the barn. At least it was shade.

Another car length. Only two more to go. There was some kind of toll booth by the roadway ahead, with a barrier and a couple of stetsoned cops inside, a couple more outside, leaning into car windows.

Then the car was waved on. I turned off my Skyrockets tape in the middle of 'It's Bad To Be A Good Girl'. My turn. The cop had a gun, an arm badge saying Border Patrol, and mirror shades.

Hello, I said. Good to be out of the sun!

He stuck his head in my window as far as his Stetson allowed, and looked around. Travelling alone? he said.

Aye, I said. Just me.

He looked at me. Where from? he said.

El Paso, I said.

Don't joke.

I'm not. A motel called La Quinta, just beside . . .

This is the El Paso road, he cut in. You couldn't get here from anywhere else. Where do you *come* from?

Oh! Scotland, I come from Scotland.

Immigration papers.

Pardon?

Show me your immigration papers.

I'm here on holiday. I don't have any immigration papers. I'm not immigrating!

You've no papers?

I paused, thinking. I've a passport.

He straightened up, looked around the barn, bent down again, pointing off to the left. Drive over the other side of the cabin, kill your engine, and DO NOT GET OUT OF THE VEHICLE.

I considered, having a quick blink at the same time, then did what he said.

I pulled up behind a battered grey truck with what looked like carpets rolled up in the back, and a Mexican-looking family in the cab. I shivered in the cool of the shade, felt a drop of sweat run down my nose and hang there. I leant over and raked through the glove compartment (no gloves, twenty-six cassettes, one can Dr Pepper) for all the papers I could think of: passport, driving licence, insurance, Hertz rental dockets, travellers cheques – no, better not show those, they might be construed as a bribe and raise the cops' ire. Worse, they might be construed as a bribe and taken away from me. Then there was my plane ticket back to London, and a copy of the *Western Swing Society Music News*. Altogether they looked to me like a pretty solid excuse for being in the borderlands, but who can tell how mirror shades alter the vision?

I tried to remember what my West Virginian friend

Pinckney had told me you were meant to do when your car was pulled over by the police. You were meant to stick your hands in the air, stare straight ahead, and bellow out like a rookie on parade: I AM A MEMBER OF THE NATIONAL RIFLE ASSOCIATION, SIR! I HAVE A LOADED WEAPON UNDER MY SEAT, SIR! A MAGNUM 44 FOR SELF-DEFENCE ONLY, SIR! GOD BLESS AMERICA AND THE CONSTI-TUTIONAL RIGHT TO BEAR ARMS, SIR!

The problem was, I didn't have a gun under the seat. The only Magnum I'd ever handled was made of ice-cream and chocolate-flavoured coating. With a tasty sprinkle of crushed nuts. It wouldn't have been much use in self-defence. And what the hell were you meant to say if you weren't in the NRA? I'M A FULL PAID-UP MEMBER OF THE WESTERN SWING SOCIETY, SIR! My shivers were turning into shakes. I was having visions of being carted over the border, dumped in the mean streets of Ciudad Juarez, El Paso's smoke-stacked twin across the river, never allowed back into Texas: passport confiscated, return-ticket cashed in, western swing newsletters torn to pieces and scattered across the desert, my sun-bleached bones slowly covered by drifting sand . . .

There was a beige movement in my wing mirror. Another cop was approaching me from the toll booth, fiddling with something at his belt. Ah yes, he was unbuttoning the strap that held his pistol in its holster. Of course. He had to be ready to draw quick and gun me down if I looked like running away, or developing a bad attitude. The DSS used to be just the same.

He stopped by my window. There were stripes on his sleeve below the Border patrol logo. A dozen paces behind him I could see the guy in the mirror shades taking up position, ready to give covering fire. The sergeant pinched the creases of his uniform breeks between thumb and first finger, hitched them up, and crouched to look in at me. He wasn't wearing shades. I wished he had been; his stare immediately started to make me itchy with guilt, even though I hadn't done anything. (*Especially* because I hadn't done anything. Three cheers for a good Calvinist upbringing.)

He cleared his throat. Now then . . .

YES, SIR!

He winced. Don't yell, he said. Just keep your hands where I can see them and tell me where you've come from.

Scotland, I said.

He sighed. Where have you come from today?

El Paso. A motel called La Quinta.

He cleared his throat again. Can I see your immigration papers? he said.

I didn't try to explain this time, I just handed over everything I had, the whole bundle of stuff.

He stood up, riffled through them, handed them back into me one by one: driver's licence, insurance, plane ticket, travellers cheques. I didn't count to see if they were all still there. Then he crouched down again, my passport in his hand.

This is what I want, he said, thrusting the passport under my nose. It was open to the page where the guy at the desk at Washington DC airport had stapled a yellow ticket-stub. That's your papers, said the sergeant. Just hand them over next time, huh?

Definitely, I said.

Definitely, he said. Now be on your way.

I can go?

Get out of here, he snapped, and turned away. I started the engine, stuck the stick into D for drive, and shot off round the pick-up, fast down the slip-ramp, fast on to the freeway, and as fast as I could along the road till I came to the first gas station somewhere in the jaggedy white mountains near Sierra Blanca. I parked the car in a cloud of dust, ran around the sand-blasted old building till I found the rest room, then dashed in and filled the pan with skitters. Prawn food-poisoning and pistol-packin' border guards made for very uneasy bowels.

Back in the car, I shoved in the Bob Skyles and the

Skyrockets tape, thinking it'd bring me back to some kind
of equilibrium.

> It's bad to be a good girl
> When you're nine miles out of town
> It's bad to be a good girl
> When that nasty man's around
>
> Now he said 'Yes', she said 'No'
> He said 'Yes you will, or that's as far as you go'
> The night was cold and the night was black
> She knew that she'd have to walk back
>
> It's bad to be a good girl
> When you're nine miles out of town
>   I mean, nine miles out of town
>
> (FLATULENT TRUMPET SOLO)
>
> It's bad to be a good girl
> When you're nine miles out of town
> It's bad to be a good girl
> When that nasty man's around
>
> Now some girls do, some girls don't
> Some girls will, some girls won't
> It's bad to be a good girl
> When you're nine miles out of town
>   I mean, nine miles out of town

Maybe I was wrong about the equilibrium. I switched it off
and drove away from the parking lot in silence.

This is Southland

Driving west Texas roads is a form of meditation. They're so flat and straight and wide that you don't have to be concentrating to stay on them. In fact, you barely need to be conscious. You can eat, drink, read a map, read a book, *write* a book, all with one finger on the wheel.

The road stretches out to the horizon. You set cruise control, slip over into the back seat and stretch out. Half an hour later you wake, yawn, rub your eyes, and clamber back into the front: the road still stretches out to the horizon.

Occasionally a semi-truck rumbles towards you along twenty miles of heat-hazed straight; or a pick-up roars past, rolls of barbed wire, a German Shepherd, half a dozen Chicanos bouncing about the back. Once or twice an hour you'll see a car with a dazed looking family inside. You wave, but no one waves back: they don't see you, they're in highway hyper-reality, they've transcended the material road.

West Texas roads are so featureless that they easily become abstractions, symbols, like the ones the Orkney poet Edwin Muir kept writing about:

> Friend, I have lost the way.
> *The way leads on.*
> Is there another way?
> *It's lost and gone.*
> Back, I must travel back!
> *None goes there, none.*
> Then I'll make here my place,
> (*The road runs on*),
> Stand still and set my face,
> (*The road leaps on*),
> Stand here, for ever stay.
> *None stays here, none.*
> I cannot find the way.
> *The way leads on.*
> Oh places I have passed!
> *That journey's done.*
> And what will come at last?
> *The road leads on.*

I'd often wondered why Muir kept going back to the road as a symbol in his poems. He returned to it as obsessively as Kafka (who Muir was first to translate into English) did to his courtrooms and castles. Then I visited the tiny island of Wyre where Muir grew up.

Wyre was the world of his childhood. Even though it was only a mile long and half a mile wide it was *all* the world: there was no possibility of travelling beyond its boundaries. To the boy Muir, the surrounding islands and skerries were as distant and unreachable as the stars. And in 1894, this indivisible, self-contained world was changed utterly: Wyre's first road was laid, bisecting the island, running down its low heathery spine, east to west. Muir was seven. He watched the road grow, walked it, took it into his world: the road that split the world but never took you out of it.

Imagine Muir growing up a Texas sharecropper instead of a north isles peasant farmer! The roads here are different: they take you somewhere, they lead you over the horizon. The road on Wyre stopped when it reached the edges of the island, the edges of the world: go any further and you'd fall off. In Orkney you have borders bred into you by the sea; in Texas the borders have to be marked out by a line of men with guns.

Approaching the town of Van Horn, I started to get paranoid. The road got busier, the traffic bunched up; I kept noticing shotgun-racks in the pick-up cabs; too many folk were wearing mirror shades, too many folk (I thought) were staring suspiciously at my outsider licence plates; AMERICAN OWNED said the sign outside the cheap motel.

I'm not used to this, I said to myself. I don't like being checked out to see if I'm a dangerous stranger from the wrong side of the borderlands. Give me the sea anyday, or a decent impassable mountain range for God's sake: at least geographical boundaries are impersonal. They just sit there and don't let you past, they don't intimidate you, stare you out, unbutton their pistol-holster.

I took the first turning off the interstate, the first road out of Van Horn, and put my foot down. In front of me was nothing but flat orange desert, and, along the horizon, a saw-edge of red mountains.

The road led on. I followed it. South, south, south. No other traffic. Just the empty road, the empty desert, the empty sky.

A speck appeared on the horizon, got bigger, solidified through the heat shimmer. A town, a village: the signs said Lobo.

Lobo was a dozen wrecked homes: a ghost town – a ghost hamlet, with no one around to avenge its death. What could you do anyway? Pour poison in the ear of the weatherman cause it hadn't rained for two years and your crops had withered? Wind whipped red dust through

the cracked windows and loose boards of the shacks on the
west, swirled it across the road, then whisked it through the
warped doors and rattling corrugated roofs of the shacks on
the east. Outside the abandoned gas station was a sign saying,
TOWN FOR SALE.

Away to my left were hundreds of rows of stunted trees, neat
lines of them stretching away across the plains. Some kind of
fruit farm or orchard. There was sparse foliage, and brown
dangleberries hanging from the gnarled branches. I decided
these were pecan groves, though I didn't really know if
pecans grew on trees, let alone on stunted, sand-blasted
cripple-trees.
    Occasionally a swirling movement would catch the corner
of my eye. I'd look around quickly, just in time to see an
indistinct mass boiling across the desert, or smothering the
far edge of the pecan forest. A drublie cloud, sometimes pink,
sometimes grey, edgeless but dense in the centre, would roll
along for a few seconds before evaporating, or sinking down,
or flattening out. I don't know what happened to the things:
they just disappeared.
    I looked back to the front, and jolted: fifty metres ahead
of me the road was filled with a vast white pile of *something*.
In a second I was inside it: a cloud of white swirling sand
and dust, so thick I couldn't see beyond the bonnet of the
Chevy. I slammed on the brakes, heard particles of grit
pitting themselves against the windows and the paintwork.
I switched on my lights, let the car crawl forward, images
of *Close Encounters* coming into my head, of the Bermuda
Triangle, of planes and ships and cars being swallowed in
strange white clouds, emerging on the other side of the world
forty years later, passengers not a day older.
    The whiteness thickened, poured across the window in
streams like an Aberdeen fog – but it wasn't a fog, for
there was no trace of moisture on the glass. The cloud
was dry as powdered bone. It streamed around the car,
energised by something or other, but strangely silent. It was
weird: there was no rush of wind, no tornado howl, just

the engine idling and the particles ticking faintly against the outside of the car.

Then another car drew up alongside me, set to overtake. I slowed to let it pass, but nothing pulled ahead. I glanced in my wing mirror: it was empty. I looked back over my shoulder: nothing in the blind spot but billows of dust. When I looked back to the front, there it was again, the other car, shadowing me. I could see its shape quite clearly at the edge of my vision.

I turned my head – and again it was gone.

Next time, I turned my head very slowly, a degree at a time, and I got a better look at the car, and at the driver – in the right-hand seat – with his head twisted uncomfortably to look forwards and out the side window at the same time. Studying the road ahead and his ghost in the red Chevy . . .

Except it wasn't *me* who was the ghost. Aye, get a grip man, *he* was the ghost, *it* was the ghost. Or whatever it was. I snapped my head round for a decent deek. Gone!

Some kind of reflection, it had to be. A trick of the light and the dust storm. Somehow the tiny particles of dust whirling about me were teaming up with the blazing Texas sunshine in a weird ghosty effect, no, a weird mirror effect: they were reflecting me and my car back on myself as I inched along. I was driving through a cloud of mirrors, looking for west Texas, seeing only myself.

Abruptly the swirling of the dust quickened, thickened, swept up my bonnet like a car wash, and instantly I was out of it, into blazing sunshine and blinding blue sky. I stopped, blinked, shook my head.

A big green and yellow tractor was approaching at high speed. The driver grinned, raised an arm in greeting, and shot past. Not a ghost. I twisted round in my seat. Through the back window I saw the white cloud, a squashed sphere a hundred metres across, rolling down the road, and the tractor-driver heading into it at full speed, arm still raised in greeting, or farewell.

Bob Skyles and the Skyrockets did a nice line in undercutting the macho-man-of-the-west image in their songs. They recorded 'The Lavender Cowboy' three years before Vernon Dalhart, and also a variation called 'The Drugstore Cowboy', focusing on a cowpunch-wannabe, all dressed up with no place to rodeo. (I remember seeing a newspaper headline from the Los Angeles *Beam* dating back to about 1944, which picked up on the same archetype: WILLS AND HIS DRUGSTORE COWBOYS HITCH HORNS TO TC AMP TUESDAY: 'SANTONE ROSE' AUTHOR BRINGS RANGE RHYTHM.) A couple of the Skyrockets' songs came closer to expressing tender feelings between tough men than just about anything else in the country and western cannon. How about this:

The pal that I loved
Stole the gal that I loved
Took away all my sunshine and joy

Nobody but he
Was a buddy to me
Since we played on the porch with our toys

I just can't believe my old pal would deceive me
Gee, but I'm heartsick and sore

The pal that I loved
Stole the gal that I loved
That's why we're not pals any more

Okay, its starting point is a very passé possessiveness, but it moves on from there. I reckon it's actually quite a revealing wee song, an honest piece of work, recorded (in San Antonio in 1938) with such regretful, understated vocals, that it really comes across as a fallible man's admission of bafflement and defeat: a confession of male frailty and pain rare in songs of the West.

An even more suggestive song is 'Way Out West of the Pecos'. At first hearing it seems like a standard celebration of the romantic cowboy image, with its saddles and sagebrush, tin stars and tumbleweeds. But it's actually subtler than that, I think. Subtle and, dare I say it, sexually ambiguous. Gay cowboy literature is thin on the ground, and man to man love songs are all but unknown in the fearfully straight culture of Nashville country. Somebody gave me a compilation tape of left-field Austin bands a few years ago, including a song called (I think) 'Last Ten Dollars', by The Two Nice Girls. The first verses went something like this:

> *I spent my last ten dollars*
> *On birth control and beer*
> *Life was so much simpler when*
> *I was sober and queer*

> *But the love of a strong hairy man*
> *Has turned my head I fear*
> *And made me spend my last ten bucks*
> *On birth control and beer*

Maybe since kd lang it's okay to be a lesbian country singer – as long as you stick to big cities like Seattle and Washington and Glasgow. I've never come across a gay country act, despite the fact that half of all country singers still dress so far over the top that they look like Village People rejects. There did use to be a gay bar in Edinburgh called Chaps. It's hard to imagine it surviving with that name in Nashville or Wichita Falls: the irate attentions of rednecked bible-bashing Roy Acuff fans would be too much to bear.

Anyway, here's that Skyrockets song:

> *Way out west of the Pecos*
> *Out on the cactus plains*
> *We don't have cold weather*
> *We seldom see clouds rain*

> *The coyotes howl*
> *And the cattle prowl*
> *And the boys sleep out on the ground*

Where a man is a man
And a friend is a friend
And they tote their guns around

There's a couple more verses, and solos from the piano and clarinet, then a final verse in which the singer imagines a campfire idyll:

I love to smell the bacon
And watch the cornbread brown
When roundup time is over, boys
We'll all ride into town

Presumably for a nice cup of tea and some scones at the Lite Bite. So much for knocking back slugs of wood alcohol in the Bucket of Blood Saloon.

Forty years later, somebody recorded a country song called 'My Wife Ran Off With My Best Friend (And I Miss Him)'. That was a joke, but, although the Skyrockets recorded a lot of humorous or would-be humorous material, they very often used laughter as a decoy, behind which they could slip in fairly subversive ideas. Did they set out to undercut the stereotypical macho cowboy image, or just to make daft jokes and break the tedium of the long taxi-dance gigs? I should've asked Cliff.

As far as I could see in any direction, the land was flat and featureless. The occasional clump of spiky grass qualified as a scenic attraction. If I'd stopped the car and climbed up on the roof, I'd've been the highest point for miles around. But I didn't want to risk it, no way: you never know when a freak lightning storm's going to brew up and bolt you.

Just ahead and a couple fields off to my right, a tree six inches wide and three thousand feet tall shot up towards the sun. That couldn't be right.

I pulled into the side of the road (though I'm sure it wasn't strictly necessary: I hadn't seen another vehicle since the tractor passed half an hour before). I got out and shielded my eyes to look upwards. A silvery blob was balanced at the top of the trunk. What was it? I cupped both hands around my eyes against the sun, and strained to focus against the glare. Eventually I made out a bulbous, bomb-shaped thing, with a three-finned tail and a little lump hanging underneath, blue against the silver of the rest. An airship! A Zeppelin! A blimp! And the trunk holding it up was actually a cable holding it down.

I followed the tether with my eyes. It was fastened to the ground just a hundred metres away, in a small fenced-in area with a small cylinder at one end and a couple of huts or sheds or kennels at the other. Apart from that the desert rolled on to the horizon.

What the hell was the blimp doing soaring away up above the flat plains of Presidio County? Something else I had no idea about. Once again I was being forced into baseless speculation.

Speculation 1. Millionaire rancher Travis Grit III got so fed up of the featureless prairie that he went out and bought himself a blimp. I'm going to get myself a picturesque view if I have to live in the clouds to do it, he said, adding, It's a long way to go for your rolls and milk on a Sunday morning.

Speculation 2. There were no clouds to live in. It hadn't rained for two years. Rafting trips down the Rio Grande had to be cancelled cause there are trickles instead of rapids, dribbles instead of falls, brown mud instead of white water. A consortium of raft-hirers wrapped a massive balloon in super-absorbent kitchen-towels, then hoisted it skywards in a desperate attempt to attract moisture-bearing clouds.

Speculation 3. Worried at the possibility of an invasion of illegal immigrants and social security scroungers from the poor towns of Mexico, local militias constructed a primitive barrage balloon, with a small armoured gondola underneath fitted with automatic weapons, cluster bombs and Rush Limbaugh rants on loop tapes. A spokesman, Colonel George Washington Himmler, said, We're going to sit up there and pick off them no-good impurities as soon as we see them sneaking over the border. Or even if they look in our direction. And if they *don't*, then we're a-going to shoot them anyways, cause they're insulting the greatest nation on God's green earth by not looking with longing upon it. Amen.

Shit. I bet it wasn't anything nearly as interesting as that really. Thank God I'll never know the boring truth.

Bright Lights and Blonde-Haired Women

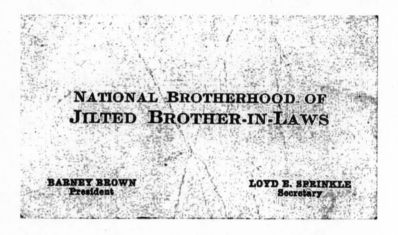

NATIONAL BROTHERHOOD OF
JILTED BROTHER-IN-LAWS

BARNEY BROWN
President

LOYD E. SPRINKLE
Secretary

Three hours later I came to the town of Marfa, and found a hotel: El Paisano. Thirty-five bucks for a suite: big bedroom, bathroom walled with mirrors and a mutant-ninja-seashell collection, kitchenette with lemon vinyl booth-seats, lounge with orange Seventies three-piece suite, orange table lamp, orange carpet (for variety the wallpaper was tangerine), and french windows opening on to some kind of courtyard.

I dropped my bag, crashed out on the settee.

Three hours later I came to, gasping for breath. The room was stiflingly hot and airless. I stumbled over to the french windows, flung them open, and stepped out onto the wrought-iron balcony. It was even hotter and more oxygen-starved there. There was a milky blue swimming pool below which should've been cooling, but the whole courtyard had been roofed in with some clear plastic stuff that seemed designed to magnify the sun's rays to skin-blistering intensity. A clammy something filled the air, half odour, half vapour: the turbid pool slowly evaporating, finding no escape through the corrugated roof, hanging about and mixing with the reek of stale chlorine, sweaty plant-pot foliage, and frying smells from the hotel kitchen whose windows opened on to the poolside. Imagine a high speed collision between a busy chip shop at midnight on Friday, and a packed laundrette on a rainy morning in February. That's what I was gasping down. It wasn't clearing my lungs, or my head. I shut the windows, grabbed my wallet, and left the room.

I'd hardly taken in the hotel lobby when I arrived, I was that tired, or something. It was vast and pleasantly dim, high ceilinged, paved with cool tiles. Big windows looked out on to a courtyard with flower beds and a fountain. It was about the first place I'd stayed in that was older than me: built in the Thirties, I'd guess, but in imitation of a Victorian elegance, with dark wooden stairs and panelling, arched doorways, worn leather settees. On the walls hung paintings of western scenes, geometric displays of Indian stone arrow heads, and shelves of books.

I always like to have a look at the books lying around hotels and guest houses: someday I'll maybe come across a signed first edition of *Ulysses*, offer the owner five quid on top of my B&B for it, and retire. So far what I've found is remarkably uniform from place to place: a mixture of the trashy, the odd, and the irredeemably dull. I had another reason for checking out El Paisano's shelves, though: fear of suffocation. The *New Grove Dictionary of Jazz* was proving rather heavy for bedtime reading; I'd fallen asleep halfway through the entry for Coleman Hawkins the other night and woken up in the wee hours with the breath crushed out of me.

Let's see. Several copies of *National Geographic* from 1978–9; two Arthur Haileys; *Little Women*; a school history of Texas; half a dozen *Reader's Digest* anthologies; *Blacking Up: The Minstrel Show in Nineteenth Century America*, by Robert C. Toll; a Hemingway novel; some theological tomes; a creased paperback *Catch 22*; a children's illustrated *Tale Of Two Cities*;

a few Zane Grey westerns; a multi-volume encyclopaedia from 1919; a collection of cartoons from the *New Yorker*; a Victorian anthology of tales of white women captured by savage, animalistic Indian tribes; *Leaves of Grass*.

Behind the desk in the lobby was a life-size cardboard cut-out of James Dean. Well, from the front it was life-size; from the side he was a good deal thinner than in real life. I asked why the cut-out was there, but he didn't reply, and there was no one else about to answer me. All became clear further down the lobby, though, where there were several wooden display cases filled with movie memorabilia. It seemed that the epic *Giant* had been filmed on ranches around Marfa, back in 1955, and several of the cast and crew stayed in El Paisano for the duration. Hence the signed photos of Jimmy, Liz Taylor, Rock Hudson, young Dennis Hopper; hence the boot that graced Liz's dainty feet, the bit that Rock's horse got his teeth into, the bandanna Jim wiped his brow on. (Nothing connected with Buddy Ray, the greatest fiddling-extra that ever lived: all his scenes were shot in Hollywood.)

Had *Giant* been filmed in, say, Nashville, there would be a continuous video showing highlights from the film, a model of an oil well gushing gen-u-ine black gold, the skeleton of Rock's trusty steed, fully articulated and motorised to gallop on the spot. Being a modest, self-deprecating wee hotel in a remote, uncommercialised town, the main attraction in El Paisano was a photo-article clipped out of *Life* magazine, which documented the shoot. A close second went to the solid gold three-boot bootlast on the floor beneath the cases. Well, when I say solid gold, I really mean solid gold-plated. Or, to be exact, solid iron, sprayed with gold paint.

I'd only seen *Giant* once, and I couldn't remember much about it. I think I fell asleep halfway through. Too many horses, ranches, high-heeled boots. I find all that stuff really boring. In films, I mean. A lot of folk assume that, because I'm into western swing, I must be into all things western: they expect to find me down the local Cowboy Club in a tartan shirt, Doc Marten bootlace tie, and chaps my mum's run up from a pair of old curtains. (Oh aye, we always had fringed suede curtains in our house.) No way. I can't stand the Grand Old Opry, which to me features all the worst aspects of country music rolled into one. I don't like line dancing at all, unlike the rest of the population of Orkney. And most of all I hate John Wayne films – I hate all corny westerns. Please don't start going on about John Ford. The only good Ford is a Model-T Ford, as far as I'm concerned. And even then, only when Laurel and Hardy are driving it/squashing it flat/sawing it in two. (Somebody told me once that Samuel Beckett was a big laurel and Hardy fan. I quite believe it, but I have a theory that he actually wrote half of their films: that one where they have to carry the piano up the endless flight of steps, and it keeps rolling to the bottom? Pure existential angst, man.) Liking James Kelman novels doesn't mean you have to like Harry Lauder and Walt Disney's *Greyfriar's Bobby* too, and liking Bob Wills doesn't mean I have to like *Rawhide* and George Bush, thank Christ. Stick that in your gun and smoke it.

I left the hotel under its six fluttering Stars and Stripes. It was getting towards sunset, and the clear skies meant the temperature would soon be plunging. I needed sustenance. In Texas that means getting in your car, so I did. But it wasn't enough, I needed more. So I drove off in search of a restaurant.

I found Lucy's. It was a bar rather than a restaurant, though it only served two types of beer. Fair-minded as ever, I ordered one of each, then asked if there was any food on the go.

Sure, said the middle-aged woman behind the bar.

Like, eh, what?

We got pizza, she said.

What kind?

Frozen.

Yeah, but what flavour?

We got two varieties: large or small.

Eh, great. I'll have a large one then. Please.

She disappeared through the back, and I heard a microwave

door slam, and the fan start up. I looked around, glugging my Coors. Lucy's was a bare place, with a couple guys playing pool at a table up the back, and no other customers. There was a juke box, unlit, and a telly on a high shelf, blaring.

Behind the bar was a handwritten sign: STRICTLY NO SET UPS. I wondered what that meant. The barmaid was back, leaning across the far end of the bar, watching a cup of coffee steam in front of her. I smiled at her.

Excuse me, I said. What's a set up?

She glowered at me. We don't do them, she said, and jerked her thumb at the sign.

I opened my mouth, then shut it, and nodded. Good, I said.

The microwave pinged, and she stepped through the back, returning a second later with a twelve-inch pepperoni and green pepper pizza, and a bottle of Crystal hot pepper sauce. I got stuck in. It was great, though a little more pepper wouldn't've hurt.

There was no sign of anybody else coming in the bar, and I was sitting eating at the counter only six feet away from her, so I thought I'd talk to the barmaid. Forward of me, I know, but after a couple dashes of Crystal hot pepper sauce I'm capable of anything.

Are you Lucy? I asked.

She looked at me over the top of her cup of coffee. Well I'm not dizzy, she said.

I nodded, swallowed, and said, Pardon?

I'm not dizzy, she said again.

Oh. Good. I stuffed another wang of pizza in my mouth, frowned while I chewed, showing it was necessary to concentrate to enjoy the full complexities of its flavour, it was that doggone delicious. Driving through the town there, I said eventually, I saw these posters – in the motel windows and stuff – SEE GHOST LIGHTS, MARFA LIGHTS FESTIVAL. What's that all about?

She sighed, laid down her coffee cup, and stretched. Nobody knows, she said – and let her shoulders slump again.

Nobody knows what? I said after a second.

Nobody knows nothing, she said. They don't know if they're campfires, or reflections from headlights . . . or ghosts. Nobody knows *what* they are. But they keep on a-shining. And the people keep on a-talking about them. Never no closer to explaining them though.

I've never seen a ghost, I said. I always wanted to see one. Or spot a UFO. Or meet a Tory voter, ha ha. But I never have. After a while you start to wonder if they exist at all.

Well, most everybody sees the Marfa ghost lights. Eight miles east of town on 90, stop at the pull in there. And wait. I don't know what they are, but they're there all right.

I finished my pizza, started in on the second beer: Miller. Maybe I should order the other pizza variety too, I thought to myself, the tantalisingly named Small. Then I could say I'd been through the entire menu of Lucy's in a sitting, food and drink. Something to be proud of. In fact, didn't such a situation crop up in *Diner* or *American Graffiti* or one of those Fifties nostalgia ads? There was some grand prize for eating the whole menu in a oner: a week's projectile vomiting, I think. I decided to skip it, and head off in search of the ghost lights. I'd no real expectation of seeing anything, but had nothing else to do but return to the Manmade Fibre Suite at El Paisano and fight for breath. No contest: give me land lots of land under starry skies above, any time.

It was pitch dark as I drove out of town, but I found the viewing-point no problem: a semi-circle of gravel edged with enormous flat-topped boulders and white-painted oil-drum rubbish bins. Out of the car, and after a couple minutes of my eyes adjusting, I was able to read the lettering on the historical marker by the light of the full moon:

MARFA LIGHTS

The Marfa Lights, mysterious and unexplained lights that have been reported in the area for over one hundred years, have been the subject of many theories. The first recorded sighting of the lights was by rancher Robert Ellison in 1883. Variously explained as campfires, phosphorescent minerals, swamp gas, static electricity, St Elmo's Fire, and ghost lights, the lights reportedly change colors, move about, and change in intensity. Scholars have reported over seventy-five local folk tales dealing with the unexplained phenomenon.

I gazed out towards the south. The land stretched out flat and dark, the Chinati mountain range silhouetted against the scatter of stars to the South-West. No sign of any ghosts. No sign of anything at all. Surprise surprise.

A faint sound in the distance rose, fell, and disappeared. Then it returned, louder: a kind of deep growl. I looked out over the plains, but it wasn't coming from there, it was off to one side: back in the direction of the town. I turned. Two white lights shimmered away along the highway, moving from side to side, closer together then further apart, bright, then extinguished for a second before blazing clearly again. The growl grew into a roar. The lights got bigger, brighter, the roaring got louder, throatier, I stared in amazement, the lights bore down on me, blinding me, the roar deafening, the lights, the lights, the lights . . . And two big Harley Davidsons cruised into the viewing area, gunned up their engines one last time, then cut out. After a second, their lights clicked off.

I blinked, sighed.

A big, broad-shouldered figure in black leather and full-face helmet separated itself from each bike, and the two of them walked towards me. They were six foot six at least. I took a step round the far side of the picnic table, the thought zapping through my head, Who eats picnics at midnight? The riders hands went up to the shadows under their chins, fiddled for a second, then, simultaneously, they lifted off their helmets.

Howdy, said the first guy, smoothing down his short blond hair with his black-leather-gloved hand.

Hi, said the second, unzipping his leather jacket an inch.

Eh, hello.

They both had neat blond moustaches as well as neat blond haircuts. They laid their helmets down on the picnic table.

Are you here for the ghosts? I said.

Excuse me? said the first guy.

We're here for the lights, said the second.

Seen anything yet?

Me? No, never. I'm probably a jinx. You'll probably see nothing either if you stand next to me.

They were both gazing away towards the mountains in the south-west. They put their heads together, muttered to each other, then turned back to me.

I'm Luke, said the first one. How do you do?

Eh? Fine! I introduced myself.

From Scotland? said Luke.

Aye!

Did you have a good St Patrick's day?

Eh . . . it was fine. Yourself?

Luke, he said.

I'm Stevens, said the other guy.

I nodded. Pleased to meet you Steven, I said.

No, he said. Stevens, with an s at the end.

And at the start, eh! Ha!

They looked at each other, smiled politely, then turned away and stared out across the dark country. They started muttering to each other again. I glanced at my watch, tried to work out how long I was prepared to waste standing out in the cold night air of the desert waiting for nothing to happen. But I couldn't read my watch: the two bikers were so tall they were blocking out the moonlight.

You on vacation? said Luke.

Me? Yeah – touring around. I'm staying in Marfa tonight.

Us too, said Stevens. Camping.

There was a pause.

You travelling alone? said Luke.

Apart from the heavily armed bodyguard three steps behind you, I wanted to say, but something stopped me: a spark in the far darkness.

Hey! See that!

What? they said together.

I thought I saw . . .

A light?

Well, more of a . . . spark.

A glint?

Well, no . . . more of a kind of . . . a flash. Over amongst the mountains.

We all stared off to the south-west. A minute passed. And another.

Ach, I said, I probably imagined it. I never see anything.

We came all the way from Houston to see them, said Stevens. Sure hope they show.

All the way from Houston tonight? On your bikes? What's that, eight hundred miles?

No, said Stevens. We drove down yesterday with the bikes on a trailer. Too hot and cold to ride all the way down. We drive down, camp in Marfa, then ride the bikes all through Big Bend. You been there yet?

No. I've heard it's bonnie, though.

Sure is, we . . .

Did you see that! cried Luke, and raised an arm to point. His leather sleeve creaked as he held the arm out towards the distant mountains.

We watched, waited. Twenty seconds later, a faint white light appeared, then immediately vanished.

Hey! said Stevens.

She! said Luke.

Another light popped up to one side of the first one. It shimmered, went out, then blazed up again, brighter than before. And the first one, or one very close to it, came alight again.

Two! whispered Stevens.

Three, I said, and pointed. Another, bigger but softer light had appeared away to one side, and lower down.

And look, said Stevens. Is that a star up there, or . . .

Near the peak of one of the highest of the Chinati Mountains was a small twinkling light. But it was *below*

the summit: no star, not unless they were drifting down
out of the night sky, no bigger than bonfires.

Suddenly all the lights went out, simultaneously, it seemed.

Wow! said Stevens.

What the heck was that? said Luke.

Ghosts, I said.

Nah!

More, said Stevens.

Two lights were burning now. Not bright and blazing, but certainly radiant, off-white in colour. They didn't
waver and flare like flames, but they did shimmer and
sway.

Is the one on the right moving? said Luke.

I stared. It was hard to say. It did seem to be swinging
from side to side, slowly, like a warning lantern.

Could be heat haze refracting the light, said Stevens.

It went out. The other one was out too, but I hadn't
noticed it go.

Listen! said Stevens.

The silence of the desert was vast and complete.

What? said Luke.

Nothing at all, said Stevens. No car engines, no train
whistles . . . nothing.

What the hell are they? said Luke.

Ghosts of pioneers, said Stevens, Lost in a blizzard in the
mountains. Indian spirits, guiding their people home. Torches
of ranchers out looking for a young boy, fallen down a mine
shaft a hundred years ago.

I have this funny feeling, I said. They can't be any of those
things, they can't be anything ghostly. I mean, I never see
anything weird, anything ghostly, I just see what's really there.
Therefore, they can't be ghosts, *because* I see them . . . I was
feeling all excited before they appeared, feeling like, well,
they might actually be ghosts or something. But as soon as
I see them I just think, nah . . . and I feel kind of . . .
deflated. I almost wish they'd never showed up: I could still
believe in them then.

I heard they've been trying to figure these things out for

a hundred years, said Luke. I can't believe it. There they are! Get over there! Work it out!

Must be some kind of gas burn off, said Stevens. Some kind of natural gas up in the mountains, coming out of the ground as the rock cools down, contracts.

A couple more lights popped up, one bright and stationary, the other fainter, wavering slightly.

I'd say they were fakes, said Luke. I'd definitely say they were a goddam hoax, if it wasn't for one thing: we're not paying to see them. If Presidio County was charging even one thin dime for us to stand here, I'd say, No way man! That's the Rotary Club over there with flashlights!

But it's free, said Stevens. It must be natural. Nothing man-made's free. It's natural gas.

Supernatural gas, said Luke. We all laughed. No, he went on after a minute, if it was gas burning – if it was anything burning – you'd find scorch marks on the hillside over there, burnt brush. No one's found that. Can't be fires.

What else then? I said. I checked the map on the way out here: if it's reflections from some town or road, then God knows where, cause there's nothing for miles.

Hell, I don't know. But I know what I'd do – look at that big sucker burn! – I'd get a goddam helicopter, fly over there and WHOOSH! Whenever I saw one down below I'd swoop down, land right on top of it: end of mystery.

Maybe it's phosphorescent minerals, I said. Or static electricity, or St Elmo's Fire.

You ever seen that? said Stevens.

St Elmo's Fire? I don't think so.

It's pretty good, he said. Emilio Estevez, Rob Lowe, Demi Moore with her clothes on . . . Funny, but a pretty accurate picture of life in the early Eighties.

Luke snorted. I hate all that bratpack stuff. And *St Elmo's*, it's just *The Breakfast Club* a couple years on, a bar instead of a school. They were just working out a formula there. It's about as accurate as a Charlie Brown movie.

Hey, don't start on Charlie Brown! cried Stevens. Pigpen

summed up the dissatisfaction of a generation! Lucy's a strong woman, man!

What! Come on!

Hey, guys, I said. What line of work are you in? Are you film critics or something?

They stopped arguing, turned to me.

We're in oil, said Stevens.

Hydrocarbons, said Luke. You got them in Scotland?

Eh, aye . . . I think so. One or two.

Get them most everywhere, said Stevens.

Hydrocarbons are at the back of everything, said Luke. Probably they're at the back of these lights too. Either that or there's a whole bunch of stoned Mexicans over there having a good laugh at all the dumb Yankees. And the dumb Scotsman. He shook a black-leathered fist in the direction of the lights and Mexico. Sons of bitches, he said through gritted teeth.

Stevens laughed. Quit fooling around, Luke.

Luke sighed, shook his head. I'm bored. Who'd've thought you could get bored seeing real live ghosts? Three minutes and I've had enough. Eight hundred miles, and all for three minutes of hydrocarbons! I could've stayed home and done an oil change on the Harley. I could've stretched that out to half an hour!

How about me! I said. I've come four *thousand* miles! Three months away from home!

All to see these lights? asked Stevens.

No, to see western swing as it should be seen! To search out the spirit of Bob Wills and his Texas Playboys!

Luke whacked a massive leather-gauntlet down on my shoulder, and squeezed. You really have wasted your time, he said.

Jesusita en Chihuahua

ACCORDION REPAIRS

W. C. Jacob

TEACHER OF
THE PIANO-ACCORDION

STUDIO 1108 ELM ST., C-3191
RESIDENCE PHONE H-5835

DALLAS

I sat by the steaming pool, breakfasting on coffee and the local weekly, *The Big Bend Sentinel*. Among the front page stories were results of the recent mayoral elections, as well as headlines like LIONS' CLUB MOP, BROOM SALE TODAY and APPRECIATION BARBECUE SUNDAY FOR TROOPS HERE. The latter had a computer illustration of a GI, looking like Sharon Stone in a tin hat. Surely not. '*No speeches, no drawings, no prizes, organisers said. Just an afternoon of fellowship to honor our military friends.*' Fidel Castro couldn't have put it better.

On page five was an interesting story all about NATIONAL PRESERVATION WEEK MAY 14–20: '*West Texas is indeed fortunate to have a number of real people whose commitment and creativity have helped to preserve historic buildings, cemeteries, and the acetic appearance of our neighborhoods and towns.*' Never mind preserving the place, real people, it's already been pickled in vinegar!

What really caught my eye, though, was a small advert at the bottom of page six for the 8th Annual Presidio Onion Festival. I remembered noticing Presidio on my map: a tiny village about fifty miles south of Marfa, down on the border with Mexico. The previous night, instead of watching the ghost lights flitting about the slopes of the Chinati Mountains, I could've been right down in the middle of them, attending the Onion Festival Queen Pageant, and a street dance featuring the Al Gusto Band. And this morning I'd already missed the Hotter Than Hell 5K Run, and the volleyball tournament. Luckily, there were a lot of treats still in store: biggest and littlest onion contest, street parade, folkloric dancers, and more music. This was not be missed.

I hit the road out of town, and drove south for an hour or so, through increasingly angular hills and bluffs, up and down steep valley sides, over dried-up river beds, past huge ranch gates that opened on to endless tracts of rocky, red land. Occasionally I'd see a bony longhorn or two tearing at an outcrop of spiky grass, but never anybody rounding them up, and never any other traffic. I did go through a village once, ranged along the banks of a dry creek: Shafter, the sign said. Something to do with mines, maybe: they used to dig up silver around here, and mercury. Imagine being a mercury miner!

Hey, Chuck! I hit a great seam here! I've got a real shovelful . . .

Ah! You're spilling it!

It keeps running off my spade, man!

In really hot weather the mercury would rise up the mine shaft, a giant thermometer.

Now Shafter was almost a ghost town: fifty adobe ruins and four gleaming trailer homes. In amongst the tumbledowns and weeds were a dozen cement mixers, each with a pile of sand and a bag of cement close by. There were no new houses being built. The only work I could see was the repointing of ruins, the consolidation of tumbling walls: the ghost buildings were being fixed in their ghost state, preserved in decay.

A little beyond Shafter I passed a Border Patrol Dutch barn.

There was nobody about, but I could see orange traffic cones piled up inside, and the same kind of booths as the one I'd been pulled in at on the road from El Paso. My stomach turned over, but I kept on driving, thinking how it was a bit strange that both these immigration controls were actually thirty or forty miles away from the border: if you're going to have them at all, then why not right on the dotted line?

A little further south and the valleys were starting to be wider than the mountains they separated. The occasional blades of grass grew into clumps, then into patches, then into fields. Irrigation ditches and pipes webbed the plains, defining rectangles and squares of bright green crops: acre after hundred acre of onions. And in the middle of the last and biggest valley – a mile or two across, with the mountains of Mexico rising up on the far side – lay the tiny township of Presidio.

I drove down the winding road into town – past wooden shacks, blocked-in trailers, a hand-painted sign advertising DAVE'S BARBER SHOP & NOTARY PUBLIC – all the time seeing absolutely nobody, neither on foot nor driving. Could a town turn into a ghost between the time it takes to place an ad in the local rag and the day of the fiesta advertised? It certainly felt spooky, the WELCOME banner flapping in the breeze over the deserted highway, the side streets empty of kids, traffic, and even dogs.

Then I turned a corner and was immediately up to my bumpers in the biggest crush of people, animals and pick-ups I'd seen in all my time in Texas. It made Wichita Falls rush hour look like the moss flows of Caithness.

Folk thronged the street, some in their Sunday finery, others in filthy T-shirts and shorts; cars, trucks and tractors were lined up nose to tail as far as I could see ahead, many of them with balloons and streamers trailing, messages written in whitewash on their windows, flowers and toys and mascots stuck on to their roofs or bonnets; children ran up and down the line of slowly moving traffic, dodging in and out, thumping their fists on the paintwork as they passed, making faces at the passengers; horses trotted along at the side of the parade, their riders done up as cowboys, or gauchos or fox-hunters; lean little dogs slept in the sun or barked at the horses; old folk sat in deck-chairs on the sidewalk, the men smoking and clutching cans of beer against their groins, the women pointing and laughing at the passing show. At me, probably! Cause here I was, pasty-faced and anxious, cruising along at one mile an hour with a white Fifties convertibleful of a dozen dancing teenagers jammed up my rear, wisps of hay drifting on to my bonnet from the tractor and trailer float inching along just in front. Up on the trailer, perched on a pile of hay-bales, were a team of infants dolled-up in black and silver fringed jackets and ten-gallon hats. Two red-string sacks of onions flanked a half-life-sized cuddly donkey crouched in front of them. (*Crouched* doesn't seem the kind of posture you'd associate with a donkey, any more than you'd expect to see cattle *prowl*, as in the Skyrockets song. But it's the only possible way to describe how the donkey was sitting there: ready to *pounce*.) Wreaths of golden onions were pinned to the hay-bales, and a yellow tasselled valance hung down the sides of the trailer, hiding the wheels – or the giant onion rings, or whatever the thing was running on. Across the back of it was embroidered FUN WITH ONIONS! with a heart dotting the i, and a couple of cheery blue-eyed, lipsticked, sexy-legged onion-people waving out.

The onion-people waved, the kids on the hay-bales waved, their proud parents waved, the pensioners in their deck-chairs waved. Everybody in the town of Presidio was waving at everybody else. The last thing I wanted to do was put a damper on the festivities by not joining in, so I stuck my hand out the window, saluted left right and centre, twirled my wrist, made o for onion shapes with my thumb and first finger. Gee, I wished I had a sizzling pan of oatmeal skirlie or a ready-mix packet of chicken dopiaza to brandish, as a fitting Scottish contribution to the celebrations!

I drove on. I didn't have much option actually: all the side streets were blocked with parked cars and rows of onlookers. A big metal barbecue had been set up on the pavement at one point, and people were queuing for ribs and burgers –

and for barbied baby onions, quite probably. Through my window came a great mingle of roasting meat, accordion polkas, exhaust fumes, shouts and laughter, flowery perfume, babies crying, horse shit, steel guitar, sweaty oxters.

I turned up the Shelton Brothers – 'Shoutin' In That Amen Corner' – trying to give the impression that it was a carefully chosen soundtrack for my half-hearted waving, rather than just what happened to be in the machine at the time. It was clear I was stuck with it, stuck *in* it: I was never going to get a proper tourist's view of the parade, because I wasn't an onlooker, I was a participant. Let's be frank: I was an impostor. But nobody else seemed to care, or even notice. As I passed a church, dozens of five-year-old boys in smart suits and ties, and five-year-old girls in pristine lace dresses all waved their white-gloved hands. What could I do? I waved back.

After ten minutes or so of toddling along, the parade seemed to speed up a little. The crowds of spectators were thinning, and there was less waving to be done. The kids on the back of the float in front of me had to sit down for fear of losing their balance and being jolted off the trailer. The donkey nodded its head as the tractor accelerated along the potholed road.

Suddenly, as quickly as I'd found myself in it, I was out of the parade. The tractor and trailer pulled off the road; the carful of teenagers was gone from behind me; up a side street horses were being led on to a transporter. The road was empty in front of me, except for a set of barrier booths about a hundred yards ahead, and a big sign saying INTERNATIONAL BRIDGE. There wasn't a pair of mirror shades in sight, however, and traffic was flowing steadily over the bridge from Mexico. It seemed that there was some kind of buffer zone: that Mexicans were welcome to cross over into little border towns like this, work here, drink here, eat onions, spend pesos – as long as they didn't try and go more than a few dozen miles north, up amongst the voters.

The street had opened out into a wide dusty space, with kitchen tables and small canvas-roofed stalls scattered over it:

a flea market. Spread across the counters were old clothes, empty coke bottles, odd lengths of corrugated iron, a bag of flour, a bag of nails, a loop of dusty dried chiles, a television with a smashed screen, oily car-engine parts, a pair of scuffed Reeboks, a hunting knife, a ball of string, several pyramids of onions.

Dogs and a few kids ran about between the stalls. There didn't seem to be anyone buying at all, just the sellers hanging around in the piece of shade closest to their wares. It looked like they'd long since sold off everything of value that wasn't absolutely essential. Then they'd sold off everything of value that *was* essential. Now they were trying to get rid of things that were neither useful nor valuable, to them or anyone else.

It was sad to see such desperation so close to the carnival. Of course, celebration and desperation aren't necessarily mutually exclusive. You often see the combination in Scottish pubs, usually just after last orders has been called.

I turned the car and drove back down the main street, which was now more or less empty. With the cars and crowds out of the way I could see that the majority of the shops there had gone bust and closed: doors were boarded up, windows grimed and postered over. The church was big and well kept, but the houses along the main street, and most of the others down the side alleys, were small and in bad repair. Most of them were made of wood and corrugated metal. Folk who had little gardens of dusty ground in front of their home filled them with old car seats, fridges on extension leads through the kitchen window, kids' paddling pools/dogs' drinking bowls. Most of the vehicles sitting about had Mexican plates and bodies that were battered and scattered. The roads were scarred too: apart from the bumpy but tarred main street, they were heavily rutted dirt tracks, gravelly in some places, dusty all over. If it ever rained in Presidio again, the place would turn into a mudbath. No immediate danger of that, though: a digital clock/thermometer outside the First Presidio Bank flashed:

11:46:50   95   11:47:00   95.5   11:47:10   96

In the outskirts of town, I drove along for a while behind a converted petrol tanker. It had a system of hoses and nozzles sticking out the back of its tank, and was spraying water on to the road as it trundled along. Presumably this was meant to keep the dust down, but it was so hot that most of the water seemed to vaporise before it ever touched the ground.

What the hell was I doing in the outskirts of town? Getting lost, that's what. Presidio wasn't a big town, but what there was of it was all on the flat, and there were no obvious landmarks to navigate by, just a grid of low featureless houses. I had the feeling that I was driving in circles, or, to be exact, in rectangles. I'd have to ask for directions. I hate asking for directions. Luckily there was nobody about, so I had a good excuse for not doing it. What I would have to do, then, was sit here and wait till somebody who looked like they might know the way turned up. Then I'd have to ask them. Or, better still, maybe I could just follow them at a discreet distance and hope they were going where the action was . . . the music, the dancing, the biggest and smallest onion competition . . .

I switched on the radio to pass the time. After flicking through a few crackling stations (reception was poor down here amongst the mountains) I caught the word ONION being pronounced with great gusto. I tuned in. It was a local station playing a festival information loop tape. Through the static, I tried to make out what was happening, and where, as conveyed in a stiff scripted conversation between two announcers. If their wee chat wasn't bizarre enough already, it was made more so by the constant fading in and out of their voices, the occasional crescendos of buzzing static like killer bees on the rampage, the interference from a Spanish-speaking channel with a liking for Barry Manilow. What I could hear went something like this:

Randy: . . . located on highway 170 east of Presidio. While you're there, ask about their bus tours into the newly opened . . .

Rosie: . . . is a full day of activities, beginning with . . . making a loop . . . finish line at the Y. Even if you don't win you get a complimentary T-shirt. Entry fee is fifteen dollars. Meanwhile, at 9 a.m., volleyball games begin at the high school gym, continuing all day . . .

Randy: . . . and going through downtown Presidio. The parade features two outstanding bands: the two-hundred member strong Presidio school band, and the . . . band from Ojinaga. There will be floats, the onion queen, her court, and more.

Rosie: From eleven is the traditional barbecue, at the American Legion hall near the Catholic church in downtown Presidio. The cost per plate is four . . .

Randy: . . . also at the Lions' Club park, a free games and crafts meet opens at noon. Inside the air-conditioned Lions' Club building is an afternoon's free entertainment. That famous hot Presidio shun, I mean sun, should be gaining momentum, so you'll want to get out of it for a time and enjoy yourself. On stage will be the fabulous . . . dancers from Ojinaga. You'll really enjoy them. And there'll be other surprises, and performances by . . .

Rosie: If you're not familiar with Presidio, to reach the Lion's Park, turn east at the . . . north at the . . . and remember at one there's steer roping at the Arandas Arena. Watch for directions at the football field.

Randy: We hope you have a great afternoon, and will be ready at 8 p.m. at the Father Daniel Benito Hall for . . .

Rosie: . . . try it for yourself: it sure can't hurt . . .

Randy: Well of course the Presidio onion is so famous worldwide, they say that the only reason they built the International Bridge here was so that the people of Latin America could get a taste of our great Presidio onions.

Rosie: Yes, Presidio is known for its sweet onions, not to mention its great cantaloupes and water melons. They'll be harvested in June and July, so be sure and come back for that.

Randy: But the weather is quite a topic of conversation around here. Former mayor Bob Anderson said he told a

Texas newspaper that Presidio has two kinds of weather: hot and hell. And so if you think it's hot today, well, just wait, because . . . sizzling . . . Presidio . . . coming soon.

Rosie: Presidio claims to be America's hot spot because, according to the *Texas Almanac*, it's a Texas hot fact that Presidio can claim the most number of days in the year when the temperature topped the 100 degree mark. And in the summer of 1962, the temperature climbed to 100 degrees or above for a season total of 107 days.

Randy: . . . the summer of 1990 – the hell summer Anderson refers to – when the gates opened on May 11 . . . and the furnace began pumping out 100 and 110 degrees . . . through most of May and the entire month of June. A sizzling 111 was reached on July 21st 1990, and remained so for three consecutive days.

Rosie: But seriously folks, the Presidio onion festival celebrates a long agricultural tradition . . .

Armed with *turn east at the . . . and north at the . . .* I soon found my way to the Lions' Club, and pulled up next to a long-snouted Pink Panther mobile. Except it was yellow.

A dozen or so women sat around in kitchen chairs under shade trees, selling coke and homemade lemonade from ice-packed rubbish bins. A couple of kids ran around spraying each other with plastic string out of aerosols. And on a patch of parched grass in front of the Lions' Club Hall was parked the trailer I'd followed through the parade. I could now see that there was a motto on the side of the valance too: BEHIND EVERY GOOD MEAL IS A TASTY ONION!

From inside the hall, a big corrugated-aluminium hangar, came the sound of loud, happy music, stamping feet, and bursts of applause. I stepped in.

There was a bandstand at one end, a few stalls at the other, and spectators sitting round the edges. All eyes were on the open space in the middle of the room, where a dozen Mexican teenagers in fancy costumes were performing an extravagantly choreographed formation-dance routine. The six boys were in stiff black jeans, red plaid shirts and red bandannas, and white Stetsons; the girls wore ribbons in their hair, white blouses, and wide yellow skirts, which flew up in the air every time they swung their hips to reveal long white flannel bloomers almost down to their knees.

It swiftly became clear that the dance was all about *seduction*.

The couples started off facing each other across the dance floor, then slowly, deliberately, they stepped towards each other. As they got close, they reached out till the tips of their fingers almost touched. But suddenly the music changed and the girls twirled away out of reach, their skirts spinning up about their thighs as they did so. The boys, enraged or aroused by the sight of the flannel bloomers, jumped forward, fierce looks on their faces, and pawed their feet, bull-like, on the concrete. The girls had stopped twirling by this time, and started to slip and slide back towards their partners, eyelashes fluttering like Venus Flytraps with the munchies. The audience all laughed.

Each boy grabbed his partner's hand, spun her round to face him. Her smile turned to mock anger. She slapped her hands together up by his cheek, and took a sharp step back. He stomped once, stepped after her. She took another step away, he another step after, till they'd crossed the whole breadth of the hall. But she made sure that each of her steps was a fraction smaller than his, so, right over at the far side they were only a hairsbreadth apart and SNAP! they seized each other in a tight embrace and came birling across the concrete, looks of rapture on their faces.

The music came to a stop, and I was away to clap, when it started up again: slow and raunchy, with the accordion making suggestive wheezes in 2/4 time. Something was happening out on the dance floor. Temperatures were rising. The top halves of the couples were motionless, but down below there was a lot of action: the guys were thrusting their hips in time to the music, shamelessly pressing up against the girls. But the girls were having none of it: every time the boys thrust, the girls pulled away, so all six sets of four legs were doing a tight little quadrille of attack and retreat, while up

top the couples were locked in a well-behaved clinch, faces
impassive. The music sped up, the drums thumped louder,
the audience clapped along and all the time the legs were
stomping back and forth more and more violently, sweat
breaking out on the brows of the dancers though still they
didn't sway or smile – till with one last roll on the tom-toms
the music exploded in a barrage of bass, drums and brass, and
the couples leapt apart, spun away across the hall, and ended
up exactly where they'd started the dance.

Everyone burst into laughter, then applause. The dancers
bowed and curtseyed, solemnly, then ran off to a corner of
the room, finally allowing themselves to smile.

The guitarist of the band leant into the mike and said
something in Spanish. There was more applause, then taped
conjunto music came on.

I looked around the hall. One counter, flanked by cardboard cut-outs of a Mexican boxer, was selling cold beer at
$1 a can. Other stalls sold souvenir mugs, cheap toys, T-shirts,
baseball cards, baseball caps with onions embroidered on the
front, and rare postage stamps. What? Yes, rare stamps, in little
cellophane packets. The guy at that stall obviously didn't have
very high hopes of great philately sales, cause he had a sideline
in filling helium balloons. Every so often he'd get bored or
forgetful and fill a balloon till it was the size of a space-hopper.
Then it would explode. No matter how often he did this,
the kids still laughed. Maybe it was because every time it
happened *he* had a look of genuine shock and amazement
on his face. I bought a beer and an Onion Fest '95 cap to
combat the famous hot Presidio shun, I mean sun, and went
outside.

It was hard to think straight, it was so hot. Everybody was
sitting resting and blethering under the wide-spreading trees.
Except me. I was right out in the furnace, making for the
food stall.

The woman spoke to me in Spanish as I approached.

I'm sorry, I said, and shook my head. Do you speak
English?

Sure, she said, and laughed. Well, American!

I was wanting something to eat, I said.

You've come to the right place.

Great. What've you got?

Onions.

I should've guessed.

Ever had a Presidio onion before? No? Well you're in for a treat. Watch this.

She took a big golden onion out of a box at her feet, and carefully placed it on the table in front of her. It was huge: must've weighed close to a pound. She held it sideways to chop off its top, then deftly peeled away most of the papery skin. Next, she took a little metal pastry-cutter with a long handle, pressed down from the top of the onion, and cut the hard core of it right out.

What's that thing? I asked.

It's an onion corer.

Oh. I should've guessed that too.

I'm going to make you a Sunflower Onion, she said. Finest thing you ever tasted. All for two bucks.

She picked up her butcher's knife again, and used it to cut the onion into vertical eighths, leaving a cross-section at the bottom uncut to hold it all together. Next was a generous sifting of seasoned flour, and then the whole thing was dunked into a deep-fat fryer sitting on a kitchen chair behind her.

Onions are good for the blood, she said. Did you know that? Good for the heart!

I have heard that.

Of course, frying stuff up like this is bad for you, cholesterol-wise.

Still, I said, Probably that just means the good and the bad cancel each other out. Except at the end of it you've had your dinner, and it's been tasty. You've eaten well and your heart's no better or worse: what more can you ask for?

Not much, around here, she said, and plunged a pair of tongs into the fryer to bob the onion right under the fat.

Three minutes later she used the tongs to fish out the onion and lay it on some paper towels on a paper plate. The eighths had all fanned out and turned golden brown, so it did indeed look a bit like a sunflower: especially one of those demented ones that Van Gogh painted. She pushed it across the table towards me, with a small foam tub of pink stuff.

Special dip, she said. Ranch with cayenne for a kick.

I took one of the brown onion petals between my thumb and finger — it fell away from the stem, it was that tender — and dipped it and chewed.

That is fantastic, I said. Finest thing I ever tasted!

She laughed. Folks here have a slogan: Presidio onions are so sweet, we eat them for breakfast instead of doughnuts.

That's snappy, I said. I'll remember that. I'll spread it around.

From where I sat, propped up against the trunk of a shade tree, I could see through the main door of the hall and watch folk dancing to the music. To begin with there'd been another display by the Mexican troupe, in blue checked shirts and red skirts this time, but by now everybody was joining in. The music was great to dance to, and not bad to listen to: bass, drums, keyboards, accordion, guitar and alto sax. About half the songs had vocals — all in Spanish, as was all the patter in between — the rest being up-tempo instrumentals: polkas, schottisches, two-steps.

I recognised 'La Cucaracha', 'La Bamba', and a particularly interesting tune called, well, take your pick: 'Jesse', or 'Jessie Polka', or 'Jesusita en Chihuahua'. I'd first encountered the tune on one of Bob Wills' Tiffany Transcriptions; it was a catchy two-part instrumental featuring twin fiddles throughout and a distinctive, banjo-like, pizzicato effect on the fiddle strings on the third and fourth verses. Bob called it 'Jesse'. I came across it again, in a very similar arrangement on a record by Adolph Hofner and His San Antonians. Adolph called it 'Jessie Polka', and recorded it in Dallas in 1941, six or seven years before Bob laid down his; it sat very comfortably alongside Adolph's other records, with their great mix of swing and Czech folk, including several other polkas. Yet another version — in fact, the first hit western swing version

– was recorded by Cliff Bruner in 1939. But 'Jesse/Jessie', it turned out, wasn't Czech, she was Mexican. For eventually I found another, much earlier version of it, on a CD of early Mexican-American Border Music. 'Jesusita en Chihuahua' was recorded in El Paso in 1928, by the Orquesta Del Norte, a large band consisting of bass, drums, guitar, piano, clarinet, flute, cornet, and two violins – which dominated the tune throughout with their plucky pizzicatos and slick, swirling, unison playing.

Now, here I was, sixty-five years later, listening to Los Latigos del Norteno (they had their name on their bass drum) playing – well, I didn't catch what they called it, but it was unmistakably the same song, with the lack of a fiddle being remedied by the keyboard player setting his machine to pizzicato and picking out the hesitant, prancing melody just as Joe Holley and Louis Tierney had for Bob Wills, as Johnny Rives and J.R. Chatwell had for Adolph Hofner, as the two unknown fiddlers had for Fernando L. Cabello, leader (and drummer) of the Orquesta Del Norte.

Suddenly I started to get very excited, for it struck me that this was as close to western swing in the raw as I was ever likely to get. Not that Los Latigos would call their music western swing; Conjunto and Norteno are the names applied to the accordion-led dance music of the Tex-Mex borderlands. (If the two names have different connotations, then they were too subtle for anyone to ever explain them to me; similarly, no one could really tell me whether either of the two names for Mexican-American people – Tejano and Chicano – was more accurate, or politically preferable.) No, it was the feel and the function of the music that were so similar to western swing. It had a steady 2/4 beat (with occasional waltzes thrown in), there were frequent improvised exchanges between the keyboards, guitar and sax, and there was a similar feeling of hilarity lurking just below he surface: the vocalist would sing an apparently serious line, only to have the sax player parp out a coarse-toned honk at the end of it, causing the singer to laugh his way through the next chorus. Or the keyboard player would play a bum note halfway through an ambitious solo, and rather than try to cover it up, he'd go completely over the top – Jerry Lee Lewis impersonating Ornette Coleman – laughing and jumping up and down, raking the keys with the backs of his hands, playing chords with his forehead. Los Latigos' main function was simple – to get people on the floor, and keep them there – and in this respect they were doing exactly the same job as Bob Wills and all the rest of the western swingers. And doing it very well. The whole hall was a mass of jiving, jigging, polking, pogoing humanity. Even I was tapping my foot in the dirt. Which was considerable exertion, considering the heat was up about the 100 mark.

I'd heard a couple of old musicians reminisce about the need to keep playing non-stop all night. Roy Lee Brown, Milton's youngest brother, told me that the Brownies often played for five hours without a break, for they'd found that as soon as they took an intermission, fights would break out amongst the drinkers and doughboys on the dance floor. Nobody ever got killed, as far as Roy Lee knew, but a lot of people got black eyes and bloody noses. Bonnie and Clyde were regular fans of the Brownies – they'd come along to the dances whenever they could, and put in requests to the radio show – but they never caused any trouble, beyond stealing hubcaps from the cars outside . . . It wasn't to stop fights that Los Latigos kept pumping out the music non-stop, it was just for the joy of it, for the joy of playing and dancing – and to fight off the heat exhaustion. I'd been at dances in Orkney, where small halls or big kitchens vibrated to the music of guitars, fiddles, accordions; there, by midnight, condensation would be running down the walls and windows, and everybody would be scarlet from the exertion of supercharged Strip The Willows and demented Dashing White Sergeants. But once you pushed through the wee-hours pain-barrier (perhaps with the help of some home-brew) you could find the dances and the hours flying past, till suddenly it was dawn, your feet were steaming, your ankles were swelling, and it was time to walk down to the pier for the ferry home.

It was mid-afternoon, in a hangar of a dancehall, with all the doors open and the air-conditioning on full, and still it was hotter than any Orkney dance ever. And still the folk of Presidio kept on dancing. This was what my Texas trip was all about: the power of the music, the way conjunto or western swing or Orkney fiddling turns desperation into celebration.

Back in 1927, when Bob Wills was in his early twenties and finding it hard to scrape a living from either farming or fiddling, he worked as a barber for some months in the town of Roy, New Mexico. To this day, northern New Mexico is known to be one of the last strongholds of old Hispanic fiddling traditions; back in the Twenties the tradition was still vibrant. So as well as cutting hair in Roy, Bob formed a band, with a mainly Mexican line-up. Apparently there were so many fine Mexican fiddlers, that Bob often ended up on drums. This nearly two decades before he outraged the Grand Old Opry in Nashville by insisting on having a drummer in his band. There's a good story in a book of reminiscences by a cowboy fiddler called Frankie McWhorter, who grew up in the same part of Texas as Bob, and was to play with him in the early Sixties. He tells the story of how Bob 'composed' his first hit:

> He was working as a barber in Roy, New Mexico, and one day a little Mexican fellow came in. Bob had his fiddle laying there and the man saw it. Bob couldn't understand Spanish and the other guy couldn't understand English, but he gestured and asked Bob if he played. Bob didn't want to, so he said no. So the man asked if he could play Bob's fiddle, and Bob said he could. Bob said, He played 'The Spanish Two-Step' and I locked the door where he couldn't get out and nobody else could get in, and I made him stay there until he taught me that and 'Maiden's Prayer'. Finally he nodded. I didn't know whether he needed to go to the bathroom or if I was doing it right, but I let him out.
> That Mexican taught him those two tunes.
> Later on he recorded 'The Spanish Two-Step' and it

was a big hit for him, the biggest thing going at the time. It was a number one record all over the country.

Bob didn't just lift melodies from the Mexican traditon – and as well as those mentioned by McWhorter he recorded such titles as 'Spanish Fandango', 'El Rancho Grande', 'La Cucaracha', 'Cielito Lindo', 'Lady of Spain', 'La Golondrina', 'Mama Inez' – he lifted a sound too, and got his horn section to reproduce it on several of his best records. It was a coarse swaggering tone similar to that achieved by countless Mexican guitar-and-trumpet street and bar bands, and very different from the more conventional hot but smooth jazz tones he usually asked for. Sometimes he contrasted the two tones: on 'La Paloma', a rhumba recorded in February 1941, two saxes and a clarinet play the melody, straight and swinging and smooth, with trumpeters Tubby Lewis and Jamie McIntosh laying on a contrasting series of throaty, almost abrasive, obbligatos, then taking up the melody line in the bridge, in a pure mariachi style. (And surely it is more than coincidence that the very next track the Texas Playboys recorded that day was a Goodmanesque big-band arrangement of 'Maiden's Prayer?')

Bob's biggest hit, the song that took him, as he liked to say, from hamburgers to steaks, was 'New San Antonio Rose', which has been covered many times since, and was one of Bing Crosby's first million sellers. It's the song Bob's most identified with around the world, and one of the select band of western songs – including the likes of 'You Are My Sunshine', 'Hey Good Lookin' and 'Crazy' – to be recognised and sung all around the world. Or, indeed, out of the world: in 1969 astronauts Charles Conrad and Alan Bean serenaded the entire world with a version of it from Apollo 12. The melody of 'New San Antonio Rose' (and its instrumental version, without the 'New' is none other than 'Spanish Two-Step', shuffled around a little and arranged, in the 1940 hit version, for no fewer than eighteen musicians: Bob Wills and Jesse Ashlock, fiddles; Tommy Duncan, vocals; Leon McAuliffe, steel guitar; Louis Tierney, fiddle and saxophone;

Eldon Shamblin, electric guitar; Johnnie Lee Wills, tenor banjo; Herman Arnspiger, guitar; Son Lansford, string bass; 'Brother' Al Stricklin, piano; Everett Stover and Tubby Lewis, trumpets; Wayne Johnson, sax and clarinet; Zeb 'Judge' McNally, Tiny Mott, Joe Ferguson and Don Harlan, all saxophones; and Smokey Dacus, drums.

A long way from a barber's shop in Roy, New Mexico? Maybe not so far. Mixing drums, strings, woodwinds and brass instruments in country dance bands was actually fairly common in Mexico, and Mexican areas of Texas, as far back as the end of the last century. There's a great photo from about 1915 of an anonymous Tejano *orquesta*, apparently based in the Houston area, whose line-up features twelve-string guitar, fiddle, flute, clarinet and trumpet. It seems very likely that Bob heard and enjoyed the music of such combos during his spell in New Mexico, and even closer to home in Texas. It seems not unlikely that he would have had such varied instrumental line-ups in mind when he came to pull together the famously heterogeneous Texas Playboys of the mid to late Thirties, and early Forties. Sure, he wanted to add jazz-linked instruments to a string-band core, but he wasn't the first to do so: orquestas had been doing it for decades.

You can't tease out the threads of influence. All you can say is, they're all in there somewhere. Hell, maybe I was over-emphasising the Conjunto influence. After all, white ranch bands mixed banjos, clarinets, mandolins, and fiddles, and black musicians, in the early days of jazz and blues, featured fiddles alongside trumpets alongside guitars alongside trombones alongside mandolins. I suppose that poor folk played whatever instruments they could get their hands on. Still, I reckoned I was on to something with the relatively under-appreciated influence of Mexican music on the formation of western swing. After all, true originality springs from a proper appreciation of tradition. And in a musical sense, proper appreciation amounts more or less to listening, learning, then lifting the bits you like. I reckoned Bob Wills had done just that with Conjunto music.

★

Then I woke up, and it was all a dream. My back was aching from resting against the knobbly tree trunk, my tongue was sweating it was so damn hot — 107 degrees on the bank's digital thermometer — and if it hadn't been for my Onion Fest baseball cap, the shifting sun would've fried my face to a crisp. All of the theories outlined above vanished from my head, never to return, and I plunged back into the Lions' Club hall to leap and twirl with the rest of the sun-crazed Chicanos.

South Texas Swing

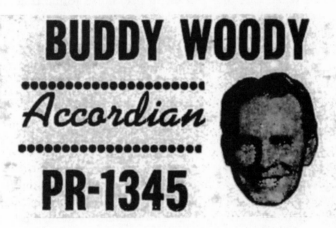

I pulled back the orange curtains to let in a little more swimming-court light. Stone the buzzards! An air-conditioner! Last night had been another swelter, and I'd been cursing the primitive cooling systems of El Paisano: a big wooden fan like the prop off a Sopwith Camel suspended over the bed.

When I'd switched it on, it started to spin very slowly, its broad blades slicing through the air like sharks in treacle; gradually it speeded up, speeded up, speeded up. Okay, it had an acceleration of nought to sixty in twenty minutes, but when it finally reached cruising speed, the fan mounting was vibrating so violently that flecks of plaster were falling off the ceiling on to the tangerine candlewick, and the column of air it blasted out was so powerful that it flattened me onto the bed. No way was I going to sleep with that thing whirring round above me – it looked likely to come spinning off its bearings any second and slice off any protruding part of me.

So I'd left the fan off and sweated and writhed all night, covers thrown back but heat closing in, dreaming feverish dreams of giant onions dancing in twirly skirts to surging sax and accordion: never mind the Butterfly's Wing Effect, imagine the Mexican Petticoat effect, and the tornadoes it must cause.

But when I awoke and set to packing, I found there was air-conditioning after all. Of course there was: James Dean's *Giant* coiffure would've melted into a mess of wilted quiff and cooking oil otherwise. I switched on the machine for a last blast of cold air as I finished sticking away my clothes, tapes and notebook. The thing rattled and roared like a cement mixer with a mouthful of bricks.

Downstairs, the lobby was quiet and cool as ever, the only sound coming from an elderly couple sitting at either end of a big leather settee by the window. The woman was reading a newspaper, and as I lugged my bag over towards the desk, I heard her say, Listen to this Chuck: If all the bees in the US were divided equally and given to America's human population, each man, woman and child would get half a million of the buzzing critters, reveals a new university study.

The man snorted. And the day after we'd be right back where we are now, he said. One guy with ten million bees, and twenty with none. It's human nature, it's in the bible.

I don't think that's the point, said the woman.

I *know* what the point is, said Chuck. It's downright communism!

I dinged the bell on the desk, a clerk appeared, and I checked out.

God had turned the sun up to eleven: walking across the elegant tiled courtyard of the hotel was like strolling through a pizza oven. I hoped I'd remembered to park the Chevy under a shade tree. Yesterday, when I'd finally tried to drive home from the onion festival, the car had been standing in the open so long that the steering wheel burnt my hands as soon as I touched it. I'd had to leave the air-conditioning on full and take a walk around the block till the temperature of the plastic had fallen enough for me to grip it, or at least pince it between finger and thumb.

I stepped through the arch, turned right, and stubbed my toes against some clunky bit of litter lying on the sidewalk. It went skittering away in front of me and stopped a metre ahead, long glinting barrel pointing straight at me: A GUN.

Jesusita.

Next thing I knew I was back at the Paisano's desk, banging on the bell and babbling away to the clerk: A gun! Out there! On the, on the . . . just lying! I kicked it, I was going to pick it up, but no no, I've seen those movies, somebody'll've been shot, and the fingerprints, see, they'll have me, so I left it, it's out there, a pistol, come on, come on . . . before I shoot someone, or myself . . .

The clerk ducked through a hatch in the counter and walked out of the lobby, with me following right on his heels, giving directions. Come to think of it, he probably did know how to get out the front door of his own hotel, but at the time I was anxious to keep him right.

There, I said. See it? I pointed over his shoulder. There!

Were those bags lying there too? he said.

No, they're mine. I dropped them.

He held up a hand for me to stay, took a step forward, and peeped over my shoulder-bag.

Ha! He exhaled.

What is it?

He leant over, snatched up the pistol, and turned back towards me.

You call this a gun? he said, and laughed.

Eh . . . yeah.

He flicked some kind of catch, then pushed the revolving magazine out sideways.

This ain't no real gun, he said.

What then? An imitation?

He tilted up the pistol so a shower of little silver bullets fell out and on to his palm.

This here's a lady's gun, he said.

Is that bad?

He shook his head, looked down his nose at the thing. Couldn't kill *shit*, he said.

I drove north out of Marfa, through deserts, pine forests, and mountain gorges.

Just past Fort Davis I slowed to gaze at a gang of vultures eating a dead deer by the side of the road. They were less curious, didn't look up or slow in tearing at the flesh of the beautiful roadkill.

I drove on, past strange rock formations, rounded and red like tumults of petrified blood pouring down hillsides towards the road.

In Toyahvale I was attracted by a sign that said ARE Y'ALL HOT, THIRSTY? and pulled in for some petrol and water. A girl came out from the wee shop to operate the pump, and it occurred to me that this was the first time in the whole of my trip that I'd been served with gas. Every other place had been 100 per cent self-service. None of this *fill your tank/check your oil/wipe your windshield?* routine like you see in the movies. Hell, round the big cities, you didn't even have to meet another human being when you paid, you just stuck your credit card directly into the pump.

A few miles further north and east was a massive sign saying LYRIC THEATRE, just inside the gate of a completely empty field: the ghost of a drive-in cinema, maybe, or the site for some Texan Fitzcarraldo's opera house, that never made it up the Rio Grande, or over Casket Mountain, or past the border guards.

By a phone booth in downtown Balmorhea lay a dead javelina – a kind of wild pygmy pig. No vultures this time, just a black shroud of flies that rose and settled as I swished past.

In Fort Stockton I took a photo of Paisano Pete, the world's largest roadrunner, a twenty-foot statue frozen in mid-scoot on a traffic island at a busy intersection. If I'd been mayor of the next town I'd've set up a thirty-foot Wile E. Coyote

immediately, and given the Fort Stockton folk a real lesson
in stupid tourist attractions.

At the Hill O' Beans restaurant, I ate green chile rellenos
with a fried egg on top, then used their payphone to call
ahead. To cold call ahead. To cold call one of the genuine
legends of western swing, Adolph Hofner, and be greeted, not
with the hesitation or reluctance I'd expected, but genuine
enthusiasm and an invitation, in a strong Bela-Lugosian
accent, to visit and talk as soon as I arrived in San Antonio.

That could be tomorrow, if I make good time, I said.

That's fine, said Adolph. Come quick! I'm getting older
every day: don't know how long I'll last!

Adolph Hofner was born in 1916, first recorded in October
1936, and was leading a regularly gigging band well into the
Nineties. In terms of sheer longevity, he has outdistanced
them all, even Bob Wills. But it's not for the sixty-year span
career that he's so notable, it's for the unique sound that he
has produced on stage and record throughout that career. For
Adolph was born in Moulton, one of Texas's many Czech
communities; he had Czech as his first language, and recorded
dozens of Czech songs – 'Dis Ja Liebe Spim', 'Strashidlo', 'Star
Kovarna' – alongside the more standard western swing fare of
blues, fiddle tunes, rags and pop.

Western swing has always defined itself, not on the basis
of any spurious notions of musical purity, but rather on
its all-inclusiveness, its willingness to accept anything and
everything that its many practitioners wanted to throw into
the melting pot. As long as the pot was heated to hottering,
and the people could dance, it didn't matter whether you
were singing in English, Spanish or Martian.

Having said that, Hofner's popularity right across Texas
and into California – where he spent several successful years
during the war – was certainly greatest in the south-eastern
part of the Lone Star State, where the many communities of
Bohemian and Moravian immigrants, and the closely related
German ones, are mostly centred. As well as the songs actually
sung in Czech, his band (they had various names: the Texans,
the San Antonians, the Pearl Wranglers – after their sponsors,

Pearl Beer) had a wide repertoire of waltzes and polkas likely to appeal to the tastes of first or second generation settlers from central Europe. Ironically, though, Adolph's greatest hit came in 1941 with a traditional fiddle breakdown, 'Cotton Eyed Joe'. This is a tune still played by just about every band south of the Mason Dixon line, and quite a few north of it. (Far north in some cases: number one in the pop charts in Britain as I drove towards San Antonio was a Scandinavian disco version of this very tune.) Another irony is that Hofner's band, which featured excellent jazz musicians such as J.R. Chatwell on fiddle, and Walt Kleypas on piano and accordion, should have had their biggest successes with relatively straight renditions of straightforward stomping dance tunes like 'South Texas Swing' and 'Paul Jones'.

Adolph was smitten with Bing Crosby and Milton Brown, and he cultivated a smooth croon – but he also yelped with joy and urged on his soloists just like Bob Wills. One of the soloists – from the early Thirties right up to the present – was his younger brother Emil, better known as Bash Hofner. The traditional explanation for the nickname was that Emil was extremely shy and bashful, but on some of the early Hofner recordings it sounds to me like Emil is just bashing the hell out of his lap steel guitar – what was he using for a slide, an anvil? Eventually, though, Bash developed a distinctive staccato sound that was sometimes harsh-toned, but always exciting, and added considerable punch to the band's red-hot rhythms.

I'd been told that Adolph – now in his eightieth year – had been ill recently, and had cut back his performances to occasional guest spots, so it looked like I wouldn't get to see him on the bandstand. But to visit him at home – or at his second home, for after sixty years on the road, the tour bus no doubt seemed more like his real home than any arrangement of bricks and mortar ever could – would be a real thrill.

I drove east – through Sheffield, Ozona, Sonora, Junction – crooning and yelping along to a tape of some of Adolph's greatest records: the Milton Brown imitation 'Does My Baby Love Me, Yes Sir', the delicately swinging 'Tickle Toe', the low down guttural 'Dirty Dog', the raunchy 'Joe Turner Blues', and the distinctive bouncing Czech tunes 'Julida Polka' and 'Na Marjanse'. A 1940 novelty song, 'Sam, The Old Accordion Man', was noteworthy, musically, for the lack of any accordion whatsoever in the recording. But the lyrics, though clumsy, touched me strangely as I thought of their singer's long, colourful career:

He just plays chords that make you feel grand
They call him Sam, the old accordion man

His dreamy chords remind you of heaven
And they're real chords, according to Dixie Land

In the evening, by the moonlight, when the sun
goes down
All the lovers, levee lovers, love to gather round

He just plays chords like nobody can
They call him Sam, the old accordion man

On I drove through Segovia, Mountain Home and Kerrville – site of a famous annual folk festival, where Michelle Shocked was discovered under a tree in the early Eighties (cross Bob Wills with Emma Goldman and you'd get a sound a bit like her excellent *Captain Swing* album). Then off the interstate for a short detour through Fredricksburg and Luckenbach – tourist traps for Germanophiles and biker-hippies respectively. Then on again through the soft rolling pastures and bluebonnet-drenched verges of the Hill Country, and pretty, prettified towns like Medina, Bandera, Pipe Creek. Till eventually, just as darkness fell, the vast sprawling neighbourhoods of San Antonio came crawling out to meet me.

Across the Alley from the Alamo

The Tune Wranglers

The Popular KTSA
Radio Orchestra of San Antonio

Back in 1929 at the height of his success, Jimmie Rodgers, America's Blue Yodeller, built himself a grand red-brick house in Kerrville, and called it (what else?) The Blue Yodeller's Paradise. However, he also kept a permanent suite at the Gunter Hotel in San Antonio, and hosted great poker and moonshine sessions there whenever he was in town. If it's good enough for Jimmie Rodgers, it's good enough for me, I thought, and went spiralling through the city centre's one-way system in search of the Gunter, eventually finding it right where I'd expected it, opposite the massive Majestic Theatre. (Unfortunately the Majestic *wasn't* where I'd expected it: hence the spiralling.)

It was too late to arrange a meeting with Adolph, so I went out for a stroll through the hot and murky streets of the downtown area, in between tall Victorian tenements and big abandoned department stores, out into a wide plaza where trams and buses whizzed past a tiny floodlit semi-ruin: The Alamo.

In the Alamo BBQ I drank beer and ate candied yams for my supper. This humble food had become the stuff of legend to me, since I'd heard Leon McAuliffe of the Texas Playboys sing about it in a 1938 roll-call named 'That's What I Like About The South'. I'd been looking out for everything listed in that song ever since I'd arrived, but hadn't come across candied yams till now.

> *Let's go back to Alabammy*
> *Let's go see my dear old mammy*
> *Frying eggs and cooking ham*
> *That's what I like about the south*
>
> *There you won't make no mistake-y*
> *And your nerves are never shaky*
> *You should taste her layer cake*
> *I say that's what I like about the south*
>
> *She's got baked ribs and candied yams*
> *Sugar cured Virginia hams*
> *Basements full of those berry jams*
> *And that's what I like about the south*
>
> *Cornbread and turnip greens*
> *Ham hocks and butter beans*
> *Mardi Gras down in New Orleans*
> *I said that's what I like about the south*

Candied yams turned out to be one of the things I liked least about the south. And turnip greens were like spinach, boiled for an hour and put through a mangle. And I never did find my dear old mammy – not surprising considering she was sitting in Aberdeen at the time, singing:

Cullen skink and curly kale
Skirlie, mince and ginger ale
Bairfit broth and creeshy meal
That's what I like about the north.

I walked out of the plaza, through a fake Mexican village
(or maybe it was a real one, so thoroughly preserved and
polished-up that it just *looked* fake) and down on to El Paseo
del Rio, the River Walk, a non-stop fiesta of bars, shops,
restaurants, clubs, water-taxis and gawping tourists that lines
a man-made meander of the San Antonio River right in the
middle of the city.

The Irish pub served Guinness, the Piano Jazz bar featured
tinkly piano jazz, Michelino's Italian Restaurant had pizza and
pasta, and the Hard Rock Café played hard rock. I wandered
along the waterside pavement, with its overhanging trees and
paper lanterns, crossing the river every hundred yards or so on
little hump-backed bridges. I crossed for variety, not to get
anywhere in particular, but there was so much on offer along
both banks that I could've crawled along the river-bottom
and still felt bombarded by novelty. Every restaurant and
bar spilled out its well-defined ethnic aroma and ambience
– German, Mexican, Chinese – but the borders were strictly
enforced, there was no mingling of cultures. I supposed
that modern marketing techniques determine this kind of
sharp-edged distinction – more of a cultural layer cake than
a well-stirred dumpling – every little retail outlet having to
have its own distinct identity, appealing to its own distinct
niche market. The parallels with the way music is marketed
are clear. Music in America is so well niched these days – each
variety with its own dedicated TV channels, radio stations,
theme parks – that once you know what you like, there's
little chance of ever stumbling across some new recordings or
artists that are going to surprise you, or shake you up. In fact, it
seemed to me that the chief result (or even the chief purpose)
of music in the States was to keep you from getting all shook
up. Okay, various sub-genres might have their provocative
lyrics – like rap's politics and chauvinism, acid house's drug

proselytising and hedonism – but all of their 'product' is so
ferociously targeted, at such a narrow demographic audience,
and all of the artists involved stick so obediently to the rigid
boundaries laid down for them by commercial management,
that there's rarely any chance of anyone hearing anything they
didn't expect to hear, and can't immediately file away in some
well-labelled pigeon-hole. There's no boundary crossing, no
transgression, no surprises. Music doesn't change people's
lives in the USA today, it confirms the life you've already
chosen, or had chosen for you.

The whole of American culture seems to me to be tending
towards atomisation. Music has become something to separate
people, to build walls between them. I love the old stuff that
brought people together, that knocked down the walls.

At the end of El Paseo del Rio was a theatre, where
theatrical extravaganzas, full of local colour, would be staged
at the allotted times. The stage was on one side of the river,
the steeply raked audience seating on the other.

I climbed away from the river, walked in one end of
an all-night drug store and out the other, passed through
a palm-treed atrium, found myself in a shopping mall. Most
of the outlets were closed and shuttered (it was nearly eleven)
but the eight-screen cinema at the top of the building was still
busy, as was the comedy club next door, and the Bake While
U Wait pretzel concession by the escalator, which sent waves
of suffocating cheesiness throughout the upper storeys of the
mall, was mobbed. The book store was closed, the make-over
parlour was closed . . . but the Rush Limbaugh souvenir shop
was open!

I'd heard a lot of Limbaugh as I drove about: his daily
show seemed to be syndicated to just about every radio
station in the country. It was meant to be a phone-in chat
show, but in reality the callers' brief contributions were
usually allowed to be no more than triggers for long streams
of right-wing political invective and social observations of
the most stereotypical and chauvinistic kind from the host.
Limbaugh was bitter and splenetic in his monologues, he
bullied and hectored anyone who dared to disagree with

him, and contradicted himself outrageously from show to
show, even minute to minute. Despite all that, he had a way
with clichés, and a booming oracular voice, and a boundless
belief in his own infallibility – 'It doesn't matter where here
and now is,' I heard him say once, 'As long as I'm there
– that made his show hugely entertaining. The first time I
heard it, anyway. After half a dozen hearings its attractions
had worn thin. After a dozen, I was filled with violent nausea
at the very sound of his voice. I think the final straw came
when someone phoned in to discuss the political problems in
Israel. Rush was very enthusiastic about that country. 'I love
Israel,' he bellowed, 'And I'll tell you why. I love automatic
weapons, and I love beautiful women. Over in Israel you
get a lot of beautiful women carrying automatic weapons.
Heaven!'

So I didn't buy any of the audio tapes available in his
souvenir shop. Nor a T-shirt with his face on it, nor a
Limbaugh for President bumper sticker, nor a *Dittohead* baseball
cap. (Rush fans call themselves dittoheads, because when they
come on the air they find themselves saying *Ditto, ditto*, all
the time – meaning they agree with everything Rush says.
Let's face it, if they didn't agree with everything he says,
they probably wouldn't be allowed on the air in the first
place.) In fact, I didn't buy anything. But I did leaf through
his autobiography. I'd been wondering, how could this man
live to forty-odds and still have so little idea about what the
world was really like? How had his towering egomania been
allowed to survive so long unchecked and untouched by any
trace of feeling for his fellow human beings?

Ah-ha! Limbaugh, it seemed, had worked as a radio DJ all
his life, had never done anything else. He'd started at the age
of sixteen, straight out of school into a station part-owned
by his father. To begin with, he spun the platters on Top
Forty shows, gradually increasing the talk quotient, and
playing less and less music, till by the early Nineties he'd
reached his present position of nationwide syndication, and
brainwide chauvinism. Not much wonder the guy was a
self-obsessed ignoramus with so little idea of reality! He'd

spent his entire adult life shut up in a dark, sound-proof room, with only the sound of his own voice for company, and everyone who might challenge his fantasies filtered out by the switchboard!

And this week's top five daft things *actually* said by Rush Limbaugh . . .

Last week's number two has fallen to five: *I think the reason why girls don't do well on multiple choice tests goes all the way back to the Bible, all the way back to Genesis: Adam and Eve. God said, 'All right Eve, multiple choice or multiple orgasms, what's it going to be?' We all know what was chosen.*

At number four, Rush on art: *I don't go to museums because they don't have golf carts. If you put a golf cart in a museum I'll go – you can drive around it a lot faster that way.*

Straight in at number three: *If we are going to start rewarding no skills and stupid people – I'm serious – let, let, let the unskilled jobs, let them, let, let, let, the, the, the kinds of jobs that, that, that take absolutely no knowledge whatsoever to do – let stupid and unskilled Mexicans do that work.*

Up to number two, Rush demonstrates his grasp of mathematics: *I'm the fourth branch of government. Why am I the fourth branch of government? Because the other two let it happen!*

But holding on at number one, it's Rush on sexual politics, and the changing place of women in America today: *Ladies, if you want a successful marriage, let your husband do what he wants to do.*

Svestkova Alej (The Prune Song)

Adolph Hofner and His Lone Star Boys!
KTSA - 12:30 P. M. - Mon. - Fri. - *Sponsored by*
LONE STAR BEER

"EDDIE"   "LEON"   "ERNIE"   "DICK"   "WILBUR"   "ADOLPH"   "RUDY"   "J. R."
DUNCAN   BROWN   LABORDE   HAYNES   MEELER   HOFNER   RIVERO   CHATWELL
STEEL GUITAR AND BASS   DRUMS AND TRUMPET   PIANO AND ACCORDION   ARRANGER   TRUMPET   GUITAR   CLARINET   FIDDLE

The Gunter has a bakery in its lobby. I bought a cinnamon croissant and two espressos for breakfast, and carried them up to my room. Sitting on the edge of my king-size bed, I spread wide my street map of San Antonio, and traced out the best route to get to Adolph Hofner's house on the south side of the city. Then I phoned up to fix exactly when I should come round.

Hello, is that Adolph?

Yeah, hi, who is this?

We talked yesterday afternoon, remember . . .

Eh . . .

You said I could come round and talk – about your music. I'm a big fan, you know.

Hey, you're the guy from Scotland!

That's me!

I got you, I got you.

Great! So, I was wondering: could I come round this morning? Does that suit?

Oh dear me.

Well, this afternoon, then?

Oh. Oh dear.

Well, anytime. You name it, Adolph, and I'll come round. I've been waiting five years to come to Texas, so a few more hours won't hurt.

There was a silence.

Are you okay? I said eventually.

Yes, yes, it's just — I'm sorry.

Why's that?

I said we could visit today, didn't I?

Yup. But I mean, tomorrow would be okay too, I suppose: I could stay another night here.

Where are you?

The Gunter Hotel.

The Gunter? Very nice! I used to broadcast a radio show from there, back in the Forties I guess. Go to the first floor and look in the ballroom there, The Crystal Ballroom, that's where we used to do our shows.

I've got a great wee radio show from the Fifties on a CD — you and J.R. Chatwell, Charlie Poss on piano and so on — it sounds like real fun, everybody goofing about. But the music's great too! That's what I wanted to talk to you about, really: was that enjoyment real, or was the whole thing just a job for you? Were the live dances the same mix of stuff as that radio show? The same fun? How consciously did you set out to produce a new sound by adding Bohemian flavours to the western swing hotpot? Or was it not a conscious choice at all, but just what audiences demanded? Did you see the other big bands — like Bob Wills' or Hank Thompson's — as rivals, or as friends and inspirations? What do you listen to now for pleasure? Still Milton Brown and Bing Crosby? How about the Mexican influence? For your '41 sessions in Dallas, did you copy 'Jessie Polka' from the Orquesta del Norte's 'Jesusita en Chihuahua', or from Cliff Bruner's version, 'Jessie'? Or somewhere else completely? And when

I say copy, I don't mean that in a bad way, I just mean
... eh ...

Hey, I know what you mean. He chuckled. That's a whole
pile of questions you have there, and I sure would like to
answer them.

Great!

But I don't think I can right now.

Oh yeah, you can't really talk over the phone. Like I said,
I'll come round. Anytime.

The thing is, I'm going away for the weekend.

That's okay, this is only Tuesday.

It's a long weekend.

Eh ... how long?

It lasts seven days.

And when does it start?

In about ten minutes. I'm just waiting for my daughter
to come round, then we're heading for the hills in the RV.
When I talked with you yesterday, I clean forgot about the
trip. Sorry.

Oh, I said. That's a ... that's a shame.

There was a pause.

Could you come next week? Adolph said.

I'm sorry, I said, I can't. I've got to be up in Turkey this
weekend, in the Panhandle, for the Bob Wills memorial.

Too bad. Well ...

Listen, I said. How about your brother Bash? Is he going
off to the hills with you?

Bash? No, no.

Ah-ha! Maybe I could meet him instead. Do you think
he'd mind?

The thing is, Bash is pretty big sick – he's just had both
his legs cut off.

An accident?

No, an operation.

Terrible. Will he be able to play again?

It's going to be hard playing lap steel with no legs.

(Was that meant to be a joke? To be on the safe side, I
didn't laugh.)

Anyway, Adolph went on, I don't think he's well enough to talk yet. In a couple of months, maybe . . .

There were noises in the background at his end. I heard a female voice in the distance, and Adolph shouting – in an even denser accent than the one he'd been talking to me in – that he was just coming. Then, That's Darlene, he said. I've got to go. Well, it's been real nice visiting with you. I sure do appreciate your interest. *Any* time you want to talk, just give me a call . . .

Closely linked with Adolph Hofner, and a Texas musical legend in his own right, was Floyd Tillman, who now lived near Marble Falls, out in the Hill Country. Born in 1914, he had started his professional career in 1933, playing take-off guitar with the Hofner brothers at their regular gig in Gus' Palm Gardens, San Antonio. He must've been hot even then, cause the brothers took a twenty-five per cent cut in their dollar-a-night pay in order to hire him. By 1936, Floyd was one of the first generation of electric guitarists, exploring the possibilities of the instrument in Houston's Blue Ridge Playboys a good two years before Eddie Durham – widely acknowledged as the pioneer of electric guitar – first recorded the instrument with the Kansas City Five.

The Playboys were a seminal group, featuring amongst others Moon Mullican on piano, Leon 'Pappy' Selph on fiddle, and Ted Daffan on steel – all important figures. Daffan went on to write such classic coronachs to love and loss as 'Worried Mind', (a hit for Bob Wills), 'Born To Lose' (one of the most recorded songs of all time) and 'Truck Driver's Blues' (the first ever trucking song, from 1939 – it's white line fever all the way from there to 'Teddy Bear'). Tillman was a distinctive, drawling vocalist, as well as a fine guitarist, but he too made his biggest mark as a songwriter, penning dozens of hits, both for himself and many other artists at the honky tonk end of country: 'They Took The Stars Out Of Heaven', 'I Love You So Much It Hurts', 'Slippin' Around'. This last named song provoked great controversy when it hit the charts in 1949, for its explicit depiction of adultery. It's not

a celebration of slippin' and sleepin' around, you understand
– the singer appears to be in a state of torment, in fact – but
apparently the moral watchdogs of the music biz thought
that even the *mention* of such behaviour was a bad thing.
Nevertheless, he became established as a writer of laconic/
yet powerful songs, and was covered by many major stars:
Gene Autry and Bing Crosby both had a hit with 'It Makes
No Difference Now', for instance, though the first and best
version (and the best version of *many* songs) was recorded by
Cliff Bruner's Texas Wanderers.

Since the early Fifties. Tillman had recorded only rarely,
and performed live even less, preferring to stay out of the
limelight and live off the royalties of his old hits while
trying to write new ones. A noble ambition. I'd never
met anyone who'd met him, but I'd heard third-hand that
he had a great fund of stories about his long and intensely
creative career. I especially wanted to hear about his Houston
years, the late Thirties and early Forties, when western swing
got electrified, got laid back, and started to mutate into
honky tonk – and he was right at the forefront of all the
developments.

I dialled his number.

Fifteen rings.

Hello? It was a woman's voice.

Is this the Tillman household?

Who wants to know?

I explained who I was, and why I wanted to talk to Mr
Tillman. She seemed extremely suspicious of my motives, but
eventually, reluctantly, she said I might visit with her husband
for a minute or two. She put the phone down. Floyd? Floyd!
I heard her shouting. There's a man from Scotland wants to
talk to you.

There was thumping and muttering; then a new voice, a
slow distinctive drawl, said, Hello, this is Floyd Tillman.

Hello, I said. It's great to talk to you.

Pardon? said Floyd.

I'm a great fan of your music.

What's that?

I love your music: 'This Cold War With You', 'Drivin'
Nails In My Coffin', 'G.I. Blues' . . .

I wrote all of them, you know.

Eh, yes. I'm a fan, Mr Tillman. I'm especially interested in
your days in Houston with the Blue Ridge Playboys – you
made some great records then.

Pardon?

'Swing Baby Swing', from 1936 – that's a great track.

What's that?

I said 'Swing Baby Swing' – you recorded it with Pappy
Selph in '36 – it's great!

Oh no, I fluffed it.

Do you think?

Pardon?

I cleared my throat, made the effort to speak slower. I
still think it's good, I said. At that time Bob Wills was still
playing New Orleans two-beat stuff – I love that too – but
you were already tuned in to what was coming next, the
honky-tonk style.

I'm getting a bit deaf, said Floyd, You'll have to speak a
bit slower.

Sorry, I said. Okay. I cleared my throat again. I was
hoping we could meet. I'm writing a book, you see, *Lone
Star Swing* . . .

What's that?

Lone Star Swing.

Lone Star Swig – is it about beer?

No, no: *Swing*. It's about music. And you're a really important figure, if you don't mind me saying so. I'd really like to
meet and talk to you about the way things were back then.

When's that?

Well, back in the late Thirties and early Forties, the
golden age . . .

No, when do you want to meet?

Oh. Well. I'm in San Antonio right now.

Not where, *when*?

When, when. Right. Well, it'd take me a couple hours to
drive up to Marble Falls, I suppose, so . . .

You mean you're in Texas now? I thought you were calling from Scotland.

No, I come from Scotland, but I'm here travelling about, talking to folk. I talked to Roy Lee Brown, to Cliff Kendrick, to Adolph Hofner. I'm going up to Turkey . . .

Listen, he said, if you're planning to talk to all those people you've got a real busy schedule. You don't want to talk to me.

I do, I do!

Anyway, it's a real small house we have here. You don't want to see it.

You're right, I don't care about the house, it's you I want to . . .

A lot of people think, just because you've had a few hit records you live in a big old mansion with a swimming pool shaped like a guitar. No sir, not me. It's just a small little house, that's all. Nothing special.

I'd just like to talk.

Pardon?

I'd like to TALK TO YOU.

It's not even real tidy right now. We've been doing some work, see, and it's a little mussed up.

There was a shriek in the background. Excuse me . . . Tillman covered the mouthpiece with his hand and spoke to his wife for a couple of minutes. Then he talked to me again. Well, sorry, it's not mussed up, it's clean as a pin. But it's just not convenient for you to come out here today: the house is too small.

I rolled my eyes to the Gunter's ceiling. That's too bad, I said. It would've been great to meet you. Maybe I could talk to you a little now though?

What's that?

Can we TALK NOW?

Now? Well, yeah, sure. But hold on, Frances is saying . . . get your address in Scotland. Yeah, we never thought nobody listened to us over there! Ha! You sure don't buy our records!

Well, I do, but . . .

Anyways, we'll take your address and . . . maybe write or something.

Great, I said. Ready? It's: 27 Alfred Street, Stromness, Orkney. Okay so far?

I think I should get a pen, said Floyd. I'll never remember all that. Frances, a pen! And paper! He put his hand over the mouthpiece again, words were exchanged, then he was back. Okay, he said, All set: shoot.

27 Alfred Street.

Frances, 37 Alpha Street.

No, 27.

I'm sorry. Frances, score that out. 27 Alpha Street.

Actually, that's *Alfred* Street.

I'm sorry?

Alfred, as in King Alfred.

Ah, King Alfred Street. Got it. 37 King Alfred Street.

No, 27.

27? Eh . . . Yep, sorry, we did have that, I just read it wrong.

No problem.

So, 27 King Alfred Street . . .

But cross out the King.

You want me to cross out the King?

Yeah, there's no King.

You said King! You got your own address wrong! Haw haw!

27 King Alfred Street, said Frances in the background. Is that it?

That'll do, I said. Great. Now. Next is the village: Stromness.

A pause.

Pardon? said Floyd.

Stromness.

Another pause.

Could you spell that?

S.

F.

No, S.

Pardon?

S. For 'Slippin' Around', I said.

Oh, S!

Yes, S. Then T.

P.

No, T.

T?

Yeah, T. *T.*

Two Ts?

Sorry. I sighed. Just the one.

Okay.

Okay. R.

R?

Yes!

S?

No, just yes, *yes*: you got the R.

I got it. Sure. So. FTR . . .

No, STR.

I'm sorry, STR.

That's it.

That's the name?

No, that's it so far, there's more. There's O, then M.

O, then N.

M.

M. Okay.

Then N.

Another M.

No, N this time.

N. You getting all this, Frances? Background mumbles. What's that? More mumbles. She says could you hurry up, we've got to go shopping.

Yeah, sorry, I said. I've not much left on my phonecard either. So, where was I?

Where was he, Frances? What's that? You were at the second M.

The second . . . ? Oh yeah. Hih! Well, put an N next.

Another one? Three of them in a row?

No, *N*, N for . . . for . . . Numptie.

Numptie. Okay.

Then E.

E.

Then S.

N S.

No, E S.

So two Es then S?

No, sorry, one E then two Ss.

Two Ss. Then?

That's the end!

Another N?

No! END!

Oh, right. That's the end, Frances.

Hold on, I said, There's the next *line* of the . . .

The robot operator's voice fizzed in my lug. You have thirty seconds left on this chargecard, it said.

I sighed.

What's next? said Frances, in the background.

What's next? said Floyd.

Just put Scotland after that.

Scotland? That it?

Yeah. That'll get to me. Eventually.

Scotland . . . What's it like over there?

Listen, I said. About your music . . .

There was a click, and the line went dead: my phonecard was done.

I fell back on the bed, the street plan of San Antonio and environs crumpling deafeningly underneath me. I folded the map up over my face, and started to chew the edges.

12th Street Rag

I drove north from San Antonio as far as the Circle K gas station at Canyon Lake. I was early, so went inside to use the restroom. The guy behind the counter gave me such a glower when I headed for the door without buying anything that I doubled back to the fridge cabinets lining one whole wall and bought a can of Dr Pepper. Outside in the afternoon heat haze, I popped it and drank: liquid candy-floss.

Back in the car, I buzzed down the windows, stuck a tape in the machine, and sat there sipping and listening: The Texas Top Hands, 1950 vintage, '12th Street Rag'.

The track opens with a chorus of high-speed precision piano playing, the fiendishly tricky sixteen-bar sprung-rag of the title, full of trills and runs and jokey hesitations – Scott Joplin on uppers. Then there's another thirty-two bars of elaborations from pianist and leader Walt Kleypas, before he nods in steel guitarist Rusty Locke for his solo.

Ah, that steel guitar rag! That electrifying electrified steel guitar! The instrument had only been invented fifteen years before, by the large and laconic Oklahoman Bob Dunn; he took the weedy Hawaiian slide guitar, amplified it, and straightaway started astounding audiences all over Texas with his unique *noise* as soloist for the top-drawing western swing band of the time, the Musical Brownies. Well before Charlie Christian had even *seen* an electric guitar, Dunn was recording outstanding jazz choruses on Brownies tracks like 'Sweet Jennie Lee', 'St Louis Blues' and 'Taking Off'. From his flurries of single notes, washes of weird chords, wild and risky improvisations, it's a straight line to Hendrix and every long-tressed fret-caresser of today.

Already in 1950, there was a whole repertoire of steel moves – from Bob Dunn's trombone-like stabs and slides, to the smoother, more elegant chordings of Bob Wills' steel-man Leon McAullife – and Rusty Locke had them all to hand. Next up, Easy Adams plays some sprightly lead guitar, receiving buoyant backing from the rhythm section: four foot ten 'Knee-High' Holley on string bass and Leonard Brown, usually a banjoist, switched to drums for this track. But the highlight of the recording, and one of the greatest jazz solos in all of western swing, is saved for last: Buck Buchanan tears in with a fiddle sound hot enough to frazzle Grappelli. He teases through the first four bars with a thrice-repeated rising and falling phrase, before finally letting the momentum of the combo rip another twenty-eight bars of dazzling bluesy improvisation out of him.

With the smell of smouldering rosin still lingering, Walt Kleypas kicks back in with two rock-steady, lightning-quick choruses, restating the melody and throwing in a few maverick licks and flicks for good measure. You think it's all over – and then, with a couple of irreverent plinking piano chords – it *is* all over.

I leant into the car, rewound the cassette, and set '12th Street Rag' going again. Good timing: out of the heat haze and into the Circle K parking lot came a big long shiny Texan car. In the passenger seat, waving, was a perjink middle-aged woman; driving was a lean man in a plaid shirt and bolo tie, greying hair swept back, dark glasses old-fashioned enough to look extremely fashionable. The passenger was Lucille Kleypas, and the driver was Walt Kleypas, one-time pianist and leader of The Texas Top Hands: a genuine dyed-in-the-wool western swing legend. I tossed my Dr Pepper can in a bin, and went over to shake the hand of the man who'd pumped the power into the supercharged, inspirational '12th Street Rag'. To my surprise, Walt paused only long enough to let Lucille clamber out, then he gunned up his engine, gave a brief salute, and headed back the way he'd come.

I'm Lucille, said Lucille.

Hello, I said. My name's . . .

I know. And that's Walt. We're to follow.

We got into the car, and set off up road after the small cloud of dust he was kicking up.

That's a nice tune, said Lucille.

It's Walt, I said.

I know it, she said, and laughed.

The route to the house was complex and circuitous; I was grateful for the guide. Canyon Lake is one of the biggest and most picturesque of all the picturesque bodies of water in the Hill Country between San Antonio and Austin, and over the past couple of decades, development after development has clotted about it: holiday homes, retirement homes, family homes, bungalows, duplexes, all laid out in a bewildering tree-studded sprawl. Bewildering to me, at least; it reminded me of the waterways of Caddo Lake.

You could get lost on the bayou for days, Oscar Plott had said. In fact you could get lost forever: going round in circles, every waterway through the trees looking the same, mist rising up off the water at sundown, gators bumping the bottom of your pirogue . . .

At least you could shoot the gators for supper, I'd said.

And now I had a supper date with the Kleypases. Lucille finished her potted history of the developments at the precise moment we arrived at their house: more good timing. Walt was waiting to shake my hand enthusiastically in the driveway, and insist on carrying my suitcase up the steps and into the house.

Within minutes we were sitting round the table, Lucille was serving up a huge Texas supper of fried chicken, potato salad, country-style beans and okra, and the talking had begun.

Grew up in Westphalia, north of here, said Walt. Family came from Germany originally.

There were very distinct German communities in Texas, eh?

Still are, said Lucille. German, Czech, Scottish . . .

I was the youngest of ten, said Walt. And we all were crazy for music: guitars and fiddles lying all over the house. In fact my older brothers had their own band, and I guess I just started messing about with their instruments.

Age of four, said Lucille.

Age of four I was getting pretty good on the old piano.

And he had this long hair . . .

I had this long hair, said Walt. I was a hippie before my time! This was in the Twenties, and me with long blond hair.

Curly too! said Lucille.

Did you know Walt in those days? I asked her.

I came down with nuns from Oklahoma at the age of six, she said.

I was eight, said Walt. When she arrived her parents took her round to show her off. Took her out to our place on the farm, the cotton farm. She was six, I was eight. That's the girl I'm going to marry, I said.

He said it right there. Eight years old! And we're still in love . . .

I helped myself to some more okra, took a drink of iced tea, and tried to redirect the conversation a bit. Walt, I said, What about music? You mentioned your brothers playing: what sort of stuff was it they played? I mean, who were your early influences?

Oh, I don't know . . . just my brothers.

I mean, were you listening to the radio back then? The late Twenties, was it? Was it kind of hillbilly stuff you were hearing? Or German bands?

Of course we didn't get married at that age, said Lucille. Did we Walt?

Sure didn't! They laughed.

We waited till I was seventeen, he was nineteen, said Lucille.

I was nineteen, she was seventeen, and we got married. Went down to San Antonio for our honeymoon. Came back on a Sunday afternoon, and in the evening I played a dance at the Modal Platform in Temple. Got paid five dollars – we thought we were rich.

We were!

That's right, because we earned maybe two dollars for two days of cotton picking on the farm.

Seven hundred pounds a day . . .

Me four hundred pounds, Lucille three hundred pounds . . .

In two days you'd pick fourteen hundred pounds between you . . .

And for fourteen hundred pounds of cotton you got paid two dollars.

So we *were* rich! Lucille nodded, happy that had been settled.

And what kind of music was it you were playing at these dances? I asked.

Would you like some more gravy? asked Lucille.

I had a radio show up in Temple, Texas, said Walt.

I'm asking the boy if he wants more gravy, said Lucille.

I'd love more gravy, I said.

That was with a band called The Bluejackets. We played in a diner called Pete's White Kitchen, and we had a radio show at noon on KTEM: Keenest Texas Entertaining Network. We were the biggest thing in Temple!

What kind of stuff were you playing there? Was it western swing by this stage? Bob Wills must've been getting well known around then.

Bob Wills? snorted Lucille. Bob Wills was a big fat slob!

That was later, said Walt.

Was it? said Lucille.

You didn't meet him till he was an old man, said Walt. He wasn't like that when I first met him.

I leant forward. When was it you met him? I asked. Was it early on?

Back around the time he quit Burrus Mill, said Walt. 1933, I guess. Fall.

So this was when Bob was stopping fiddling with The Light Crust Doughboys, the band sponsored by the Burrus Mill Company? When he struck out and formed The Texas Playboys?

That's it: he wanted me to be a Texas Playboy. But he came to see us playing with the other Doughboys – Tommy Duncan was there, he was a fine singer.

He was a gentleman, said Lucille.

They were a four-piece band, but Bob wanted to build it up. And after the show their manager asked me to come along to Green Terrace in Waco on the next Wednesday. Bob would sign me up to play piano with his new band.

Cause Papa Calhoun would've been tearing it up on the piano with the Brownies by this time, eh?

Walt threw back his head and laughed. Boy! I remember . . . Milton Brown was playing in Temple, and I lived three-quarters of a mile up the road. During the intermission I took Derwood Brown and Papa Calhoun home, gave each of them a big jar of homemade wine. Boy, did they grin during the second half!

But listen . . . I said.

Let me clear these plates, said Lucille. Would you like some pie?

Yes, yes, I'd love some pie. Thanks. But listen, Walt, what about Bob wanting you to join the Playboys?

He looked away. Well, I was just sixteen, see, and my daddy wouldn't let me go.

Good thing too, Lucille said, pausing on her way to the kitchen. Or you might have ended up a big fat slob like Bob Wills.

So no regrets, then?

Walt looked back. I played with a lot of fine musicians, he said.

The Texas Top Hands! '12th Street Rag' is one of my all-time favourites!

Walt nodded. That name was Lucille's idea. We wanted something western-sounding; cowboys were big then. A top hand is the best worker on the ranch. And we were meant to be the best band around, so . . .

You made some great records, I said. 'Bear Creek Hop', 'Little Brown Jug' 'You're Killing Me'.

Before that I was with Adolph Hofner, said Walt. Have you heard of him?

Sure! I nearly met him a couple days ago, in fact, but it fell through. A CD of his old stuff was released in Britain recently, it's great!

Released in Britain? Boy!

You're on one of the tracks, 'Sagebrush Shuffle', from 1942: great stuff. And you're on the cover!

I'm on a CD? Goddam!

I love the way you play, it's really ragtimey, or something, like a brass band I sometimes think – the way you kind of go oom-pah oom-pah down on the bass notes, then put in all those syncopations up on the high notes, those trills.

You like that?

Too right. Nobody else sounds like that, you know. That 'Sagebrush Shuffle's got a brilliant piano solo: you go really really quiet one moment, then get loud all of a sudden, then quiet again. Not many folk have delicacy as well as power, but you do.

Lucille came back from the kitchen with pie and ice-cream.

That was during the war, said Walt. I was with Adolph for a year or two, but he wasn't called Adolph then.

He changed it because of Hitler, said Lucille. *His* name was Adolph too, you see.

I remember one time we were playing in Fredricksburg, west of here, said Walt. Boy, we were lucky to escape with our lives. There was a mob, they decided Adolph had to be a German sympathiser because of his name. We had to climb out a window in back to escape!

But Fredricksburg puts itself over as a big German community, I said. Signposts and restaurants and everything!

That's for the tourists, said Lucille.

Adolph changed his name after that, said Walt.

What did he change it to?

He cut out the *A*: made it Dolph Hofner.

Dolph? I said. I think I'd've gone further than that if mobs were chasing me! I'd've made it Uncle Sam Hofner or something!

After pie we moved over to the settees. Lucille nodded to the piano against the wall and whispered to me as we walked over: He'll play if you ask him.

I'd seen the piano as soon as I came in; I'd been hoping I could pluck up the courage to ask for a tune or two.

Walt, I said. I'd love to hear you play something, if you don't mind.

He grinned, stepped quickly to the stool and sat down. What do you want to hear? he asked, rubbing his hands together. Anything! Name it!

How about '12th Street Rag'?

Boy, that's a tricky one, but . . .

He fluttered his fingers above the keys, then plunged in to a full-speed version of the tune I'd been playing all day. Halfway through the first chorus he hit a couple of bum notes, stopped playing, and looked round, shaking his head. I've got this arthritis now, in my fingers . . .

Getting old, said Lucille.

Eighty this year, said Walt.

Lucille grinned. Married sixty of those, she said.

Still in love! said Walt, grinning back. They gazed into each other's eyes.

Play something else if you like, I said. I mean, anything would be great.

Anything! he cried. Just name it!

Well, I don't know. You choose.

He closed his eyes for a moment, then turned back to the keyboards and started in on the turn-of-the-century parlour standard 'O'er The Waves'. After that he played and sung 'Make The World Go Away', a Sixties hit for Nashville crooner Eddy Arnold. From there Walt went straight into a medley of his own 'Westphalia Waltz' and the classic barrelhouse 'Down Yonder'.

I like the mix of stuff you're doing, I said. It's classic western swing: a bit of old time, a bit of pop, a bit of a blues.

It's all just music, said Walt. You had to play everything in the supper clubs. *Anything* they asked for you had to have a shot at it. And I guess I did okay, cause that's where I made my money. Adolph Hofner made a lot of money, but where is it now?

Long gone, said Lucille.

I met him two or three years ago at a show, said Walt. When are you going to give it up? I said to him. You're too old, you can hardly move! No money, he said. Got to keep working.

Well, you're still playing great, I said. You're singing's good too.

He grinned, and turned back to the keyboard. 'Tennessee Waltz!' he cried, and sang it.

How about one of those old fiddle tunes? I said.

'Cotton-Eyed Joe'!

How about a Bob Wills tune?

'San Antonio Rose'!

By the end of that, the best known and biggest selling south-western melody of all, Walt's fingers were well and truly limbered up. Without further ado he trilled the opening phrase of '12th Street Rag' high up on the keyboard, thumped out the answering chord down at the bass end, then whisked through a note-perfect rendition, with a generous helping of inventive new jazz licks thrown in.

No doubt about it: Walt Kleypas was still a real top hand.

Let's Count the Stars Together

The spare bedroom was luxurious and I slept like a logbook, reliving in my dreams the past week's driving: through cactus-studded deserts, jagged mountain ranges, San Antonio's sprawl, Canyon Lake's convoluted lanes. I awoke to find Lucille making a big breakfast – even though we'd done nothing but sleep since the last big meal – and Walt dusting down a bizarre contraption, consisting of two wooden painted maracas attached to a metal bass-drum pedal.

What do you think of that? said Walt, grinning.

I'm not sure, I said. What is it?

It's my rhythm section, said Walt, and laughed. Watch.

He went to the piano, placed the maracas to the left of the foot-pedals, then started picking out a Latin tune on the keyboard: 'La Paloma', I think.

Now listen, he cried. Rhumba!

And he started pressing the contraption's pedal in time to

the melody so the maracas shoogled rhythmically, one going up as the other went down, and the beans inside swished along so effectively that I half-expected Carmen Miranda to sashay in with a pound of bananas on her head. Instead, Lucille came out of the kitchen, a coffee pot in one hand, milk jug in the other, and hip-swayed across to the table, fluttering her eyelashes.

Over breakfast, Walt explained that, after leaving The Texas Top Hands in 1952, he'd led his own band for a couple of years. Despite continuing success, he'd gradually become disillusioned with the touring musician's lifestyle. The long hours of travel, the late nights, the frequent absences from home while on tour or at recording sessions, wore down his initial enthusiasm. For the life, if not for the music. What made matters worse was the fact that he also handled all business matters for both the Top Hands and The Walt Kleypas Band, so rare non-performing evenings would be taken up with paperwork instead. And still it was hard to make ends meet: the expense of paying wages, transport and accommodation costs for a five or six-piece band was crippling.

From the outside you don't really appreciate that, I said. It all looks effortless and fun to the audience.

We *did* have a lot of fun, said Walt. Some places we went back to year after year, like the fair at Bandera, we always had good times there.

I've seen a photo of the Top Hands playing at Bandera, I said. There's a huge crowd, you're playing the accordion, and all the band have these funny goatee beards.

Walt and Lucille hooted with laughter. We used to grow those specially every year for Bandera, said Walt. I can't remember why . . .

I liked that beard, said Lucille. I could get a kiss and my teeth cleaned at the same time.

Walt shook his head. But still, you get tired of it all after a while, never seeing your family. Well, some guys maybe liked it, but I got to where I just about hated it.

So in 1955 he went solo. More than that, he went

north-west, to hunting resorts like Sun Valley in Idaho and West Yellowstone in Wyoming. There he played in lounges, supper clubs, and restaurants. (Didn't Hemingway hang out in Sun Valley for a lot of the Fifties, slaughtering anything that flew, crawled or swam past his increasingly bloodshot eyes? Yes he did. Funny to imagine Walt tinkling away over in the corner of the lounge as Papa beat his chest and knocked back triple daiquiris at the bar.)

I just played the piano to start with, said Walt, But then I got to thinking: a bit more rhythm might be good. Especially in the clubs. So I got this little twenty-inch bass drum, it fit in beneath the piano real neat, just to the right of the pedals.

He was a regular thumper, said Lucille.

And then, said Walt, All that Latin stuff started to get popular. People were asking for rhumbas and bossa novas and sambas.

So you bought your maracas!

That's it, said Lucille. They were a hit.

And then I got a Solovox, a kind of electric organ with a little bitty keyboard. Like those synthesisers people have now – but this was 1962! And that was on a stand by the top end of the piano. I could play a bass line on the piano, then reach over and do melody effects on the Solovox.

Stomping away at the rhythm section with your feet the whole time?

Yeah! Shit! I remember one time I was playing away – one hand on the piano, one on the Solovox, one foot on the drum, the other on the maracas, and my knee switching the Solovox on and off . . . and singing! – when the boss walks up. I said to him, Just don't ask me to sweep the floor, boss, cause I know where you'll stick the broom handle!

We laughed. Sounds like you were a regular one-man band, I said.

Yes sir, said Lucille. And that's when the trouble started. The union! She glowered. They banned Walt.

Well, they gave me a little trouble.

That's right: they banned him. Said he was playing four

instruments, and there was only one of him. So he was doing three men out of a job!

Walt shrugged, munched on a waffle. Anyway, he said after a while, The winters were too bad up there. I was glad to come back to Texas.

Did you get into western swing again when you came back?

No, no. The supper clubs were where the money was. I'm not talking big bucks, you understand. I'm just talking about a good regular income for the family.

We have three children, said Lucille, Two boys and a girl. Well, they're all grown now, of course.

They're older than we are, said Walt.

Lucille patted the back of my hand. I wish they were as interested in their father's music as you are, she said.

Maybe they just take it for granted, I said. For me it's exciting: I mean, I've come all this way, I've tracked you down . . . But for them, I suppose it was just what Dad worked at.

It was a job, said Walt, nodding. I went out, I played, I came home.

How about practising?

I don't mean to be big-headed, said Walt, But I've never needed much in the way of practice. I guess when you're playing five or six hours a day, you just learn as you're going along.

Same as writing, I said.

Sure, said Lucille. You wouldn't write a book for practice, throw it away, then write another one, would you? That would be an awful waste of time.

Walt had a long career in Houston supper clubs like the Cork Club (in the Shamrock Hotel), Bud Bigelow's, and the Outriggers' Club. At one point he was booked into Lionel's Flame Room – the first bottle bar in town, Walt called it – for a fortnight's engagement. He ended up playing there for five years. He had a grand piano with a glass top, and sixteen stools ranged around it. People would sit and drink and talk as he played, occasionally making requests.

One strange request came late at night, when everybody except a particularly wealthy and miserable customer had gone home.

He was sitting there by himself, said Walt. He'd been there all night, drinking himself stupid, breaking out crying every so often. And now there was just me and him at this big glass piano. So I got talking to him. Turned out his son had graduated a week ago. That's great, I said, You must be proud. Yeah, said the guy. But I bought him a Ferrari for a graduation present. What does the s.o.b. do? Crashes it that same day and gets himself killed. I didn't know what to say, so I just played. Then the guy says, Hey, buddy, can you do something for me? Sure, I said, If I know it. Buddy, could you go through to the kitchen and get some black-eyed peas and cornbread for me?

I raised my eyebrows. And did you?

Sure, I felt sorry for him.

Because of his son?

Because of his whole life. All that money, and still not happy! He said those peas and cornbread were the best food he'd had in years. Walt shook his head – in disbelief, maybe in disgust.

The best things in life are free, said Lucille. You can't buy love, no matter how fat your wallet is.

I used to hate rubbing shoulders with those rich bastards, said Walt, suddenly gloomy. So much money and so little sense.

Lucille reached across the table to take his hand. We might not be rich, she said, But we got each other.

Married sixty years, said Walt, perking up.

Still in love! cried Lucille. They smiled at each other.

The Kleypases gave me directions on how best to drive into Austin. Apparently the best way was not to go there at all, thus avoiding the nightmarish traffic. But I was determined to have a look at the state's capital, so they finally gave me some tips. They also told me about the Driskill Hotel, a grand and historic place right in the middle of town, on Sixth Street, famous for its music clubs and buskers. That sounded like the place for me.

Walt insisted on carrying my bag to the car for me again, then he dashed back inside the house. Lucille gave me a hug, and Walt reappeared.

I'd like you to have this, he said. He held out the pedal-operated maracas contraption.

I can't, I said. It's yours. All those years you played it! Sentimental value and all that.

No, said Walt. I want you to have it, to remember us by.

I took the contraption, gave each of them another hug, then drove off. Walt and Lucille were waving, arms around each other as I turned the corner at the bottom of their street. Married sixty years. Still in love.

Tired of the Same Thing All the Time

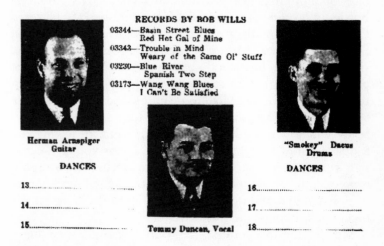

RECORDS BY BOB WILLS

03344—Basin Street Blues
Red Hot Gal of Mine
03343—Trouble in Mind
Weary of the Same Ol' Stuff
03230—Blue River
Spanish Two Step
03173—Wang Wang Blues
I Can't Be Satisfied

Herman Arnspiger
Guitar

DANCES

13.................................

14.................................

15.................................

Tommy Duncan, Vocal

"Smokey" Dacus
Drums

DANCES

16.................................

17.................................

18.................................

Austin calls itself the Live Music Capital Of The World, and 6th Street (formerly Old Pecan Street — nice to see that confusing old poetic name being replaced by a nice clean number) is the city's acknowledged entertainment hotspot, its Basin Street, its Broadway. So I booked in to the grand old Driskill, designed to 'loom like a palace over surrounding structures', and immediately headed out into the balmy evening in search of live western swing in the political and musical heart of its home state.

6th Street was buzzing. It was ten o'clock and the pavements were hoatching: strolling couples, serious leather bikers, groups of half-drunk girls, teenage boys cruising past in open-topped cars, sidewalk artists trying to stop folk trampling on their chalk Hendrixes and Monroes, vendors yelling about their hot snacks, cool jewellery, souvenirs. Grinning youngsters stood at club doorways thrusting flyers into the

hands of passers-by, dragging them inside if they showed
the slightest interest; at other club doors (and sometimes at
the same ones) bouncers barred the way, checking IDs and
frisking for weapons, bottles, or just for fun.

Late night drugstores and delis thronged with customers:
students buying sandwiches, short Mexican ladies with big
bags of shopping, bearded men in ragged coats clutching
bottles in brown paper bags. A busker thrashed at a battered
Gibson jumbo with great enthusiasm, reminding me of
Derwood Brown, Milton's younger brother and trusted
rhythm guitarist. Derwood's playing was so forceful, violent
even, that strings were constantly snapping. A boy (sometimes Roy Lee Brown) had to be employed just to sit in the
wings and restring guitars, so a fresh tuned one was always
ready when Derwood reached out his hand for it – maybe
a dozen times a night. There were a few young Tejano
kids running up and down 6th, a scattering of drooping
hippies, one or two strutting drugstore cowboys. A pair
of policemen wandered through the crowds, knee-length
night-sticks swinging at their sides.

Most of the folk looked like tourists though: spending a
few days in the capital, desperate to have a good time, to hear
some music, to get drunk. They'd eaten at the Texas Chilli
Parlor or Don Limon's Tex Mex, and were now pounding
the entertainment district, pouring into Headliners East to see
the Solid Senders, then out of there and along the street to
see Stumble at Babe's, then out and round the corner to the
Elephant Room on Congress to see Rez Abbass, then down
to the Continental Club for Toni Price and Doak Short.

I let myself be swept along from one bar to the next,
downing a Bud in each, watching college football on big
screen tellies, dodging flying beer and staggering tourists,
hearing band after band playing Stevie Ray Vaughan-style
heavy metal blues. Guitar solos would grind into action as
the barman prised open my beer, and would still be screaming
away when I drained the last drop. (Mind you, that wasn't
always a very long time: the thrusting Strats and flailing red
bandanna tails spurred me on to drink quick.) I'd stumble out

into the street – only marginally less hot, sticky and crowded than the bar – and turn left or right or walk straight ahead through the crawling, cruising honking traffic. It didn't really matter where I went: there was always another open door, heavy blues pounding out, neon beer signs flashing, drunk tourists whooping and spilling beer.

Oh, Bob Dunn! Look what you started! It's a long way from your awesomely inventive electric steel – your delicate fills, your sudden lunging slides, your subtle tremelos, your trombone impersonations, your frenzies of splintered melody – to this streetful of screwed-up angst-ridden faces hunched over their wailing Fenders. I'd like to imagine you saying, like the Arkansas Traveller, You can't get there from here. But you can, they can, they do. Everything you did, Mr Dunn, was thrown out with a casualness, a lightness of touch, above all a sense of your playing's contribution to the overall sound of the band, that was the antithesis of what rules on 6th Street now.

After a couple of hours, I felt I had listened more than enough. And still I hadn't heard much worth hearing. There was no western swing revivalism of the type pioneered in the early Seventies by Austin residents Asleep At The Wheel, no Willie Nelson-style outlaw country of the sort that boomed here so resoundingly in the mid to late Seventies, no introspective, intelligent songwriting of the type that Townes Van Zandt and Steven Fromholz excelled at, no idiosyncratic, skewed, satirical country from the likes of Ray Wiley Hubbard (author of 'Up Against the Wall', 'Redneck Mother') or Kinky Friedman and his Texas Jewboys; there was no Tejano, no hard-core honky-tonk, no swing (the club called Jazz was playing only CDs when I dropped in). In short, the great mix of musical genres and styles, the great kirn of voices and accents, the great joyous collision of all the musics of America – and quite a few from beyond – that Austin had been famous for, were gone. All I could find, all along 6th Street, and for blocks around, were averagely talented white boys playing overblown versions of 'Flood Down in Texas' and 'Crossroads' and not much else. They achieved extreme heaviosity, but failed to move me at all – except out the door.

I paused to wonder which club I should try next, then was overcome with the sudden powerful urge to give up on 6th Street completely: even Pete's Peanut Bar could not tempt me to stay a moment longer. I zigzagged through the traffic and crowds one more time, ducked down an alley past a gym, a multi-storey car park, and a museum in honour of sometime Austin resident O. Henry, and passed into the quiet, dark streets beyond.

The abrupt change in atmosphere reminded me of somewhere I'd been before, but it took me a couple blocks' walking to remember where. A few years before I was travelling down from Orkney to Edinburgh, and I stopped off on the way at Keith, in Moray, for the annual Traditional Music Festival. The main street of the small distillery town was jammed from end to end with crowds of locals, visitors, folk music fanatics, pipers, fiddlers, folklorists, travellers, bodhran-players, bothy-balladeers, hamburger salesmen, and – above all, encompassing most of the above – serious drinkers. The road was sticky in places with great puddles of spilt beer, littered thickly all over with discarded plastic pint-glasses. The sound of hundreds of people tramping up and down over splintering, crackling plastic glasses was like a ton of brittle bones being masticated in some giant beast's maw. Couples copulated up close. Fights broke out here and there, ending as soon and suddenly as they'd begun when one or other of the protagonists slipped drunkenly on a shard of plastic glass and fell to the ground. Music poured from every pub door, from open house windows, from buskers, from wandering pennywhistlers and squeezeboxers on their way to the next session, and from the cassette players of archivists and BBC producers playing back the recordings they'd just made.

The thing that struck me – standing there in the middle of 'The Mason's Apron', 'The Mucking of Geordie's Byre', 'The Nuptial Knof', 'MacPherson's Rant', 'The Bonnie Ship The Diamond', 'Deil Among the Tailors', and a hundred others – the thing that struck me was the strange but certain feeling that nobody was really listening to the music.

For one thing, they were all too drunk. Ninety per cent of them had started chucking down the heavy and whisky ten hours before, when the pubs opened and the sessions started, and kept at it all day. (For my money, that's why the best music had come about one-thirty in the afternoon: the level of alcohol in the musicians' bloodstream was perfectly balanced at that point: it had loosened the fingers but not completely disconnected them.)

Mainly, though, folk weren't listening to the music because they didn't want to, they didn't need to. What really mattered was the *idea* of being at Keith Traditional Music Festival. They liked the idea of a weekend of carousing and music: they could look forward to it for months before, they could recollect it in sobriety for months after. While they were there, of course they would enjoy it. The folkies of the North-East of Scotland had whipped themselves into such a frenzy, were possessed of such a firm determination to enjoy themselves – wholeheartedly, ferociously, suicidally – that no other outcome was ever possible. The actual music could've been dull, clumsy-fingered, tuneless (it was often all three) but that didn't matter: it was the idea of the music that was more important than the actuality. As long as there was a vaguely melodic racket going on in the background, then everybody could keep on knocking back the whiskey, swaying in time to nothing at all, yelling at each other what a great time they were having.

That's exactly what it was like on 6th Street, Austin, Texas. All these visitors had come to the Entertainment Main Street of the Live Music Capital of the World. Goddarn it they were going to have a good time! From the minute they put on their Ralph Lauren Polo T-shirts and their DKNY mini-dresses and stepped out of the Driskill, they were going to drink, dance and be merry, and nothing was going to stop them. Not even over-priced drinks, tarted-up tourist-trap bars, and third-rate, mind-numbing, body-and-soul-less imitation-blues.

Walking through the empty backstreets, in the general direction of away from 6th Street, was also strangely like Keith. In both places there was a sharply defined boundary between fun-zone and dead-zone: as soon as you stepped out from the loud, brightly lit crowded area, it might as well never have existed: all was quiet, dark, deserted. I remember being almost shocked in a Keith backstreet to pass an uncurtained window and glimpse a girl inside watching TV: life *did* still go on outside the festival! For some reason, I immediately identified with the lone telly-watcher rather than the boisterous crowds a couple hundred yards away. Likewise, I immediately felt myself relax when I walked into a small, almost empty Mexican restaurant somewhere down near the river.

I ordered a San Miguel and some crabmeat tortillas in chocolate mole sauce, and sat there wondering if there was something wrong with me. Everybody else seemed to be content to focus on the *idea* of having a good time. Why did I have to make things difficult for myself by needing to genuinely feel like I was *having* a good time? But then the tortillas came, and they tasted so utterly weird and wonderful that I stopped worrying and just ate.

Good Time Cake-Walk

SGT. PEPPER'S
J. P. HAYES, CHILE CONNOISSEUR

P.O. Box 49565 Austin, Tx 78765 512.482.0449

Late next morning I walked from the Driskill up to the pink granite dome of the state capitol, famous for being seven feet taller than the US capitol in Washington, but more notable, in my opinion, for the involvement of several dozen Scottish scumbags in its construction in the 1880s. Following the engagement of virtual slave-labour in the shape of 500 convicts, the original Texas stoneworkers went on strike, and held out resolutely for fair employment practices. Stand up the brave blacklegs of Aberdeen! Lured by the promise of four dollars a day, sixty-two Aberdonian masons came to Austin, broke the strike, and laboured for six years on the building. Three cheers for the international labour market! (For that, of course, is what allows me, another Aberdonian, to come to the States and, with the help of my team of convict fact-checkers, put a dozen travelogue-writing Texans out of work.)

All around the grand pink building were lawns, flower-beds, shade trees and security guards. I walked on, and gradually the security guards thinned away to nothing. I was now strolling through the lawns, flower-beds and shade trees of the University of Texas. Forty-nine thousand students attend the place, (I did a quick head count), and most of them were sitting on the grass, talking, sleeping, snogging, even reading.

I checked out the James Michener collection in the Huntington Art Gallery (crap writer, great taste in art: Carl Andre, Mark Rothko, Robert Rauschenberg), and also had a good look at their Guttenberg Bible. Very nice. Enough to make me consider converting to Christianity. Or typesetting.

Upstairs was the Harry Ranson Humanities Center. This is the place where the manuscripts of such folk as Dylan Thomas, Anne Sexton, D.H. Lawrence, Tennessee Williams and George Bernard Shaw reside. I never made it beyond the lobby. There I found display cases of *really* interesting stuff. Who needs the manuscript of *Women In Love* when you can look at the author's New Mexican bead mocca-sins? I'm talking about literary artefacts on the order of Katherine Mansfield's handbag, Carson McCuller's cigarette lighter, Charles Dickens' monogrammed dinner plate, Evelyn Waugh's pen, Compton Mackenzie's pipe, Anne Sexton's chequebook. Like many writers' chequebooks, Sexton's was worth far more money after her death than it was ever able to command during her life.

Stepping over the prone bodies of tens of thousands of students soaking up knowledge and UV rays, I wandered through the campus till I came to The Drag, a wide shopping street of secondhand bookstores, record shops, folk art galleries, cafes, guitar shops, delis, and The People's Renaissance Market: a bunch of pavement stalls selling clothes, jewellery, collectable comics and marshmallow cookies.

I bought a cassette by Tom Morrel and the Time Warp Tophands, a two-volume set of Tolstoy's letters, a Little Jimmy Dickens LP featuring his hit 'May The Bird of

Paradise Fly Up Your Nose', and also a sheaf of small magazines: poetry broadsheets, events guides, underground insurrectionist rags, short stories printed on rice paper, oddball personal commentaries, secret diaries, obsessives' confessions. I found a seat in a coffee shop, ordered a raspberry bagel and quadruple espresso, and started reading.

The relatively straight-laced *Austin Chronicle* had an interesting section entitled, THINGS YOU THOUGHT DIDN'T HAPPEN ANY MORE:

> Michael E. Marcum, 21, was arrested for theft of six 350-pound power company transformers in Stanberry, Mo., in January. Marcum said he needed the transformers for the time-machine he was building. He said he wanted to transport himself into the future a few days, find out the winning lottery numbers, and then return to buy a ticket.

I thought that, if I had a time machine, I would go back in time, perhaps to late 1934, and visit the Crystal Springs Ballroom on the west side of Fort Worth. There I'd have the unalloyed pleasure of seeing the Musical Brownies at their dancefloor-shaking best. An added treat would be seeing the dancers' looks of astonishment as new recruit Bob Dunn lashed out with his astounding steel guitar sounds, then fell off his stool, blootered. Suddenly something occurred to me: was it a depressing reflection of my mental tendencies that I instinctively wanted to travel *back* in time? Shouldn't I have been filled with the youthful, optimistic lust for the future? To put it another way: was I a sad old bastard? Quite likely. Tough queso. Personally, I don't see the point in travelling forward in time. We're all going there anyway: what's the rush?

Next up was a bizarre, badly photocopied fanzine called *Boji For The Mentally Ill*. In addition to various odd stories, abusive letters, and froth-mouthed rants, mostly about violent death and strange sex (also violent sex and strange death) there

were some great record reviews written by someone called
Mrs McFeelme:

Doo Rag *Hussy Bowler*
Scary carny freaks eating corndogs while they man the
pig races! Extremely appetising. YEE*FUCKIN*HA!!!!
Portishead *Dummy*
Just go and buy this right now. Don't ask any stupid
questions. All I can tell you is it's so sweet it drips.
Blonde Redhead *Blonde Redhead*
Sexually charged and throbbing. Big, mean, fatty bass.
This is the way drugs would make you feel if they didn't
inevitably start to suck.
The Chimpanzees *El Chimpo Grande*
This is thoroughly annoying in the best possible way.
Diarreah Naoko's vocals reach an impossible pitch and
stay there. This suits the subject matter just fine: lost
noses, cannibal families, stealing, vomiting, sperm and
ovum . . .

The lost nose song sounded especially interesting: a thrash
version of Gogol's classic short story on the same theme? Or
was the title a sly reference to the western swing standard
'El Rancho Grande'? That's sung mostly in Spanish: on
one Texas Playboys recording, Bob mutters to Tommy
Duncan during an instrumental break, What are you talking
about boy? I don't know, replies Tommy, and cracks up,
laughing all the way through the final verse. Good old *calzone!*
shouts Bob.

Office Number One was good. A well-laid-out A4 newspaper, I spent the bottom half of my coffee trying to
work out if it was serious or not. The lead story in issue
20 was, PARAPSYCHOLOGISTS DISCOVER CANINE
EMPIRE:

A group of Stanford parapsychologists discovered a gate
to the long-sought-for astral plane last week. A party of

six explorers ventured into the plane and discovered it was heavily populated by canines.

Remember, said T. Mya, leader of the expedition, Entities with sufficient skill merely use their vision and will to alter the environment in the astral plane; in other words, dogs don't need opposable thumbs to build homes there.

That couldn't possibly be serious, could it? Well, considered in tandem with another newspaper, *Emergence Quarterly*, which certainly was serious, I couldn't be too sure. *EQ* featured reports of SIGNS AND MIRACLES FROM ALL OVER THE WORLD, including a 'column of light created by the Master Jesus (York, England)' which looked incredibly like a camera wrist-strap dangling in front of the lens. The new messiah, Maitreya, was quoted on page two as saying, Those who search for signs will find them. A man of wisdom indeed.

The second lead story on *Office Number One* settled my internal debating: THREATS AND VIOLENCE INDUCE SCHOLASTIC INCENTIVE:

Children who fail to develop according to the academic standards of public schools will be beaten with cane poles under new legislation adopted last Friday. Legislators, educators and parents developed the plan at a weekend retreat outside of Houston.

'Since there are no wars going on,' said Teacher Sarah T. Rod, 'We're asking the army to provide soldiers to beat students who fail in school. When students conform to our scholastic standards, we'll stop beating them.'

Governor Bush also announced plans to implement the incentive procedure into areas of the private sector that seem to be flagging.

'With a properly motivated work force, we could reduce the deficit in no time,' remarked Buck Moore, an economic analyst for the governor. 'Of course, we'd have to charge higher taxes to pay for these new services.'

Response to the new military incentives has been favorable. Hundreds of students have volunteered to help improve their teachers in order to raise the over-all standards of their education. They are hoping to use leather thongs to thrash teachers until lessons are presented in a comprehensible, easy to grasp manner.

'We want to give something back to the system that has given us so much,' said student Martha Karr, in an expression of benevolence common in many classrooms working under the program.

My doubts were settled: of course *Office Number One* was entirely serious. After all, hadn't just such a programme of incentives been operated all through my schooldays in Scotland?

I got another espresso (just a double this time: had to watch my caffeine intake) and a cinnamon bagel with cream cheese, then wished I'd read *15 Minutes* first. This single A3 sheet (presumably it takes fifteen minutes to read – or is that to produce?) had a very profound motto under its masthead – **To each his own, it's all unknown** – and an invaluable Gerg 'n' Zub Fast Food Review Special on page 2: BUSTING THE BUFFET. Of their ten commandments for getting the most out of chain-gang restaurants' regular buffet-deals, I particularly liked number 9:

> **Don't be ashamed of your gluttony**. This point should prove relevant to women who have been raised to eat like a lady. Don't buy into the media lies designed to turn you into an anorexic waif. Any man worth his bulk will love a woman who can hold her own at the trough, and if you have trouble finding a man like that, please give us a call. Please.

And number 10 led on nicely from there:

Eat slow. The advent of fast food has bastardized the beautiful art of eating into just another stupid bodily function, like sex. Fight back by taking your meal nice and slow. Talk to the people you're with. If you're alone, bring a book. Remember, eating isn't just a meal – it's your Best Entertainment Value!

I had been about to leave, but now resolved to stretch my coffee and bagel crumbs for another ten minutes. *The Quarterly Newsletter of the Bay Area Spoonless Society* was next. This detailed the exploits of a group of Californians dedicated to eradicating the diabolical utensil from American homes and restaurants. It included tips for outwitting the Spoon Nazis, a spoon-related crossword, and an interview with fourteen-year-old Jake Ceely of Hawthorne, New Jersey, headlined BURY 'EM ALIVE!

B.A.S.S. – When did you first realize that spoons were the ridiculous tools of oppression?
JAKE – About a week after I realized they sucked.
B.A.S.S. – I understand that you recently buried the family spoons in the backyard. How did your parents react?
JAKE – They flipped. I got a big lecture. They told me I shouldn't steal spoons.
B.A.S.S. – People with old-fashioned values might consider what you did to be a crime. Do you view it as this?
JAKE – No. It's a revolution.

My final publication turned out to be a publicity flyer. What good fortune! It was in the form of a calendar listing all the bands appearing at one of the most famous honky-tonk dancehalls in all of Texas: The Broken Spoke, motto, We ain't fancy but we're darn shure country! I'd just missed gap-toothed country swinger Alvin Crow, and also noteworthy songwriter Gary P. Nunn, but tonight I could cruise down to 3201 South Lamar and see Charlie Robison. Any relation to

Carson Robison, long-time guitarist and arranger for Vernon Dalhart? I didn't know: great-grandson would be about right. I'd ask the man himself, tonight at 9.15!

On my way back to the Driskill, I stopped off at an odd shop called Terra Toys to buy some postcards. I had a few hours to kill before Spoke O'Cloke, and thought I'd better get in touch with the old country. As it turned out, I didn't even have to write the cards to do so.

The young guy behind the counter had a shaved head, a rivet through his bottom lip, and baggy surfer shorts on. He flipped through the cards I'd chosen, fingers flittering over the till, then stopped at an old sepia photograph of a cowboy in boots and hat, flying off a bucking bronc. Surprise and disgust creased across his face.

That old nostalgic crap! he said.

Pardon?

All this horse and Stetson stuff. It's garbage! Nobody dresses like that in Texas anymore.

You're joking, I said. Everybody does. Well, not everybody: not you. But out in the country you can't get moved for Stetsons!

No, he said, Not any more. It's just in the movies, or at the line dance clubs where all the fat-assed secretaries go. Nobody *seriously* wears high boots and ten-gallon hats any more.

You're not from round here, are you? I said.

Sure am, he replied. Born and raised in Austin, grad student at UT now. The only place to be.

But listen, I've been out west – Presidio, Wink, Fort Stockton – and everybody there's wearing . . .

You'd have to be crazy to go out there, he interrupted. There's *nothing* there.

Well, how about Fort Worth, Wichita Falls, El Paso?

Like I said . . . *nothing*. And *nobody*. Austin's it.

He dropped my cards into a paper bag, hesitating over the cowboy one as if considering dropping it in the bin instead – then pressed the total button on the till. Three dollars, he said.

Handing over my change, he paused, looked me up and
down. Where are you from? he said. Ireland?

No, Scotland, I said. I'm Scottish. I've come here to track
down Bob Wills and his . . .

Scottish? From Scotland? Hey! Did you ever hear of a band
called The Proclaimers?

The twins? Aye, sure! I've seen them loads of . . .

They are just fantastic. Those voices!

Yeah, it's good that they sing in their own . . .

Listen! He leant across the counter, eyes glistening. You
can maybe solve a mystery for me. You know their album,
Sunshine On Leith?

Aye.

Well, what is Leith?

Eh . . .

Like, is it a mental thing? A state of mind?

That's what it is exactly, I said. It's a town too, though, a
port. But above all it's a state of mind.

He nodded. I thought it was.

Yup, and you are in it.

I am?

Yeah, you are truly in Leith, as they say.

Hey! Great! You've made my day! I'm in Leith! He did
a little shuffle behind the counter. How about you, he said.
Are you in Leith?

No, I replied, I have been in Leith, but now I'm involved
in a different mental thing. Now I'm in a Lone Star State
Of Mind.

He frowned. What's that?

A song by Nanci Griffith.

Who?

Not *who*? but *where*? was the question that occupied me as I
reeled back to the hotel. Where were Austin's western swing
bands? The music had been played here just about as long as
anywhere – right back to the Thirties and Forties when local
bands like Delores and the Bluebonnet Boys and Jesse James
and All The Boys were knocking them dead all over town,

and laying down some great records too. There were also contemporary musicians worth listening to, I'd been told: the aforementioned Alvin Crow and his Pleasant Valley Boys, at the country end of swing, for instance. And Wayne Hancock, working hard at reincarnating Hank Williams. And the most popular new name on the scene, Don Walser, a portly retiree who yodelled and yelped along over a swinging honky-tonk backbeat.

None of the records I'd heard by these folk were anywhere near jazzy enough for my liking, but I'd still have loved to have seen them live and had my prejudices overturned. It was not to be. None of them was performing in Austin during my stay, nor anywhere else that I passed through on my travels.

Maybe I should have veered off the Bob Wills trail for a while, and tried harder to track down these guys. But my time was limited. And anyway, the spirit didn't move me.

Maybe I should also have veered off towards the Gulf Coast, and spent some time in Houston. I could've tried to find Cliff Bruner, maverick swing fiddler, and the last surviving Musical Brownie. Maybe I could have learnt some more about the intriguing pioneer western swinger, Shelly Lee Alley. I could perhaps have talked to his son, Shelly Lee Alley Jr (no mean musician himself, and a preacher to boot) and his stepson, Clyde Brewer (a professional multi-instrumentalist since his early teens with great bands like Link Davis and his Bluebonnet Playboys, and his own Original River Road Boys.) I could maybe have had a look at the early stomping grounds of Buddy Ray, maybe sought out folk who played with him in groups like The Texas Wanderers and Dickie McBride's Village Boys. Maybe I could have slipped into the Houston City Auditorium, where, back in 1941 or so, Buddy and the other Village Boys found themselves the only white folk watching Jay McShann and his big band – featuring Charlie Parker on sax. Due to segregation laws, they couldn't sit in the auditorium, so had to sneak into the orchestra pit and soak it all in from there . . .

Maybe I could've have done a lot of things in Houston. But the spirit wasn't moving me in that direction either.

The Wheel of the Wagon is Broken

I drove south over the river in high spirits, singing along
to Emmylou Harris live at the Ryman Auditorium. She
was doing a great thumping version of Steve Earle's 'Guitar Town'.

> Nothing ever happened round my home town
> And I ain't the kind to just hang around
> But I heard someone calling my name one day
> And I followed that ghost down the lost highway

Yes siree, that was me, following the ghost of Bob Wills – and
Hank Williams, Spade Cooley, Jimmie Rodgers, Bill Boyd,
Bob Dunn, Lefty Frizzell: a whole posse of ghosts – down
the lost highway to the Broken Spoke, 'home of the best in
live country band music and chicken fried steak'.

I found the place no bother – some distant echo of all the

great music that had ever been played there drawing me in like a beacon through the dark streets of Austin – and I pulled into its generous parking lot, slipped into neutral, and sat there for a moment, feasting my eyes on its classic honky-tonk frontage: weathered clapboard walls, a long fenced-in front porch, two enormous wagon wheels flanking the sign above the door. A dozen or so cars were already ranged in front of the porch, so I pulled in just beyond the far one, easing the nose of the Chevy forward into the vibrant light of a neon beer sign hanging from the veranda.

A middle-aged couple in baggy shorts, shaven heads and lip rivets walked up the front steps. No, sorry, that was just a trick of the gloaming: the gent held the front door open for the lady to enter, and the light spilling out from inside illuminated them in all their plaid-shirted, high-booted, ten-galloned glory. I grinned, and got out of the car to follow them in.

Beg your pardon.

Somebody was hissing words at me from the shadows by the Spoke's front porch. I gazed into the darkness, but couldn't make anything out. I locked the car and turned round it towards the steps.

Beg your pardon, sir.

This time the words were more of a rasp than a hiss. I frowned at the shadows, and after a few seconds a small hunched figure began to emerge, shuffling across the dirt of the parking lot. She was wearing a calf length nylon skirt and a torn padded anorak with the hood up. A sinewy hand, very white where it emerged from the dark sleeve of the coat, gripped a polystyrene cup, shaking it slowly from side to side as she lurched towards me. Whatever was in it didn't spill over.

What can I do for you? I said.

Beg your pardon, sir, she said. Can you help me?

Help you do what?

She stopped. You know, just help. She moved her cup from side to side again. Now I could hear a faint clinking coming from inside.

Oh! Sure! A bit of, eh . . . I reached in my pocket and

took out what I had there – no coins, I'd swapped all of those useless wee blighters for notes at the Driskill reception – just a palmful of crumpled notes. I transferred a couple of scrunched up singles to my other hand, stuck the rest away again. Here, I said.

She held my gaze, didn't reach for the money, nodded at her cup.

Oh yeah, sorry. I flattened the two notes out a bit, noticing that one of them was a fiver for God's sake but too late to insult her now by pocketing it again and anyway I was in a hell of a good mood, and dropped them in her cup.

She looked at me, her eyes dark but brilliant in the light from the beer sign, rasped, Thank you, sir, Jesus is watching, and took a few scuffling steps backwards into the shadows.

I gazed after her. I had no idea if she was standing there, just out of vision in the dark, or if she was already sprinting away round the back of the Broken Spoke to the nearest licensed grocers with my six dollars. But it didn't really matter. She was somewhere. And I knew where I was: three steps away from the front door of the world's most famous honky tonk. With thirty-something dollars. Everybody was happy. Especially me. I went in.

The Broken Spoke was split in two. The front half had a bar down one side, with small tables scattered about, a few punters sitting at them. There wasn't much talking, just a lot of guzzling: long-necked beers and chicken fried steaks. At the far side of the room was a partition with a door in it: the door was wedged open, and through it I could see a polished wooden floor with a small stage at the far end, empty except for a drum kit and a couple guitars on stands. I strolled over and leaned in at the booth by the door to the dancehall.

Hello, I said.

Hi.

I was wondering, I said. What kind of music is it tonight?

It's country, she said. It's all we ever have: country.

Great, I said. Good. But is it, like, western swing, or straightforward honky tonk, or a bit bluegrassy, or what?

She sighed, looked at me with scorn. Like I said, it's
country.

Right. Eh . . . how much?

Four bucks.

I reached into my pocket again, glancing into the empty
hall as I did so. Sorry to be a pain, I said, hesitating, But when
does the band start?

She didn't look at her watch. About twenty minutes.

Right. Well. I'll just have a drink and come back then. I
mean, there's no point in sitting around . . . I nodded towards
the empty tables circling the dance floor.

She shrugged. You do what you like. That's what the
Spoke's all about: what you like.

I know, I said. Great.

I went to the bar, got a Bud, and took a slug, looking around the wood-floored, wood-walled, wood-ceilinged
Broken Spoke. It really was like being inside a covered wagon
(assuming the cover was wooden), or maybe a coffin – it
was quiet as a grave. Okay, quiet as a grave with a sound
system playing Dwight Yoakam's greatest hits. The bar and
dancehall combined looked like they could hold a good
few hundred folk, though there were no more than twenty
scattered about right now.

The world's largest honky tonk (like Versailles is the
world's biggest country cottage) is Billy Bob's Texas in
Fort Worth. It can accommodate several thousand dancers,
has its own shopping arcade, a choice of cafes and bars,
and an indoor rodeo show. I hadn't made it there, (nor
Disneyland), and didn't expect to. Anyway, it was hard to
imagine the atmosphere of some of the smaller halls I'd seen
being bettered.

Maybe the best was the community hall in Oatmeal, in the
Hill Country west of Austin. Floyd Tillman lives close by, but
true to form he wasn't there the Saturday night I visited. In
fact, there was nobody of any reknown at all, just a shifting
line-up of local guitarists, fiddlers, and mandolin strimmers,
swinging together in approximate but infectious versions of
classic tunes by Bob Wills, Eddie Arnold, Hank Williams,

Patsy Cline. Up the back was a table with sandwiches, sausages and coffee for anyone who liked to help themselves. A phalanx of community-minded Oatmeal ladies stood behind the table, filling up any gap on the sandwich tray as soon as it appeared from an apparently inexhaustible supply at their backs. The gentlemen of Oatmeal stood outside smoking, passing a bottle, or practising a lick or two on their guitars before taking the stage. And quite a few folk sat at the long tables edging the hall, listening and drumming their fingers, nodding their heads and even tapping their feet. The old guy next to me had a banjo case open in front of him, but had been waiting for an hour or so for the right moment to take his instrument out. I leant over to him.

This is such great dance music, I said. Why's everybody sitting? Why don't they get up and dance? It's hard not to!

He laughed. Most of these folks is Church of Christ, he said. They don't believe in dancing.

Because it leads to sin?

Hell no. Just because. They don't approve of sex either – cause they've heard that can lead to dancing!

Other classic Texas venues, where dancing *is* allowed: Fischer Dance Hall, built by a one-eyed carpenter in 1875; Gruene Hall (pronounced Green) never closed since 1878; Luckenbach Hall, built to hold 350 dancers, despite the fact that the hamlet's population is only 3; the Farmer's Daughter in San Antonio, where Ray Sczepanik's 1990s version of The Texas Top Hands still perform regularly; the Debonair Danceland Westernplace in Dallas, winner of the Best Named Venue Prize 28 years running; the Stampede, Big Spring, which I'd visited . . . a few days ago? A few weeks ago? In another life? And many others, wherever the music swings, the laughter rings, the beer flows, the fists fly, and the boots two-step across a hardwood floor . . .

Across the far side of the Spoke's bar was another doorway, with a sign saying MUSEUM next to it. I strolled over, long-neck dangling between first and second finger in traditional fashion, and walked into a mini-wonderland of country music memorabilia. LPs signed by Ernest Tubb;

instruments touched by the hands of various gods of the
plectrum; photos of the Spoke's owner, James White, with
Willie, Waylon, Kris, Nanci, Townes, Butch . . . everybody;
signed posters for Leon McAuliffe and his Cimarron Boys;
battered old felt hats, beautifully sweatstained; classic 78s by
pioneer artists; all crowned by a cigar butt – half-smoked
by Bob Wills! I bet the British Museum doesn't have one
of those!

I wandered through the display cases, marvelling and sipping Bud. After a while sounds of tuning-up and mike-testing
started to drift through from the dancehall, then, after a
second's silence (last mouthful of beer?) Charlie Robison and
his band bounced into a fine steely version of Webb Pierce's
1953 tear-in-the-beer honky-tonk classic 'There Stands The
Glass'. I headed across the bar, filling up now, reckoning
on buying another Bud and nursing it through the band's
set. I didn't want to miss anything. The barman raised his
eyebrows, and I opened my mouth to order.

There was a loud crash outside, a rending of metal, then
a pause. Someone standing on the porch gave a yell. A big
engine revved, tyres bit into dirt and gravel, and a vehicle
drove off at great speed.

Ouch! said the barman. He stepped to the end of the bar,
and leant over to look out the window, cupping a hand round
his eyes to see out into the darkness. Bad one, he said, then
walked back towards me, shaking his head. Now, what can
I get you?

What happened? I said.

Some knucklehead in a Montero just tried to park on top
of somebody else's car out there, he said. Another Bud?

Eh . . . what kind of car?

Montero.

No, the other one.

It's a red Cavalier, said a guy in a leather jacket, coming
in the door. Hurt pretty bad.

I lunged across the room, flung myself out the door, got
entangled in a party of pensioners occupying the whole front
porch. Excuse me! I shouted, elbowing my way through,

leaping down the front steps, and sprinting to the far end of the lot.

BASTARD!

The rear door on the driver's side was stoved in, a massive dent in the middle, trim hanging loose, white paint scoured all the way across it and up over the wheel arch.

BLOODY BASTARDING HELL! I shouted, and jumped up and down, thumping my fist against the roof of the car, scuffing the dirt with my heel. If I'd been wearing a hat I'd've trampled on it.

Hey boy, someone called from behind me.

I looked around. The team of pensioners were all lined up along the porch still, watching me.

What? I said. Did you see it?

No, but I heard your language, said an old man in a white Stetson: the sheriff, maybe. You better watch it boy, there's ladies present.

WAAHAHAHAHAAA! I wailed again, and turned, walked swiftly to the far edge of the parking lot where it led on to South Lamar. So much for Jesus watching out for me! I looked up and down the street. There wasn't a Montero in sight. Come to think of it, I wouldn't have known a Montero from a Model-T. But even if I could've, and if it had been there, what could I have done? I could have shouted, I suppose:

Hey, ya big Montero driving bastard! You've ruined my trip of a lifetime! Here's me meant to be driving all over your state, tracking down your musicians, writing up all about the wonders of your honky-tonks and dancehalls, and all you can do to help is smash my car and drive away! What now? What'll I do now, eh? *Walk* the rest of the way? Make like beardy whatshisname in *Paris, Texas* and stroll into the desert in the general direction of Turkey? You big Texan bastard ye!

And what would he reply? Blam! Blam! Blam! Three bullets to the chest, quite likely.

I trailed back to the car, looked it over as closely as the light from the neon signs would allow. It wasn't so bad, maybe. At least the window wasn't broken. And there were no hydrocarbons piddling out of ruptured pipes, as far as

I could see. I pulled at the handle of the damaged door.
The hinge creaked, resisted, then came open with a metallic
scraich. I wheeched the door back and forth a few times: no
problem, just a grating noise, and a stiffness, a resistance. Who
needs a back door, anyway? Those axe-wielding hitchhikers
would just have to walk from now on. Or sit in the front.

So it wasn't so bad after all. Bastard. Why did I feel so
crap then? I could hear good country music leaking out of
the Broken Spoke, but the last thing I wanted to do was to
go in and try to enjoy it. Enjoyment was impossible now,
quite out of the question. Getting my car bashed was a real
personal injury. And the bastard driving away was the insult
added to it. I felt like I'd been stabbed.

Don't get me wrong, I wasn't a fanatical car lover. Not at
all. In fact, back in Scotland I didn't even own one. I only
learned to drive in order to come on this trip. If you'd
asked me five minutes earlier what I'd thought about my
Hertzmobile, I'd probably have replied, Not much. But now
I felt wounded, distraught. I suppose that over six weeks
and ten thousand miles of driving, I'd got attached to the
goddarn thing. More than that, I'd started to identify with
it, to blend with it, like that guy in a Flann O'Brien book
whose atoms get mixed up with those of his bicycle. The
car was the only unchanging thing on my trip. The scenery
changed, the food changed, the people changed; I'd slept
in a new motel, or on a new settee, every night till I'd
become quite indifferent to my surroundings: the Driskill
could've burnt down and it wouldn't've bothered me. But
I spent most of the day, most days, in my Chevy, and it
had become almost like a mobile home from home: with its
sound system to play all my latest western swing discoveries,
its heater for mountain nights, its air-conditioning for desert
days, its handy cup holders by the parking brake for coffee
or Dr Pepper, its reclining seats for siestas at the roadside . . .
Even the colour of it! Bright red: a bold colour, a joyous
colour, a colour for moving forward, for keeping keeping
on, for never retreating. Like Hugh MacDiarmid wrote in
his poem, 'Why I Choose Red':

I fight in red for the same reasons
That Garibaldi chose the red shirt
– Because a few men in a field wearing red
Look like many men – if there are ten you will think
There are a hundred; if a hundred
You will believe them a thousand.
And the colour of red dances in the enemy's rifle sights
And his aim will be bad – But, best reason of all,
A man in a red shirt can neither hide nor retreat

Now all that nobility, that purity, that heroism, was broken, sullied, splintered.

I slammed the damaged door shut. It bounced back open. I slammed it again, harder. There was a clash of metal on metal, and it rebounded and whacked me on the knee.

Shit.

I leant against the door, forcing it into its socket, shoogling to try and make the snib catch. It resisted fiercely: something had been bent or twisted or banged out of shape. I remembered a story about Bob Dunn, who, spectacularly drunk one night while touring with The Texas Wanderers, got his jacket sleeve caught on their bus's handle. Enraged, and too far gone to try to work out a logical solution, he ripped the door off its hinges, threw it away, and calmly climbed aboard. That kind of brute force was beyond me, though, certainly after one bottle of pissy Bud, so I would have to resort to logical thought, last refuge of a desperate man.

Thought 1. The widest open door is the least liable to intrusion, wrote Hugh MacDiarmid. Oh yeah? On a Whalsay croft in 1934, maybe, but not exactly sound advice for a traveller through the inner cities of the USA sixty years on.

Thought 2. This thought required the assistance of a friendly barman. I hoped the Broken Spoke had one in stock.

I walked in. The music sounded bloody awful. I'm sure it wasn't really, but that's how it sounded to me right then. I attracted the barman's attention. By weeping on his counter.

Somebody's smashed into my car and ruined my life, I said. Can you give me a piece of rope?

He eyed me. Rope? What do you want that for?

To tie the knackered door shut! I cried. I'll tie the inside handle of that one to the inside handle of the one opposite, slip it tight, make it fast. I can't drive up to Turkey with the door flapping open in the prairie winds for God's sake! *That's* what I want a rope for!

Ah, right, he said, and started rummaging about in a cupboard at the back of the bar. No problem. Glad to oblige. He laughed. The way you looked when you came in there, hell, I thought you were fixing to hang yourself!

Hell, I said. I wish I'd thought of that.

I Can't Be Satisfied

James Robert Wills was born on 6 March 1905, just outside Kosse, Limestone County, east central Texas. His parents were poor cotton-farmers, as their parents had been before them. Bob's maternal grandmother was part Cherokee, and it's been said that his dark-eyed good looks came in part from that Indian blood. There were also several fiddlers in his mother's family. On the Wills side, the fiddling was even more important when it came to establishing a sense of identity and pride. Bob's dad, known by everyone as Uncle John Wills, might have been a pretty poor farmer, but he was an excellent breakdown fiddler, as were his own father, his uncle, and other close relatives. Folk said that the Willses were the best fiddlers in Limestone County, maybe in the whole of the Brazos River country.

That's why the photo in the Kosse junk shop caught my eye. A wiry, leather-faced man in dungarees stood with a

fiddle under his chin, bowing arm held stiffly at the ready.
Behind him, a wooden shack, a wagon, an open gateway. The
fiddler squinted into the sun. The earth under his boots was
dusty and rutted, with little white flecks here and there across
it: cotton.

I fished out the photo from its place at the back of a shelf
of knick-knacks – little china dogs, souvenir ashtrays from
Texarkana, a saucer of assorted brass buttons – and turned it
over. But there was no name there, no date, nothing. Still.
Even if it wasn't a Wills, it certainly gave every appearance
of dating back to the time when the King of Western Swing
was first picking up a fiddle: the black and white of the photo
had decayed to brown and cream, the surface was creased
and wrinkled like . . . the face of the elderly woman in the
easy-chair behind the counter.

Excuse me, I said.

She looked up from the pile of old *Reader's Digests* she was
fingering through. Yes?

I took a step towards her, held out the photo. There's no
price on this.

She peered over the top of her glasses, first at the photo,
then at me.

How much, do you think? I asked.

Not for sale, she said, and looked back to her *Reader's Digest*.
Increase Your Word Power: RUSSIFICATION.

I got it off the shelf over there, I said. Are you sure I can't
buy it? It was just in with everything else.

She sighed. It's just for show, she said. Lord, Lord – do you
expect me to sell *everything*?

Well . . . in a shop . . . yes.

Young man, she said, glaring at me over her glasses again.
Some things just *can't* be sold. Now put it back where you
found it.

When Bob was eight, the whole family left their failed farm
in Limestone County and walked five hundred miles north,
sleeping rough, headed for what they hoped would be a more
prosperous farming life in Hall County, in the Panhandle.

They worked their way north, picking cotton for a little money or food on the way, sometimes sleeping in farm shacks, sometimes under their wagon of chattels and fiddles. The journey took them two months.

I'd taken the notion to retrace that epic trek. I was aiming to do it in about eight hours. It was Bob Wills' music that had drawn me to Texas in the first place, and the annual Bob Wills Memorial Weekend in the town of Turkey, Hall County, was going to be the climax of my trip. Either that or the anti-climax. The point was, Turkey was going to be the *end* of my trip. For the return leg of my plane-ticket was booked for a week's time, and it couldn't be changed. If I didn't make the flight – from Washington DC, fourteen hundred miles away – I'd have to work my way back across the Atlantic, picking cotton maybe, up through Canada, across Greenland, down into Iceland, Faeroe, and home.

No, my journey around the Lone Star State was coming to a close. So far I'd followed my nose, following whims, followed contacts from one town to the next, from one old western swinger to the next. What better ending to my trip than to follow in the footsteps of Bob Wills himself? I would drive from Kosse to Turkey, fling myself into the celebrations there, and that would be an end to it.

A long, slat-sided six-wheel trailer was parked under the Kosse water tower. Inside were two beautiful skewbald horses, neatly coiled lariats hanging from their saddles. For a second I imagined myself opening the rear door of the thing, leading out the horses, and galloping off out of the town before anyone could stop me. Hi ho Silver, away! But no, even Texan horses don't have stereo cassette players fitted in their saddles, and I couldn't ride all the way to Turkey without a constant soundtrack of hillbilly jazz – it just wouldn't be *right*.

So, hi ho Chevy, away!

The Willses' great hopes for their new life in the Panhandle came to nothing. They stayed poor as ever, each year a struggle to earn rent-money from the sandy wind-blown soil of their farm in the Red River Valley, between Turkey and Memphis.

If it hadn't been for the family's musical abilities, they might have starved many times.

Bob started out on mandolin and guitar, providing rhythm backing for his father's fiddle breakdowns. But by the time he was in his mid-teens, Bob was fiddling in his own right for paying audiences at dances and parties all over Hall County and beyond. He worked in Uncle John's cotton fields for years, on and off, but his heart was clearly in music. In his early twenties, worried that heavy farm work might end up damaging his fiddling fingers, he trained as a barber, and worked at that trade for some time in Amarillo, New Mexico and back in Turkey. Of course, a fiddle was always on hand.

It seems that a bottle was usually on hand too. Contemporaries of Bob's speak of him as being a well-known carouser in the streets of Turkey – a small town that bulged and bustled at harvest-time with hundreds of poor whites, blacks and Mexicans seeking work in the huge fields of the area's cotton, peanut and watermelon farms. Bob's musical abilities were well known, as were his pride, his cussedness and his determination to make some kind of mark, even if just by being the drunkest fool in town.

That wasn't how he did it. Not quite. Bob left Turkey in 1929, in disgrace (in his own mind at least) after a night in jail for rowdy behaviour. He headed for Fort Worth – known sarcastically (by outsiders) and affectionately (by natives) as Cow Town – a busy, trade-propelled city, full of saloons, dancehalls and men on the make, as well as cattle markets. Registering as a barber, he made an impact, almost immediately, as a fiddler.

Bob teamed up with other musicians his own age: first with guitarist Herman Arnspiger, and soon after with inspired singer and band leader Milton Brown. First they were The Aladdin Laddies; then, after a change of sponsor, The Light Crust Doughboys. Soon they were the most popular band in Fort Worth, making radio broadcasts as well as playing at dances. In 1932 they even made a record.

And by 1933 they had split up. Milton went off to form the innovative and influential Musical Brownies. Bob started building his own band, based at first in Waco. After a shaky start there, the band moved north to Tulsa, Oklahoma, where they acquired their name, The Texas Playboys, and started laying down the foundations of an incredible forty-year career. By this time, Bob was playing with more than fiddlers and back-up guitarists. The Texas Playboys of this era featured piano, saxophone, trombone and drums as well as the standard stringed instruments (and amplified steel guitar – at this stage still a very non-standard stringed instrument, despite the growing legend of Brownies' steel man Bob Dunn). Clearly, they were not playing old-fashioned front-porch breakdown fiddle tunes anymore.

I was passing through a village called Kirk. And yes, it had a kirk in it. (Not much else, in fact.)

Kosse had sounded vaguely German to me, and the area I'd been driving through had featured a good mix of mid-European names (Groesbeck, Riesel, Otto) and Indian/Mexican ones (Tehuacana, Mexia, Navasota). But Kirk was undoubtedly Scottish, especially as a sign pointing to the next town, a mile or so the west, told me it was called Mart. What next? Public Hoose? Imagine some pioneer from Aberdeen or Arbroath setting down here and looking around with a town-planner's gleam in his eye: Well, first things first; we need a kirk for our prayers, a mart for selling our beasts, and a pub for getting pished in. (If you didn't have a pub, the first two would be useless: you'd have nowhere to spend your siller, and nowhere to commit any sins that would warrant praying about.) Get bigging!

Unfortunately for this theory, the next town wasn't Public Hoose, it was Prairie Hill. Ah well, onwards and northwards.

Since his youth, Bob had been a huge fan of blues and jazz. There's a story of him riding from Turkey to Childress, a round trip of sixty miles, to hear Bessie Smith sing. He always claimed to have picked up a feel for the blues – as well as actual songs and tunes – from the black migrant workers he picked cotton alongside.

While playing with Milton Brown, an avowed pop and jazz lover, Bob developed his ideas about combining these more modern sounds with the traditional fiddle style he had learned from his father. Realising that more than a guitar and fiddle was needed for the range of effects he wanted to achieve (and that the increasingly urbanised and sophisticated audiences wanted to hear), he started to add brass and woodwinds, and also to employ other fiddlers and guitarists who could play hot jazz solos. Interestingly, Bob could never play jazz fiddle himself: he loved it, he could hear what he wanted, but the old melodies and fingerings were too deeply ingrained for him to be able to fly free of them into improvised take-offs. Merle Haggard called his Wills revival LP, *A Tribute To The Best Damn Fiddle Player In The World*, but that reflects Haggard's generosity more than reality. The reality is that Bob was a very limited musician. His intonation could be wobbly, his pitch sometimes only approximate – especially in his later years – and his sense of timing was idiosyncratic to say the least. Like another early country giant, Jimmie Rodgers, Bob had the habit of extending or cutting short melodies as the feeling took him, starting in on a new variation of the tune before the band had finished the old one. (Rodgers performed solo most of the time, so his lingering and lunging-ahead didn't cause too many problems – though guest instrumentalists Louis and Lil Armstrong, backing him on 'Blue Yodel #9' from 1928, clearly have a lot of, eh, *fun*, keeping up with him.) Bob couldn't stick to meter, or bar lines, to save his life. But he didn't let it bother him. For Bob, music was all about expressing emotion, about ebullience and blues, about *soul*. Once, when a trained musician in his band complained about his free and easy way with the rules of timing, he replied:

That's the way I feel it. That's the way I do it whether it's right or wrong, and that's the way we're going to do it. If the Lord had written the first music, I wouldn't question you at all, but a man wrote the first music and for all you know, I may be smarter than he was. If you don't want to play it like this, put your fiddle up and be gone.

★

Interstate 35, the main route from Austin and San Antonio in the south to Fort Worth and Dallas in the north, thunders over the roofs of the little town of West. It reminded me of South Queensferry outside Edinburgh, where I lived and worked as a janitor for four years. Queensferry had the two Forth bridges above it. Every day dozens of trains and thousands of cars and lorries would go roaring by just above our heads, exhaust fumes and grit and flakes of rusty iron from the rail bridge settling down on the village. Only once in a blue-fugged moon would a car turn off the motorway and come down the hill into the old streets by the water's edge. It was like living in a town that the rest of the world had forgotten: half Scotland's population was rushing by a hundred yards away, and there was us, the Ferry folk, quite invisible.

West had an attraction that made quite a few interstaters stop, though: it had kolaches. Kolaches are Czech pastries, sweet, crumbly, and filled with fruit. West had a lot of kolaches. It had thousands of the darn things: with blueberries, peaches, apricots, apples, even prunes. It had seven bakeries, all of them stuffed with kolaches.

Guess what I had for lunch? That's right: sausage, kraut and Czech fries in Sulak's Diner.

Then I drove on, under the interstate, veering west out of West.

Above all the Texas Playboys' music was for dancing. Bob was a master at keeping folk on the floor by careful variation of tempos, by constant mixing of popular tunes of the day with old standards, and by the rock-solid beat his rhythm section was exhorted to lay down. (You got to put their feet down and pick 'em up again, Bob used to tell them.) The Playboys were probably the first string-based band to include drums, and also one of the first to really exploit the possibilities of amplification. They had, said trumpeter Danny Alguire, a beat that wouldn't quit. If you couldn't dance to it, you couldn't *walk*.

By 1935, the year of the first Texas Playboys recording session, Bob Wills was leading an inventive and multi-styled band capable of everything from 'Crippled Turkey' to 'Darktown

Strutters Ball'. They had started with old-time string-band music, but now sounded (and looked) more like hot jazz musicians. They drew huge audiences wherever they played, had a hugely successful radio show on KVOO in Tulsa, and sold tens of thousands of records. By the late Thirties (and especially after Milton Brown's early death following a car crash), Bob Wills was certainly the most popular and creative band leader in the south-western states.

Whitney was close to the shores of Lake Whitney, one of the most popular water-recreation areas in central Texas. The town itself, though, was tranquil – slumberous in the afternoon sun. Big Victorian wooden houses sat in the middle of neatly blooming gardens. Tall oaks gave welcome shade. Every few minutes a car would drive in slow motion down the dirt road under the trees. It was idyllic.

I parked in the brick-paved main street, and walked up and down the raised sidewalks, no doubt spoiling the idyll for everyone else. Sorry, I said, then felt bad for having spoken aloud.

What was the place like eighty-four years ago? I wondered. As quiet and empty as this? No: I knew for sure that there was at least one person here in 1911. For it was in Whitney that Tommy Duncan, vocalist with the Texas Playboys from 1932 till 1948, was born. At least, Charles Townsend's biography of Wills says Duncan came from here; other books, and a couple of folk I asked, all said he came from Hillsboro, about ten miles to the east of Whitney. But my route to Turkey didn't take me through Hillsboro, so tough! I'm with Townsend on this one!

Hell, I've no idea what Whitney was like eighty-four years ago. But in 1995 it was warm, easeful, and very laid back. All qualities shared by Tommy Duncan. His voice was the epitome of mellowness – flexible and flowing, emotionally expressive but never melodramatic. It made Nat King Cole sound like Little Richard. In his youth, Duncan was a great fan of Emmett Miller, the blackface minstrel with the distinctive yodelling delivery; it was his accomplished singing of a Miller classic, 'I Ain't Got Nobody', that got him his job with the

Texas Playboys. He was also adept at Jimmie Rodgers-style blues, however, and the influence of singers as diverse as Fats Waller, Bessie Smith and Bing Crosby was undoubtedly important too. But the early influences shouldn't be over-emphasised: by the late Thirties Duncan's singing style was as sure and confident, and as immediately distinctive, as that of his near contemporary Frank Sinatra.

And this was despite the relative lack of emphasis that the singer's job carried in Wills' band. Vocals were very rarely the main feature in any song. Quite often, Duncan would step up to the mike for just a couple of verses, or even one chorus, almost as if his throat was another instrument due its occasional solo. That performed, he would modestly retreat into the background again. All through the Thirties, the Playboys' repertoire (similar to every other western swing outfit) consisted of classic blues ('I Can't Be Satisfied' 'Empty Bed Blues', 'Bleeding Hearted Blues'), pop hits ('I Wish I Could Shimmy Like My Sister Kate', 'Lady Be Good', 'I Can't Give You Anything But Love'), and jazz standards ('White Heat', 'Wang Wang Blues', 'Four Or Five Times'.) (Plus fiddle breakdowns, which were invariably instrumental.) In these days, it was how you played the songs that mattered, how hot you cooked them, not whether you were the first to play them or not.

For various reasons, though, more to do with commerce rather than art, the late Thirties and Forties saw record companies expressing stronger and stronger preferences for original material. In addition to this general trend, the Texas Playboys came under pressure from the film studios, who demanded new western-themed songs for the B-movies they were appearing in. Professional songwriters like Cindy Walker ('Dusty Skies', 'Miss Molly', 'You're From Texas') and Fred Rose ('Roly Poly', 'Good Time Cake-Walk', 'The Devil Ain't Lazy') started to supply the band with specially composed material. This resulted in the lyrics getting foregrounded more and more: it was the words and their melody that were interesting and novel. The jazzing of the tunes, the hot solos, never disappeared – but they did increasingly take second place to the vocals.

For me this explains why a lot of the post-war Wills stuff sounds dull compared to his earlier recordings: the songs were getting in the way of the music. It's also why Wills is almost completely ignored by jazz fans today: his later material, with its surface dressing of prairie pintos, Cherokee maidens and little cowboy lullabies, leads to him being written off as just another country and western hat-act. Big mistake: Wills' CDs should be filed next to Cootie Williams, not Hank Williams.

The early Forties saw Bob Wills making some of his most remarkable recordings, with a fifteen-piece orchestra featuring extended horn and woodwind sections. Some of these tracks are as smooth and swinging as the best of Benny Goodman or Count Basie. Around this time, too, Wills' compositions began to be covered by other artists. Bing Crosby's million-plus-seller version of 'New San Antonio Rose' spread his name all over America, and brought in huge royalty cheques.

But paralleling all the musical triumphs was a series of personal disasters. Bob was a very heavy drinker – almost certainly a binge alcoholic – and around this time started to get a reputation for missing gigs while drunk. The official biography, by Charles Townsend, tends to play down the less pleasant side of his character, but contemporaries and band-members speak more openly of Bob's mixture of womanising and insane jealousy. His first marriage, to Edna Posey, whom he courted in Turkey, ended in 1935 after nine years. His second, to Tulsa music teacher, Ruth McMaster, lasted only three months, ending with her divorcing him for extreme mental cruelty. The third lasted longer – five months. Bizarrely, it was to Mary Helen Brown, widow of Bob's best friend and mentor, Milton Brown; it was almost as if Bob's early adulation of the smart and sophisticated singer had reached its ultimate conclusion. Very shortly after their divorce, Bob and Mary Helen remarried; this time it lasted only a few weeks. Bob's fourth wife, and fifth marriage, came about a month after his second divorce from Mary Helen; it was to Mary Lou Parker, a seventeen-year-old from Pawhuska (he was thirty-four at this time). It seems Wills had in mind a kind of *Pygmalion* routine, whereby he could mould this innocent and naive girl into his ideal woman. The ideal woman would be one who could put up with his mood swings, his sudden profound depressions, his drinking, his jealousy, his flirting, his idealisation of previous wives, his sarcasm, his insecurity, his hypochondria, his temper tantrums. After three months of marriage, an annulment was granted.

If Bob decided to get married, said Mary Lou, He got married. If he decided to get divorced, he got divorced. He was not in the mood to be married any longer. Really, that's all it had to take with Bob.

Two days after the annulment was granted, Mary Lou discovered she was pregnant. This led to a dramatic courtroom reconcilement between the couple five months later, during a dispute over the terms of the annulment. It seems that Bob got enraged at his lawyer's questioning of his wife, at his insinuations about her morals and the question of whether the child was really Bob's. Wills leapt up and shouted, You shut up! You can't talk to Mary Lou like that! I won't have it! Soon after the couple were whispering to each other, and within minutes they were announcing that they were going to give their marriage a second try. The second try lasted thirteen stormy months, before she was granted a divorce for gross neglect and extreme cruelty.

In 1942, Bob married Betty Anderson. Only nineteen, she was tough and understanding beyond her years, and managed to build a marriage that lasted until Bob's death thirty years later. It would be naive to think that it was ever easy being married to Bob Wills (thank God we only have to listen to his records) but Betty seemed to calm him to an extent, and to be able to put up with his failings better than anyone else. They had four children. Ironically, just as Bob's home life started to get happier and more settled, his musical career began to fall off in terms of creativity and innovation.

Bob served briefly and unhappily (for all concerned) in the army during World War Two, and plunged back into his musical career as soon as he was allowed. By 1944 he was touring with his biggest band ever, a twenty-one piecer featuring three fiddlers, two lead and two steel guitarists, three trumpeters, four sax men, a trombonist, two vocalists, a bassist, a pianist, and two drummers. This was a huge line-up, even for the big-band era. Other top names of the era – Chick Webb, Jimmie Lunceford, Duke Ellington – typically led groups of thirteen or fourteen musicians. The massive Playboys combo must have been thunderously sweet.

Unfortunately, it never recorded, and didn't last long. Following the end of the war, changing fashions and economic conditions meant that – along with almost all other big band leaders – Bob had to cut back drastically on personnel. He did continue to lead good small combos for several years, including the outstanding line-up that recorded the extensive Tiffany transcriptions (for some aficionados this hard-driving, blues'n'bop-oriented group was the best ever incarnation of the Texas Playboys.) But Bob was never able to organise another big orchestra. And the great musicians who passed through his bands didn't seem to hang around for very long.

Duncan was sacked from the Playboys in 1948, having complained once too often about having to take the flak from disappointed fans for Bob's drunken absences from the bandstand. Several of the Playboys followed him, and, under the name Tommy Duncan and his Western All Stars, they toured and recorded into the early Fifties, with some success. Excellent sidemen like Joe Holley on fiddle, Millard Kelso on piano, and Jimmy Wyble on guitar – all dedicated jazz men – helped make the records Duncan recorded at this time much more interesting than the stuff his ex-boss was laying down. Tracks like 'Sick, Sober and Sorry', 'I Reckon I'm A Texan', and 'Grits and Gravy Blues' were all marvellously relaxed, with Duncan's languorous, smoky vocals floating over great guitar and trumpet soloing. These records are little known, even to fans of his work with the Texas Playboys, but I love them. Duncan habitually wore a doe-eyed mournful look, but his voice had (as guitarist Eldon Shamblin put it) a ripple of happiness right through it.

★

It was past lunch-time, but all of the shops in Whitney seemed to be closed or comatose. All that was open was Larry's Barber Shop. I decided to commemorate my visit to my favourite singer's home-town (allegedly) with a haircut.

There was nothing alleged about the haircut that Larry's assistant, Wanda, gave me. None of these hippyish number-twos for her! This was going to be right to the bone!

Were you born here? I asked her as she cut a swathe from the nape of my neck to my widow's peak.

Nope, she said. Dallas. Been here five years. She buzzed the clippers round my ears. Sometimes I think that's five years too long.

My scalp had quickly come to resemble the toe of a big suede boot. I like the feel of the place, I said. Laid-back, you know.

Five years is a long time in a redneck town like this, she said, gazing longingly at my eyebrows.

I think that's enough off now, I said. Thanks. Great.

Know the last time anything happened here? she said. 1949. Ha! The Battle of the Street Benches. All the old rednecks wanted to sit out along Main Street all day, spitting and swearing. The town wanted to smarten the place up; they said the old men had to spit in their homes, not on the street. War!

Yeah. Whitney made it on to the national news, can you believe it? They interviewed Larry! The place was a tourist mecca, for a week or so. She wheeched the sheet from under my collar, gave me a piece of tissue. And I missed it: forty years late for the one interesting thing that ever hit Whitney. I don't know . . .

So what happened? I asked. Who won? Do the old men still sit there and spit?

Nah. They're all dead.

Shame, I said. Maybe I could have asked them about Tommy Duncan.

Well, don't ask me, I hate all that redneck music. Now Barry Manilow, he's a real fine singer. Six bucks please.

As I stood to get the dosh out of my jeans pocket, a little

brown plastic tub on the counter by the mirror caught my attention: OSAGE RUB. Hey, the first track ever recorded by the Texas Playboys was an irresistible stop-time jive called 'Osage Stomp'. Where did that name come from? Could Osage Rub be a locally produced toiletry – some kind of linament or hair-tonic – that Tommy had had clarted over his skull as a child. Could he have recalled the name much later, and used it as the basis of a catchy, wryly observed celebration of life in his home-town?

No. 'Osage Stomp' is an instrumental. The boy from Whitney doesn't appear on it.

Have a nice rest of the day, said Wanda.

The departure of Tommy Duncan, combined with several disastrous ventures into running ballrooms and ranches, make the early Fifties a depressing period to contemplate in Bob Wills' career.

Come to think of it, the late Fifties were much the same, and the Sixties even worse. Wills received more and more recognition, it's true, from both civic and musical authorities (including – inappropriately as he saw it, as he'd always considered himself well outside the Nashville mainstream – induction into the Country Music Hall of Fame). His personal appearances were still extremely popular, whether with later, unstable but still sometimes exciting, incarnations of the Texas Playboys, or with various pick-up bands. But his recordings were often desultory, even tuneless, affairs. Part at least of the blame for this must lie with whoever made him record in Nasville. You just have to listen to the records to have Bob's opinions confirmed: the musicians and producers there had no understanding of, or feeling for, Texas swing. He recorded far more towards the end of his career than he had in the early days, but far less of it bears listening today. Certainly he was a long way from the cutting edge of popular music, which he'd occupied for fifteen or twenty years from the early Thirties onwards.

He suffered from increasing bad health from the early Sixties, finally dying after a series of strokes in 1975, at the age of seventy. Ten or more of his compositions had become – and remain – country standards, and the influence of his pioneering of drums and amplification has been (for better or for worse, viz. Garth Brooks) enormous.

Just as I entered the town of Hico, my accelerator pedal fell off, leaving only a thin rod poking up through the floor of the Chevy. Now, in Britain this would have been bad enough, with three foot-pedals to choose between. But being the States, the car I'd hired had of course been an automatic, and had no clutch; the disintegration of the accelerator left me with only the brake pedal to play with. Useless. I stopped in a broad side street, and scrabbled about in the footwell, trying to snap the pedal back on to its fitting. I felt myself getting hot and flustered as I struggled with this advanced piece of automotive mechanics, especially as some nosey bastard was standing right behind me, looking over my shoulder, no doubt laughing his head off.

Eventually the goddarn thing snapped into place, and I stood up, whipping round to face out my audience.

It was a life-size statue of a guy in a cowboy hat, pointing a long-barrelled revolver down towards the crossroads. BILLY THE KID, said a plaque:

William Bonney did not die in a shoot-out with Pat Garrett at Fort Sumner, New Mexico, in 1881. He escaped, led an adventurous life throughout the South-West, eventually retiring to Hico with his wife. We knew him as Ollie Roberts, as Brushy Bill – but his real identity was far more historic. It was HERE that Billy the Kid died, December 27 1950.
Hico town motto: EVERYBODY IS SOMEBODY.

I wonder who I am? I thought to myself as I headed out of town. I haven't met anyone who knows me for weeks and weeks. Everyone I talk to takes my word for what my name is and what I'm doing and why. If I ever forgot those things,

I'd be really stuck: there'd be nobody to remind me. I could be wandering about Texas for ever.

The last house in Hico had a hand-painted sign in its front yard: HAMSTERS AND GUINEA PIGS FOR SALE. Right next to it, a plaid-shirted man with a furious expression on his face was using a huge axe to hack at something small sitting on a tree-trunk chopping-block.

On through Smith Springs, near Stephenville – where Milton Brown grew up, and lies now under a pink granite headstone with radio masts and a big old diamond-shaped microphone carved on it.

On through Mingus, where Derwood and Roy Lee Brown had a regular Tuesday night gig in 1946, at the Eagles' Hall. *Of Course You Want To Hear Us And Dance* was their slogan at the time, but unfortunately not enough people did, and before long this last incarnation of the Musical Brownies was wound up. Derwood moved to Colorado to work in the oil fields there, and Roy Lee went into the fire department.

On through Strawn, Caddo, Breckenridge, Woodson, Throckmorton, Munday, Rhineland, Benjamin, Guthrie.

On past Grow to Paducah, *not* the home town of the long-running Grand Old Opry comedian The Duke of Paducah, with his hilarious catchphrase, I'm going to the wagon, these shoes are killing me. Turn left at Paducah and thirty-two miles of nothing but cottonwood-studded prairie till Matador, with Bob's Oil Well standing at the crossroads in the middle of the town.

On, on, on. The final leg now. On over Middle Pease River, Tom Boll Creek, North Pease River and Quitaque Creek. On over the flat brown prairie. On towards a small huddle of trees, wooden houses and farm stores in the middle of vast red fields. On through the city limits, past the big steel signpost, three metres high, four across, with its tableau of metal fiddlers and guitarists welcoming the weary pilgrim to: **TURKEY TEXAS, HOME OF BOB WILLS.**

Crippled Turkey

ADMIT ONE PERSON
——— TO THE ———
MERCHANTS GOOD-WILL FROLIC
——— AT THE ———
CASA BLANCA: MON. & WED., MAY 26-28
This Ticket Through Courtesy of

Pete Baggett

Adm. $1.00 or One Ticket/Jack Ream & His Music

I'd phoned ahead and arranged to stay with John Moen's friends, the Montgomerys. I'll have a look around the town before I come by, I'd said. That won't take you long, June Montgomery had replied.

Turkey was a small place. **Pop. 503** said the bullet-pocked sign at the city limits, but it felt like less. The streets were wide, and the houses, uniformly squat and brick, sat well back in big yards of sand or parched grass. Even the smallest wooden shack had twenty metres between it and the next building. Of course, it could've been that Turkey was denser in its boom years, and just had a lot of abandoned buildings knocked down. The main street, for instance, had quite a few gap sites, as well as a fair number of dead businesses: boarded up groceries, filling stations with the pumps ripped out, and the Gem Theatre, long abandoned, but with a ginger-wigged shop-window dummy sitting in the ticket-booth out front.

There were maybe a dozen shops still operating along Main
Street – Turkey Automotive, R&T Welding, Two Js China,
Lacy Dry Goods, The Peanut Patch ('For Gifts Made of
Peanuts') – but most of them looked like they'd seen better
days. The red-brick Hotel Turkey was spruce, with two big
plastic tepees and some llamas in its back garden; Bob Wills
is supposed to have played in the dining room here before
he left for Fort Worth and eventual stardom. And there were
several churches, all with car parks as big as a small Church
of Scotland parish.

Cruising around the near-empty streets reminded me,
fittingly enough, of Kosse. And it made me think of a sepia
panorama photo in a long frame, that had been hanging on
the wall of the junk shop there. (Something else the lady in
the easy chair wouldn't sell me.) It was taken from the top of
the water tower, one Saturday night in 1915, and it showed
Kosse looking like Cowboy Babylon. Model T Fords were
lined up at the roadsides in their dozens. There were scores
of horse-drawn carts and gigs. People thronged the sidewalks.
Drug stores and bars had crowds of bottle-toting men and
laughing women gathered at their doors. Kids played in the
street. And what was Kosse like now, eighty years later? Like
most of the folk in the picture: dead. Turkey was, if anything,
more run down than Kosse. But it did have one great amenity
that nowhere else in the world could claim: the Bob Wills
Museum and Community Center.

I'd seen a few good museums on my travels: the masterpiece-
stuffed Kimbell in Fort Worth, The Broken Spoke's music
memorabilia in Austin, Donald Judd's vast sheds of minimalist
art in Marfa. The best one, though, was undoubtedly the Creation Evidences Museum, a little south of Fort Worth. **EVI-
DENCE HERE! MAN & DINOSAUR TOGETHER!**
declared a garish roadside sign. And underneath, in smaller
letters: **Not responsible for accidents**. It boasted exhibits
such as 'iron hammer embedded in Creataceous rock', 'fos-
silised human footprint discovered in the same limestone bed
as dinosaur footprints' and 'the only double-yoked dinosaur

egg in existence'. There was also a startling display of life-size dinosaur heads, mounted on the wall like stuffed hunting trophies. My favourite exhibit, though, was the Bombardier Beetle, a big shiny-carapaced thing pinned to a board in a glass case; its caption card, typed with great force of feeling, was what made it special:

> Bombardier Beetles shoot combustible materials from their rear extremity when threatened.
>
> This life form demands a Creator and Design.
>
> They could NOT have evolved without EXPLODING.

The basic premise of the museum, outlined in a vibrant super-realist mural entitled **CREATION in Symphony**, was that, before The Flood, man and beast (including dinosaurs) lived together in peace and harmony. Oh yeah, and humans were ten feet tall. Then God had punished us with forty days of rain – he must still be punishing the Outer Hebrides – and bodily shrinkage.

The curators were experimenting with a special biosphere, a hermetically sealed glass tank; through manipulation of the micro-climate, they were all set to recreate paradisical pre-Flood conditions on Earth. The biosphere hummed and gurgled behind some hospital screens in a corner of the museum. I'd tried to sneak a look, hoping to see a frog as big as a hog or something, but all I'd glimpsed was an old aquarium with some pond-weed in it, when the attendant rather brusquely directed my attention back to her guided tour. She went on in great detail about Earth's Pre-Flood Internal Nuclear Reactor, and how this had provided the heating for the Garden of Eden. She had pointed out Eden on the mural; Adam and Eve, modelled by a young Ronald Reagan and Pamela Anderson, their modesty protected by palm-fronds, patted a brontosaurus on the rump.

Well, the Bob Wills Museum wasn't quite as mind-blowing as that – how could it be? – but it did have a lot of worthy stuff: photos of Bob as a barefoot child, as a dungareed cotton-picker, and as a cigar-chomping star; old posters advertising dances and personal appearances; a Light Crust Doughboys shirt with a blue lyre logo; several hats and saddles; a model of the steel and granite monument that stood on the edge of town, and the Playboys' PA from the Forties – two twelve-inch speakers in scuffed wooden cabinets, and a couple of boot-sized metal mics. My favourite exhibit, though, was a black, flower-embroidered shirt in a glass case; again, it was really made special by its caption-card:

Late 1950s, Bob's father found this shirt in Flint, Michigan, and bought it for Bob. Bob's reaction was . . . Papa, you know I'm never gonna wear that shirt! And he never did.

If the story wasn't special enough in itself, it's made more so by the strange but true fact that Bob's father died in 1952 . . .

I chatted for a while with Vida, the elderly volunteer curator, who answered all my questions much more fully and enthusiastically than the creationists had done. In fact, she was just about hopping with excitement at the prospect of how many visitors she was going to be getting over the weekend: her own once-a-year Flood. Turkeydoon awakes!

I picked up a Bob Wills Day bumper sticker and a timetable of events for the next two days, then headed off to find the Montgomerys' place.

Arch and June welcomed me into their bungalow like a long-lost son.

You just come in and make yourself at home! said Arch in a thick north Texas accent, his voice so crackly with age that it sounded like his words were being played back from an ancient 78. I don't care where you're from, I don't care what colour you are, you're welcome here!

June was a good deal younger than Arch's eighty-five years, but just as welcoming. She sat us both down at the kitchen table and served up a grand dinner of fried chicken, cream gravy and freshly-baked biscuits.

You just help yourself, said Arch. I don't care where you're from, you just eat your fill.

June bustled about, helping me to help myself. Soon I felt more at home than I had since leaving Orkney many weeks before. As we ate, I noticed a line of instruments – electric guitar, tenor banjo, semi-acoustic guitar – propped up against the wall at the end of the seating-area.

I didn't know I was staying with musicians, I said. John Moen told me you were great folk, but he didn't let on you were western swingers too.

We used to swing, said June, and laughed. Getting a little old now: the spirit's willing but the flesh is weak. Especially his.

You just help yourself boy, said Arch. You go ahead and pick a little – I can see you're itching to.

I took my coffee over, perched on the front of an armchair, and strummed on each of the instruments in turn. They were all worn with decades of playing, the wood of the fingerboards burnished dark by however many millions of chords Arch had fretted over the years.

I reckon Gibsons made the best guitars around, said Arch. They've sure lasted well.

I picked out the intro of 'Steel Guitar Rag', Leon McAuliffe's signature tune, on the beautiful cello-bodied semi-accoustic. The same notes I always played on my guitar at home, but somehow they sounded better, more *Texan*, than ever before.

You had them long? I asked.

That one you're a-cradling, he said, I got that in '42.

Wow!

Yeah, but the electric's not so old. I only got that in, oh, '55 or '56.

Still, forty years old! Look, you've worn right through the plastic guard with your pick.

He could play the gold horns off a brass billy goat, said June.

How about the banjo?

Got that in '34. Still going strong. Stronger than me! My fingers are getting weak . . .

The oldest one's hanging on the wall there, said June. Next to . . .

. . . my wedding photo! I looked at it for a while. How did you get that?

She laughed. John sent a copy.

The guitar on the wall, a narrow-waisted Spanish acoustic, had a bouquet of dried flowers sticking out of its soundhole, and only a couple strings. It was battered and chipped, and had obviously seen even more action than the others.

When did you get that one, Arch?

Got that in 1923. Had that sucker seventy-two years.

It's an antique!

Yeah, said June. Just like us!

Hometown Stomp

RECORDS BY BOB WILLS

03451—Get Along Home Cindy
       Right or Wrong
03424—What's the Matter with the Mill
       She's Killing Me
03394—Steel Guitar Rag
       Swing Blues No. 1
03361—Fan it
       Sugar Blues

"Sleepy" Johnson
Banjo

Joe Ferguson
Bass Viol and Vocal

DANCES

DANCES

7..

8..

9..

Jesse Ashlock, Fiddle

10..

11..

12..

It cost me eight dollars to get into the Friday night dance with Bob Wills' Texas Playboys. The cost of my whole trip looked like it was going to add up to about eight hundred times that amount. But *this* eight bucks was the eight that really mattered.

I arrived in the auditorium of the old high school just as they finished their introductory theme tune – 'Eagle Riding Papa' getting yet another outing, sixty-five years after Bill Broonzy and his pals had first recorded it – and was immediately bowled over by two things: the noise and the stomp. The Playboys were loud, they were loose, they were really swinging hard: the rhythm section pounded out the 2/4 Wills beat – lifting up the dancers' feet and setting them down again – while the fiddles, sax, steel and piano tore into wild exuberant solos left right and centre. They really were *getting like a coal miner*, as Tommy Duncan used to tell them to: *low down and dirty*.

The auditorium was a cavernous dimly lit box, high notes echoed and blared against the ornate plaster ceiling, the Playboys were crammed on to a tiny pallet stage – but nobody seemed to notice that they weren't in Cain's Dancing Academy, Tulsa, or one of the other grand, luxurious, well-sprung ballrooms of Bob's heyday. Least of all the dancers. There were a few bleachers for seating up one end, but hardly anyone was sitting: the whole hall was a shuffling mass of close-dancing couples in boots, Stetsons, brightly coloured shirts, dresses and jackets in gingham, denim, and fringed suede.

At last, after a month of listening to records and tapes, after weeks of modestly rewarding visits to hear live music in nursing homes, coffee bars and living rooms, here was what I'd come to the States in search of: western swing in its native habitat, performing its original, heaven-blessed function – making several hundred Texans two-step around a dancehall on a Friday night. Where more fitting than in the home-town of the King of Western Swing?

And who more fitting than the Texas Playboys? They were great. After hearing so much almost-good almost-western-swing on my trip, I'd been prepared for disappointment. But they were better, hotter, fresher than I'd ever imagined was possible. During 'Right Or Wrong' (an Emmett Miller yodel that Tommy Duncan made his own) I threaded through the steer of dancers (all ages, it seemed from eight to eighty) and stood with fifty or so other fanatics, just *watching*. Here's who I saw:

Tommy Perkins. Drums. Played with Bob in the early Fifties, as had most of the guys. Featured for years in Billy Jack Wills' band.
Truitt Cunningham. Bass, vocals and leader.
Clarence Cagle. Piano. Played with Johnnie Lee Wills for a long time.
Curley Lewis. Fiddle. Another Johnnie Lee Wills veteran.
Glenn Rhees. Tenor and soprano sax. Bob changed his

name to Don Rhees at one point in the late Fifties, to
avoid confusion with a vocalist with a similar first name.
Then, when the vocalist left, Bob unceremoniously
changed the name right back again.
George Uptmor. Fiddle.
Benny Garcia. Lead guitar. One of the top West Coast
jazzmen in the Forties and Fifties, with bands like Spade
Cooley's and Tex Williams'.
Eldon Shamblin. Rhythm guitar. Joined Wills way
back in 1937, and arranged many of the Playboys' best
recordings.
Bobby Koefer. 'Clown Prince of the Steel Guitar.'

There were also guest appearances by: **Johnny Cuviello**
on drums, **Jimmy Young** on fiddle and Bob Wills
impersonation, **Louise Rowe** on vocals, and **Glynn
Duncan**, Tommy's brother, the vocalist whose name
had erased Glenn Rhees from existence for a while.

All the band wore white shirts and snap-on ties patterned
and textured like a black and white Friesian cow hide. They
all kept an eye, or half an eye, permanently fixed on Truitt
Cunningham, for he had adopted Bob's old role as leader,
nodding in the next soloist – usually with no more than half
a bar's notice – urging on their flights of improvisation.
   And they really did fly. On 'Silver Lake Blues', a traditional fiddle tune, Benny Garcia poured out an extra-
ordinary bop-harmonied guitar solo. On 'Blues For Dixie'
the fiddlers got into a honky-tonkin' bluesy groove behind
Cagle's percussive piano boogie. And on *everything* Bobby
and Glenn tried to outdo themselves – and each other –
on the inventiveness and intensity of their take-offs. Best
of all was the old classic, 'Spanish Two Step', swung very
fast and hard, where the steel and sax riffed in unison
before shooting off wildly in acute angles to the original melody, shattering the weel-kent tune into a thousand
jagged fragmented notes . . . before turning on a dime and
– suddenly, casually, wondrously – bringing all the pieces

together again into a smooth seamless whole for the final unison chorus.

Bobby Koefer did high kicks of joy off the front of the stage as the audience whooped and cheered, and Glenn Rhees held his sax aloft and offered it round the hall as if to say, Come on, anybody, beat that! Then he caught Bobby's eye, and both of them burst out laughing.

They played 'Brownskin Gal', 'San Antonio Rose', 'Take Me Back To Tulsa', 'My Confession', 'Faded Love', 'Silver Bells', 'Steel Guitar Rag', 'Corrine Corrina', a magnificent rollicking 'St. Louis Blues' . . . Then, suddenly, they stopped. It was all over.

What? Already!

I checked my watch. It was past midnight: they'd been playing for more than three hours.

The lights came on in the hall. The Playboys started packing up. Some folk stood around chatting, others started drifting out. Quite a few crowded around the bandstand, shaking hands, asking for autographs, or just talking.

Talking! This was my big chance. But I stood rooted in the middle of the dance floor, I just couldn't do it: I just couldn't go over there and *talk to the Texas Playboys*! I mean, what the hell would I say to them? For me, speaking with these guys would be like speaking with, I don't know, Dostoevsky maybe, or Greta Garbo, or Ghandi. Their music had been so other-worldly, so transcendent, so superior to any kind of verbal communication, that the few feeble phrases that formed themselves in my mind shrivelled and died as soon as I imagined mouthing them aloud: Hello, I really enjoyed . . . I liked the way you . . . That's the best . . . Can I touch the hem of your . . .

So I turned away and left the hall, and took an hour to walk the half-mile home. I dawdled, I took detours, I danced with my shadow, and I stood motionless for minutes on end replaying all that wonderful music in my head one more time, before it started to fade.

Smile Darn You Smile

First thing in the morning, June introduced me to her neighbour, Byron Young, a slight, bespectacled man, one day short of his seventy-fifth birthday.

Back when Byron was mayor, said June, He started off this whole Bob Wills thing. You ask him!

Oh, it wasn't me, said Byron. There was a whole crowd of us.

What about the monument? said June. Didn't you organise that?

Oh, a lot of people helped with that. Forty of us signed notes for four hundred dollars. Wasn't just me.

I imagine Bob must be pretty popular around here, I said. He's put the place on the map. I mean, *I* certainly wouldn't be in Turkey if it wasn't for him. He's a legend!

Thing is, said Byron, It's different for folks round here. Cause we remember him as a man, just like you or me. We grew up with him.

Did you know him when you were a kid?

Sure. Well, we used to live right close to him. When I was real young, about eight or nine, I used to see Bob and his dad and his friends playing. I don't mean playing like kids do, I mean playing their instruments. They used to play out behind my daddy's filling station, back in those great big cottonwoods, down in the west end of town. And so we'd all gather up and listen to it. In fact I drilled a hole through the wall at my friend's house so we could watch them better, while they were playing their music. I wanted to *see!*

And this was before he was famous, eh?

Well, he was famous in Turkey, I guess. For various things, good and bad.

And after he *was* famous all over the South-West, did he come back here?

Sure, he always called Turkey Texas his home. He used to come through the town whenever he was playing nearby. He'd have the tour bus park up on Main Street, and they'd get out and have a concert right in front of Ham's barber shop where he used to work.

And did the whole town turn out to see him then, a kind of prodigal son?

Well, a lot of people, knowing his past history, they didn't want to listen to his music a whole lot. My dad didn't. But I always did: I'd slip off and listen whenever I could. But in the end the whole town would be gathered, more or less. The street would be blocked up from side to side.

Nowadays, said June, The street would still look empty if every single person in town gathered there.

We laughed. I suppose it used to be a lot busier, I said, Back in the days when a lot more folk worked the land? It's the same where I come from.

Oh sure, said June. You wouldn't recognise it.

I know the town looks bad, said Byron. There's worlds of them all over the United States, you know. The big cities get bigger, and the small towns get smaller.

So what was it like when Bob was growing up here? When you were growing up?

You may think I'm crazy, but at one time – back when the pavement was laid in '27, '28 – we were a busy little town: fifteen, sixteen hundred population. We had four drug stores, about eight grocery stores; we had four or five doctors, we had a hospital. What else? Four barber shops, two car dealerships, two tractor dealerships. It was a busy place. It was booming. And on Saturday night, when all the farmers came to town, they would start coming in and parking up around our filling station. Even the ones still with teams and wagons! They'd park up behind our place, then down front of our place, and we'd have to close early, cause they'd have our drive jammed up solid.

It was a genuine boom town, said June.

Not any more, said Byron.

I drove downtown, parked just off Main Street. It wasn't exactly blocked, but people were starting to gather, set up their lawn-chairs, find themselves shady places under shop awnings. The parade would be starting soon. But I had time to visit another historic site first: Ham's barber shop.

There was no sign up outside, but Arch had told me that Ham's was the only barber still operating, so this had to be it. I walked in. The shop was cool and clean, floored in black and white checks, and with two big swivelling leather chairs in front of the mirrors. I wondered which one Bob had worked at. That would be the one to sit in, no doubt about it. There were no other customers, I had my pick.

A burly middle-aged man in a blue sleeveless shirt sauntered through from the backshop. Howdy, he said. What can I do for you?

I'd like a haircut, please.

He shook his head. Don't think so.

Pardon?

I can't cut your hair. It don't need it.

Well, just a trim then.

He laughed. There's no hair there to cut off! When did you last have it done?

Eh, yesterday.

Hoo! Well, what can I say? You're scalped!

I had it done in Tommy Duncan's home-town, I said. I thought it would be nice to have it done in Bob Wills' home-town too – especially in the very place that he used to work.

He looked at me, laughed again.

This is Ham's isn't it?

Sure. I'm Harold Ham. Pleased to meet you. He held out a big soft hand, and we shook. It was my daddy taught Bob to barber, he said.

Wow! See what I mean? It would be *great* to have a haircut here!

But he just laughed.

Get out of here! he said.

The parade crawled down Main Street:

Men on horseback waving Stars and Stripes,
other men in golf buggies with more Stars and Stripes,
a couple in drag on a tandem,
women on horses with lone star pennants,
Miss San Antonio Rose in a red dress as big as the wagon she was sitting on,
six guys leading a buffalo,
the Khiva Temple band playing 'Yearning' as they jolted along on a specially adapted trailer,
a man from an insurance company in a jet plane the size of Miss San Antonio Rose's dress,
a woman on horseback wearing a Lone Ranger mask and a black cape,
a man on a miniature tractor, steering with his knees so he could blow his nose,
the Bob Wills Queen, struggling to smile and hold her split skirt down in the wind,
a team of fez-wearing oldsters, formation driving motorised pedal cars,
the Texas Playboys sitting and waving on a float adorned with giant musical notes,

a group of bearded bikers on Harley-Davidsons with
fezzes *and* flags,
more cowboys,
and cowgirls,
a van from a bail bond company,
and a guy with a pushcart selling balloons shaped like
dinosaurs.

But not, unfortunately, one shaped like Bob Wills. I'd've
bought one of those.

I adjusted my Presidio Onion Festival baseball cap, but it
was no use: wherever the peak's shade was, the sun still got
me someplace else. I'd heard that cases of ear cancer had
increased tenfold in the States in recent years, since everyone
had started wearing caps instead of wide-brimmed hats. But
fashion had not hit Turkey yet: Stetsons were definitely the
headwear of choice. I went back to the car, and fished my
black Wichita Falls Wal-Mart cowboy hat out of the boot.
If I was ever going to wear it anywhere, it was here, today.

TOP TEN THINGS TO DO IN TURKEY, TX.
ON BOB WILLS DAY

10. Listen a while to the Old Time Fiddlers' Competition
in the auditorium. Here 'Big Taters In Sandy Land' played
so many times that, by the end, you could do a passable
rendition yourself, even though you've never picked up a
fiddle in your life before.

9. Examine a wood and felt doll Indian made by a gushy
lady in the gift tent. Every doll has a birth certificate, she'll
assure you. Every one signed by hand!

8. Stroll out to the ballpark, and look at the little concrete jail
that young Bob got locked up in now and then. Remember a
story Byron told you: Bob was in there with the local doctor
one time, and another fellow got thrown in too. Well, this
one starts demanding to see the health officer: the facilities are
too bad, there's no water, no restroom . . . Anyway, he yelled
and demanded, demanded and yelled, till finally the doctor

said, Hey, just cool it, *I'm* the health officer, and I'm in here
with you! On your way back towards the centre of town, get
puzzled for a moment by an apparent climatic freak. Then
laugh at yourself as you realise it's not snow lying in the grass
at the side of the road, but wispy bolls of cotton, blown in
from the fields, escaped from the gin.

7. Visit the Hotel Turkey, meet and greet with Scott and
Jane, who've just had two dozen Brazilian ranchers staying,
and now have two dozen Texas Playboys. At least the
Playboys speak English, sort of, says Jane. Note the sign
which reads: *Please no smoking in the rooms for the Historical
Preservation of the Hotel.* Resist the temptation of taking up
smoking just to make a point about *their* English.

6. Buy from charming Lisa at the souvenir stand a selection
of live Bob Wills tapes, a genuine Fifties Bob Wills poster,
and videos of two very bad Bob Wills westerns from the early
Forties. Talk with Pat, Lisa's brother: Turkey could be called
a one-horse town, he'll tell you. But at this time of year we
all pull together, try and put on a good show. That's what
it's all about. The show must go on.

5. Have a drunk cowboy poet grab your arm in a pincer-like
grip, then recite endless drivel along the lines of:

> Now the night was dark and the moon was bright
> Way out on the windswept prairie,
> When two cowpokes got in a fight
> On account of a girl called Mary.
>
> The one said, Heck, I'll break your neck
> If you don't quit your messin'.
> Mary's mine, and soon we're gwine
> To get the preacher's blessin'.
>
> Young Tex was not to have his way
> For Billy made to draw,
> But Tex was quick, his holster slick,
> And blaw de blaw de blaw de blaw de blaw de blaw
>   de blaw de blaw

4. Stand at the city limits, watching tumbleweeds tumble, and the deep blue sky turn pink along the horizon, as the wind whips up the desert dust. See a giant green John Deere tractor harrowing a field the size of a small Scottish county. Say, in an Aberdonian accent, Aye min, you'd fair get a hease o neeps in that park!

3. Buy a bowl of chilli and beans from the Muleskinners Barbeque – *Remember, all proceeds go to help the crippled children of America!* – and sup it while wandering through the maze of RVs, caravans and trucks lined up out back of the old high school. Listen to a dozen or more groups of amateur pickers, jamming through songs by Bob Wills, Hank Williams, Chuck Berry. Burn your mouth on the chilli, and go back to the Hotel Turkey for a beer to cool you down. Reel in astonishment and grief when Scott tells you, Sorry, this is a dry county; you'll have to go to Estelline, thirty miles east, if you want liquor.

2. Meet a youngish Belgian guy, who at first seems interesting, but then depresses you by telling you all the places you *should've* gone to hear western swing: Sunday nights in the Longhorn Saloon, Fort Worth, are pretty good, yeah, Tom Morrell on steel. And in Dallas there's The Light Crust Doughboys, they're still going strong, yeah. (Did you know Marvin Montgomery wrote 'Red River Valley' sitting in the dining room of this very hotel? says Jane. No he didn't, you say. Yes he did, said Jane. No he didn't, you say, It was written long before he was even born. Look, says Jane, Whose hotel is this anyway?) *What?* continues the Belgian. You didn't go down to Houston to talk with Cliff Bruner? He's playing better than ever, you know, yeah. And – I don't believe it – you never went up to Tulsa, Oklahoma? But Bob Wills is buried there, yeah! You *are* going down to the western swing gathering in San Marcos next week? You're *not?* But Herb Remington is playing! Yeah! What do you mean you have to go home? You've seen nothing yet, *nothing* . . .

1. Rush back to the park in plenty time to get a good seat, right in the front row, right out in the full glare of the afternoon sun. Within spitting distance of guest MC Dr

Charles Townsend when he announces: We didn't come
here to stay, we came here to play! The Texas Playboys are
on the air! And watch the same line-up doing much the same
songs as the night before, but don't let that worry you, cause
now you can sit back and relax, soak it all in, get a really good
look at the band in action: you can trace the interplay of horns
and strings, watch the fiddle players stepping forward together
in unison for their harmony parts, see new ideas emerging in
the head of Glen Rhees, watch them change shape under his
fingers, see them roar out of his sax and fly away over the heads
of the massive sun-drenched crowd. Oh yes, *this* is definitely
what it's all about. Sing it Mr Duncan, ahhh-haaa!

> *Smile, darn you, smile*
> *You know this old world is a great world after all*
> *Smile, darn you, smile*
> *And right away watch Lady Luck pay you a call*
> > *Things are never black as they are painted*
> > *Time for you and joy to get acquainted*
> *Make life worthwhile*
> *Come on and smile, darn you, smile*

After the show I went one better than number one: I plucked
up courage and hung around the back of the stage as the band
put away their instruments, and started to climb down. Then,
when the chance came to shake hands, and to exchange a few
words with one or two of them, I grabbed it. I introduced
myself to Glen Rhees and Bobby Koeffer, and complimented
them on their double act.

Oh we're quite a team, said Glenn.

I think we can go places! said Bobby, and they both
laughed.

Where were you thinking of going? I asked.

Scotland! yelled Bobby, kicking his boot in the air.

I laughed, then asked them how long they'd been playing
together.

We've worked on and off since 1950, said Glenn.

On and off, said Bobby. Not steady, but at different jobs.

Most of the guys here today can say the same thing. We're Fifties vintage. Fine wine!

And when you play the music now, do you try and play it note for note the same as you did in the early Fifties?

Glenn nodded. That was the idea when this group was organised; we were going to play the authentic Bob Wills stuff like he did it.

No, said Bobby. I'd have to disagree there, Blub. We don't play the same notes, because *he* never played the same thing twice. That was not his style. He wanted you to play what you *felt*.

Well yeah, said Glenn. That's right: freedom! Freedom to do what you wanted to do, that was Bob's thing.

When we're playing, we don't know what we're going to do next, said Bobby. You may have noticed that!

I laughed.

Bob always practised that. He'd say, Blub — he generally called me Blub: I was pretty blubbery in those days — he'd say, When I give you a chorus, I want you to play *everything you ever heard*. Right Bobby?

That's right. There was nothing laid back about it. You were there to work and put your heart into it.

A bunch of old friends appeared and started slapping the guys on the back, and goosing and whooping, so I sidled away, and looked for another Playboy to talk to. I was getting into this interviewing lark now. I found Johnny Cuviello, a whippet-thin fellow with a razor-sharp white moustache and a store of nervous energy, whose ten-minute drum solo on 'Texas Drummer Boy' had just about stolen the show. I asked him to tell me a little about the composition of that song.

We were in a hotel room, Herbie Remington, the steel man, and myself, he replied, And I decided to write a little song. This was 1947. I wrote the first line, Herbie picked it up and made a little more of it, and then I decided, well, we'll do a little drum solo. So I asked Bob Wills. And he said, Sure, let's do the drumming, that's okay. And that was 'Texas Drummer Boy'. And we recorded the thing in two takes.

And . . .

And today it's legendary, it's a classic, it's very hard to purchase! If you buy one you are *very* lucky.

And just in case I couldn't find one to purchase, Johnny thrust a photocopy of the original 45 into my hands.

There had been drum breaks before, I said, after thanking him. Even drum choruses, on things like 'Lady Be Good'; but I suppose that 'Texas Drummer Boy' was the first western song actually built around the drums?

Well, Dr Townsend says it was, but it wasn't, cause back about a month before that, we tried out another one: 'Drum Session'. We laid that down in the Whitley Building in Chicago Illinois. But it was never released, see, so it's been forgotten. But that was *all* drums – that was really wild!

In those days it must have been more amazing, because very few western bands had drummers, eh?

Yeah, that's it. I hadn't played country music much: I stuck with the commercial music. Benny Goodman kind of stuff. He had a drummer. Tommy Dorsey had a drummer, Harry James had a drummer. I listened to all of them. And that was what I played, too: big band style. And then Bob Wills came into Fresno California, my home-town, and he was looking for a drummer. So I went up to the studio, and they let me practise with them. Well, I *thought* I was practising. Actually they were making records, transcriptions, for the radio. And when we got through Bob said, Will you join my band? I said, Sure will, I'd be glad to.

And that was you in!

Yeah, except I didn't have the outfit, because I was still playing with a pop band. So Bob bought me boots and a hat. Went on the road for a year and ten months. Then one day I was waiting outside my house – that's what I did, I waited outside my house and they came along in the bus and picked me up – and one day the bus never came. And it never came the next day either. And that's how I found out I wasn't a Texas Playboy no more.

Gee, I'm sorry Johnny. That's a terrible way of operating. You must have been . . .

Pissed?

Upset.

Oh well. I enjoyed it, but you get real tired. You've got to *really* love music to be on the road. You sure don't get no money. You have to do it for a love of music, and a love of the people. That's why Bob did it. Money was not his angle. When he died, he died just a gentleman.

As I shook hands with Johnny I asked him where his name came from. Was it Italian?

He grinned: he'd been waiting for this. Half Irish, half spaghetti! he cried.

The Playboy I most wanted to speak to was Eldon Shamblin, pioneer electric guitarist. He'd first joined the band in Tulsa in 1937, and had been responsible for many of their arrangements as well as rhythm and occasional lead guitar for many years, finally leaving in 1954. He had probably done more than anyone – with the exception, of course, of Bob – to mould the innovative sound of the group in their glory days. Shaking hands with this plump, bespectacled, wry old man – with his Fender Stratocaster and his Texas Playboys belt buckle – was, for me, shaking the hand of a minor deity.

Wills was a very dynamic performer, he told me, when I asked for his views on his old boss's amazing popularity. That's what made him so great. He had a good personality, and he *entertained* people. They'd stand thirty deep out front of the bandstand, from maybe fifteen minutes before we started playing; and they'd stand there for four hours and never move. He just *hypnotised* them people.

Was that something he had to work on?

No, I think it was just his personality. Just natural. Like he played the fiddle – self-taught, natural.

You mean his impact was more down to personality than music?

Well of course you needed the music. We wouldn't be here today if it wasn't for the music itself. But there's a lot of good musicians about. Bob had something extra: he was a dynamic performer, and people just loved that, you know. They loved him. And I guess that's what it takes. He could draw them people right in.

But surely the music drew people in too?

Well yeah. But it was the fact of Bob being there that attracted people. Him being on the stand would guarantee a good time, no matter what the music was. Whether it was 'Big Beaver' or 'Ida Red'. Bob used to say, It don't make no difference what you play, if it's got a good beat to it, and it's danceable. Sure enough, that's the way it was.

Am I right in thinking that, despite the mixture of stuff you played, you saw yourselves as basically a jazz band?

Basically a dance band, I would say. But we all loved jazz. We had the combination to play any of that big band stuff. Seven or eight horns, plus fiddles, steel, whole rhythm section. We did a lot of Woody Herman tunes, for instance. At one point we even hired a whole bunch of musicians off the Herman band.

So you didn't see yourselves as country at all?

I don't think so. I don't think Bob listened to country music much.

But you still ended up on the Grand Old Opry, didn't you?

Yeah, that was a blast.

What happened?

Well, Bob used to like drums. But at the Grand Old Opry back in those days they wouldn't let you use drums. Everything had to be acoustic too, and everything we had was electric. Ha. Plus drums! So they told Bob he couldn't use the drums, and he just told us, Pack 'em up boys! If I can't have the drums, I ain't going to play a damn note. So they gave in. That was what he believed: hold out for what you want. It was the same the first time he was recording for Columbia. That yell he had, you know – Ahhh-haaa! – the guy who was doing the recording said, Bob everything was going good, but I can't have that hollering. Made Bob mad. He says, to hell with it. If I can't holler then we ain't going to hit another lick. He stuck with his word and finally got what he wanted. And that is what you *have* to do. Cause if you ain't careful, they'll tell you how to eat! But Bob was a strong-willed old boy, and that is what it takes in this life. You can't change every damn thing to suit somebody else!

A television crew appeared, and started setting up to interview Eldon. Not being strong-willed enough to tell them that I was here first, bugger off, I thanked him and wandered away again. Bobby and Glenn were standing by themselves off to one side of the stand, drinking coke and chatting. When Bobby saw me pass, he yelled, Hey, Rob Roy! Come and see this!

I glanced over my shoulder. He did mean me. What is it? I asked.

Look.

He gave me a colour photo of himself, completely naked except for a three-foot long piece of cane, or bamboo, or something like that, which sheathed his penis and jutted out horizontally in front of him. He was standing outside some kind of hut, holding a little briefcase, and making as if to walk off – all with this three-foot prick sticking out in front. I must have looked surprised, because Bobby and Glenn roared with laughter.

A Texas Playboy on his way to work, said Bobby, and they laughed even louder.

What is it? I asked.

Well if you have to ask . . . said Glenn.

No, said Bobby, I'll tell you. I stayed out in New Guinea for a while, out with the Indians there. And this is what they wear for going into battle – pretty cool, eh?

I should think it's pretty cool, I said, You don't have any clothes on!

They laughed some more.

Show business, said Bobby. There's nothing like it.

Yeah, said Glenn. Where else would anyone give us a job?

Tell me about Bob and putting on a show, I said. Eldon was saying that it was Bob's personality that was stronger than his music, in a way.

He *was* a great show man, said Glenn. He was a master at it. I have never seen anybody with the charisma that he had. He was born to be a band leader.

He just had to do what he wanted, that was the main thing.

He did. He knew how to get it out of you. Whenever he stepped up there and pointed and gave Bobby a chorus, or me a chorus, he would just make you want to play like you never had before. He would just stand up there and give you a talking to, all the way through your solo.

He made you play better than you could play.

He got out everything that you had in you, is what Bob did.

Yeah, and some stuff you didn't know you had in you!

Talking of finding unexpected things, I said, Well, on the steel sometimes, Bobby, you really sounded like a trombone!

Trombone? Yeah, good. That's because it's Dixieland type music we're playing. So I quite often play a horn part. And then the fiddles might play the high clarinet part.

Bob loved Dixieland, said Glenn. He sure did.

That is where Bob's beat came from, said Bobby. Dixieland. There was a lot of good fiddle bands before Bob, and they had good rhythm. But it wasn't as swinging or as solid till Bob added the drums to the band. And then when he added horns on top of that – that's western swing!

And that's why we're here today, laughed Glenn. Yes sir!

I looked around at the crowds of folk still sitting out in front of the bandstand, at the hundreds of RVs and trucks, and the fans queuing up to talk to the Playboys. What would Bob have thought of all the folk gathering in Turkey in his honour? I asked.

Oh he would love this, said Glenn. He would be in Heaven here, I guarantee you, said Bobby. This is Bob's cup of tea!

Glenn nodded. Course, he probably wouldn't have *tea* in his cup . . .

Still Waters Run the Deepest

I went back to the Montgomerys, and sat at the kitchen table, drinking coffee and telling them how the day had gone. June was very interested in everything, but Arch was a bit distracted. I wondered if maybe he didn't share his wife's fondness for western swing, or if he'd maybe just seen far too many of these weekends to work up any more enthusiasm for my benefit. Or maybe he was just tired: June had told me that he had difficulty sleeping, and often sat up half the night, sometimes trying to read, mostly just sitting.

Suddenly, though, Arch sprang into life.

I'd been mentioning how I was keen to try and find the house down between the rivers where the Wills family had lived, and played, back in the Twenties. I'd asked around town, but had had no luck so far. A couple folk had told me it was pulled down years ago; a few more said they had no idea where it was; and one or two muttered about how it was on private land, and how I shouldn't go trespassing without asking, and how they couldn't tell me who to ask because the owner didn't live in Turkey, but away in a city somewhere they didn't know where, Dallas maybe, or New Orleans, or London.

That house is out by 657! cried Arch. What they talking about, pulled down? I saw it just the other day – drove past it.

Can you tell me where it is then? I said. I'd love to have a look at it, imagine what it was like in the old days.

I can tell you that too, he said, and laughed. You don't have to imagine nothing.

Really? Were you ever there when the Wills family were there?

Sure, a hundred times!

Arch knew the Willses real well, said June.

Played with them too, said Arch. Some of them, anyways. Uncle John, Bob . . .

You *played* with Bob down between the rivers? I gasped.

I've got to go to the bathroom, said Arch. You just make yourself at home till I get back.

He hauled himself to his feet and paced away out of the room. I turned to June. This is brilliant! I said in an undertone. I'd no idea! How come you never mentioned that Arch played with Bob Wills?

June laughed. You never asked.

Ho! What else should I ask? Were you ever a Hollywood movie star, June?

Didn't you see me in that little old thing with Clark? Rhett! Tara! I swear I'll never go hungry again . . .

Arch shuffled back into the room. You making yourself at home? he said. We're glad to have you, yes sir. He worked himself into a sitting position above his chair, then plonked down on to it. He looked at both of us, grinning.

You go ahead, said June. You ask him all about it. He likes to talk. Don't you Arch?

What's that?

Tell us about where you were raised and all, said June. And

about the music, and the Wills family. All those old stories I get tired of hearing.

Arch laughed, smiled at his wife, then turned to me. I was born in 1910, in Fisher County, just south of Rotan, he said. You been there?

Nearly, I said. I passed through Swenson, right next door.

Well, Rotan's my home-town. But I left it when I was a boy. Family moved to south of Turkey, to farm there.

Was it a musical family? I asked. Any relation to Marvin Montgomery of The Light Crust Doughboys?

No sir, not that I'm aware of. But we sure were a musical family, the whole lot of us. I could play banjo by the time I was five.

How about the Willses? They were a musical clan too, eh? Did you know them?

Sure: everybody knew the Wills family. They lived on the other side of town from us, though, to the north. The road to Memphis used to run right by their door – it's shifted a little aways now, the 657 – and any time you passed you could go in there and there'd be music going on. More music than work, I reckon!

And were they known to be good musicians? I mean, were they famous for it at this stage?

Well, Uncle John, he was a real fine breakdown fiddler. Bob wasn't as good as his father to tell the truth. I accompanied Uncle John at a fiddle contest in Childress one time – and we won! Well, *I* didn't get a prize, but Uncle John got first prize: a beautiful fiddle, pearl inlay all over the back.

You played with Bob too, though, said June. Tell him that: that's what he wants to hear about.

Do you want to hear about that?

Do I? Yeah!

Well. I guess the first time I played with Bob was . . . at the start of . . . '28. A blackface minstrel show came through town – these weren't black folk, you understand, these were white folk with painted faces, that's why I call them that – and Bob persuaded them to let him play and sing a little. Dance too! Did you know he was a dancer? He danced that buck and wing pretty good!

I heard that, I said. I don't exactly know what it is though.

We're too old and stiff to show you now, said June, and laughed.

Anyways, said Arch, He danced and he fiddled, and I backed him up on the banjo.

That's amazing, I said. Did you play with him again after that?

Not directly, cause I went off to school in Canyon, see. But I came back in the fall, and just before Christmas I was getting a haircut in Ham's barber shop. And who was the hairdresser? Bob Wills. Arch, he says, Would you play with me for a dance on Christmas night? Okay, I said. And I did. It was in an empty grocer's shop, just along from Ham's.

On the corner of Third, said June. It's Affiliated Food now.

So we cleared it out and a *crowd* of people came. It was packed. We played *all* night!

What did you play?

Mostly pop songs. Just whatever was popular. Pop, a few jazz tunes maybe.

But what instruments?

Well, Bob was on fiddle of course, then there was somebody on guitar, and me on banjo. Till I broke a string, and I didn't have any spares, so I switched to guitar. That one there.

He nodded towards the wall, and the battered, stringless, historic wreck of an instrument hanging there.

I could hardly speak. That's amazing, I said at last. I can't believe . . . I mean, it's fantastic! Here you are being so hospitable and all, putting me up in your house, and now I find that you played with the Great Bob – probably further back than anyone else alive!

Ha. He wasn't so great in those days.

I suppose not. But still. You were there right at the beginning, right at the start of his career. Why didn't Charles

Townsend talk to you for his biography? There can't be many
folk around who played with Bob and the Willses way back
in the Twenties.

There's a lot of people Dr Townsend didn't talk to, said
June. Mind you, there's some people didn't want to talk to
him. Least not about Bob Wills.

What, is there still bad feeling? Not about him drinking
and so on?

Well, not just that, more like . . . the way he treated people.
One lady I know, she used to live next door to Bob Wills and
Edna and their baby – this was after Bob left his father's farm,
set up house in the town. And when Bob struck out, when he
went to Fort Worth and left his wife and baby – no warning,
just like that! – this lady heard poor Edna crying so hard next
door, that she never could forgive Bob. After a while Bob
called on Edna and Robbie Jo to come down and live in Fort
Worth, but it was too late by then, the damage was done.

What, between Edna and Bob?

No, between this lady and Bob. She could never even
listen to his records after that, she hated him so.

Arch, I said. After this Christmas dance, did you play with
Bob again?

Sure, sure. Hey, I was fixing to be a Light Crust Doughboy
at one time!

You're joking, I said. When was that?

That was in 1932, the fall, I guess. I got a message that
Bob wanted to try me out – they needed a guitar or a tenor
banjo, see, and I could do both – so I headed on down to
Fort Worth.

That would have been after Milton quit, I said, And he
took Derwood with him, their guitarist.

When I got down there, Arch went on, It turned out
the audition was really a broadcast. WBAP. Bob on fiddle,
Tommy Duncan on vocals, Herman somebody on guitar, me
on banjo.

Herman Arnspiger, I said.

Could be. Wilbert Lee O'Daniel was hanging round too
– I don't remember what the heck he was doing.

I think he was the sponsor, I said. Through Burrus Mills.

Could be. Got to be state governor later, you know.

He was a crook, said June.

Anyway, we didn't rehearse or nothing, just tuned up and went on the air.

That must have been pretty scary!

Well, the thing was, I'd learned all their tunes perfectly. I'd practised – could play them better than they could!

But you didn't get the job?

Arch shrugged. Nope. Don't know why. They never did tell me.

Because you could play them better than them, said June.

Arch laughed. Well, maybe.

So was that the end of it?

I'd nowhere to stay down there, I remember that. Nowhere to stay and no job! So Bob took me out to his parents' house for the night – they'd moved down after him by this time. And the next day I started back to Turkey, and the farm.

That's a bit . . . sad, I said.

No, sir, said Arch. I'm glad. I wasn't then, but I am now. I wouldn't be here today if I'd gotten that job: I'd be in the ground. All those musicians doped or drank. That's why they're dead and I'm alive.

He laughed a brief, wheezy laugh, and gazed off across the kitchen.

I think that's enough, whispered June.

It's the Bottle Talkin'

Bob Wills Day

Welcome, Visitors
We're Glad You're Here!
VALLEY PEANUT GROWERS

I'd got so involved in Arch's reminiscences that I was late for the dance. Tonight, Jody Nix and his West Texas Cowboys were to be pickin' the folks' feet up and puttin' them down again.

As I trekked up the dirt road towards the old high school – past overflowing trashcans, the Cowboys' gleaming blue and silver tourbus, and someone trying to tip over a portaloo (with someone else inside protesting, not surprisingly) – I could hear 'Milk Cow Blues' booming out from inside the auditorium. It was another hot night, and all the windows and doors in the hall were wide open. I paused for a moment as I threaded through the rows of parked cars, and picked out the searing fiddle and the hard-edged steel, and felt my cheek-bones vibrate to the seismic beat of drums, bass and guitar. The Cowboys were tighter than the Playboys had been, but far less jazzy; they were right at the honky tonk end of the western swing spectrum.

Hey!

I looked round. A couple guys in hats and moustaches were standing at the back of a big long car, the boot gaping open. It was completely full of cans of beer.

Are you selling? I said.

Hell no, that's illegal, said the first guy.

I just thought . . .

But I'll tell you what, said the second guy. Why don't *you* give *us* a gift of a couple of bucks, and then *we'll* give *you* a gift of a couple cans of Coors?

It's a deal.

I popped one of the cans and drank. It was pish. But it was ice-cold pish. Spot on.

A jeepful of screaming kids bounced past at great speed, followed – at no great speed – by some kind of dune buggy. The buggy's engine was dead, and three guys – including one wearing a crash-helmet with massive steer horns sticking out of it – were pushing it along. Another guy was sitting steering; he raised a bottle in salute as he passed us, and yelled, We're out of gas, and we don't care!

The guys who'd sold me the beer sniggered.

That pretty much sums up Bob Wills Day, said the first one. A bunch of drunks acting ignorant.

Yup, said the other one. It's a fine way to be.

They locked up their car and headed off for the hall. I didn't feel like going in. Not yet, anyway. I sat on the guys' back bumper and sipped my Coors.

The Nix band was playing 'Jole Blon' now, the swing-inflected Cajun classic written by a Wills-infatuated Louisiana fiddler called Harry Choates. As well as being heavily under the influence of Wills, Choates spent his life more or less permanently under the influence of whiskey. His appetite for moonshine and self-destruction matched that of renowned country kamikazes like Hank Williams and Charlie Poole, and in fact he managed to out-Babylon them both by dying drunk in police cells at the age of twenty-eight. Hank didn't die till he was twenty-nine, and Charlie stumbled on till he was *thirty*-nine – goddarn nancy boy.

I drained my first can and chipped it towards a pile of rubbish lying underneath a nearby bin. My second can was balanced on the wing at the rear of the car. I reached over for it, the car tilted on its spongy suspension, and the can fell off. Bloody hell. I got down on my knees, and started raking about in the darkness under the car's exhaust.

Howdy, everything okay?

An elderly couple had stopped just in front of me, and were standing looking down, concern on their faces.

Eh, aye, thanks, I said. I just dropped something. But I'll get it later. I stood up.

You here from abroad? asked the woman.

Yeah: Scotland.

Really, *we* were in Ireland just a couple years ago! Y'all having a good time?

Great.

You coming in to dance?

Och, I can't dance. I'm hopeless.

You just need practice, said the man. I used to be the same. Tripped over my own feet. But we've been coming here twenty-four years now – since the very first one – so I've got pretty good.

The woman laughed, jabbed him in the side with her elbow.

Was it just like this back in the early days? I asked.

More or less, he replied. It used to be rougher: more hippies, less students . . .

Oh yeah, said the woman. It did used to be rough. They used to cart the drunks away in cotton wagons.

All these hippies would meet down by the monument, said the man. They'd be doping and smoking marijuana . . .

There's some of them down there tonight, said the woman. We saw them as we come past.

The man shook his head. Used to be terrible down there, he said. Everybody drunk, doped up. Hippie chicks running about half naked, mud wrestling . . .

Two minutes later I was down at the monument, a thirty-foot

pink granite obelisk engraved with significant scenes from the life of the Great Bob, and topped with a big steel fiddle. His most famous tunes were meant to play constantly from concealed speakers, but the batteries must have run down or something. So I hummed 'Time Changes Everything' to myself as I climbed a fence and made my way down through the cottonwoods.

At first there were tents pitched in amongst the trees, and people sitting quietly around campfires, smoking and drinking beer. Young kids ran about waving sticks at each other, and at me, though whether the sticks were fiddles or rifles I couldn't be sure.

A little further on a pick-up truck, covered in brown sludge an inch thick, was stuck half-in and half-out of a mudhole. A group of guys, also covered from head to toe in mud, were trying to push it out of the hole. The engine revved, the wheels spun, the guys shoved, and the sludge flew. Then the truck rolled back, all the guys tumbled over into the mudhole, and laughed hysterically.

Further on still there was a huge bonfire, with a couple hundred student-aged folk standing gazing into it, or standing swaying to the music, or just standing. Bottles of whiskey were getting passed around, and every so often somebody would toss an empty one on to the fire. A stage had been set up against a couple of the biggest trees, and a four-piece group was thrashing away in front of a banner with their name on it. The Rocket Scientists.

I'd heard their music, faintly, from just about up at the old high school. Sounds carried far over the flat land in the still night air. Their sphere of influence, and Jody Nix's, had met just outside the Bob Wills Museum. Now the Cowboy sounds were inaudible, and I could listen to the Scientists' blend of grunge and Southern rock uninterrupted (apart from the baying and hooting of the audience.) It was identical to the kind of thing you might hear in Austin, or London, or Thurso. The only strange thing was that they were singing a song about milking cows. And all the kids in the audience were wearing white Stetsons; I don't know about London, but they're scarce on the ground in Thurso.

Hey, buddy!

A girl in a stripy shirt was offering me a bottle of Jack Daniels.

Thanks, I said, and took it. Can I have a scoof, like?

That accent! Where *you* from? New York?

I laughed. No, Scotland.

I lifted the bottle to my lips, then looked at her, raised my eyebrows. She nodded. I took a swallow.

I came to find out what Bob Wills was all about, I said.

What it's all about? She grinned, flung her arms wide. It's about coming down here, kicking it up, and having a *good time*.

What, like dancing and stuff?

Maybe. Mostly by tipping the bottle.

Oh yeah?

Yeah! Tip the bottle till it runs out! Then get another one! She took a big drink, passed it back to me.

Do you like Bob Wills music? I asked, before taking another slug.

I don't know, she said. Ain't heard that much of it. But I'm happy to come down here and honour a great man.

By getting drunk?

Oh, we don't honour him by getting drunk. We do that every weekend! It's just an excuse. We just all get together to do it this weekend!

The Rocket Scientists had slipped into a Stevie Ray Vaughan-ish heavy boogie, and couples were dancing around the clearing in a style that mixed the pogo with the two-step.

Hey, said the girl. Let's dance. She tipped the bottle till it was empty, dropped it to the ground, then pulled me on to a patch of open ground.

I'm not a great dancer, I said.

I am. I'll teach you. She put one hand on my hip, the other out to the side for me to grab. Okay. she cried. Let's go!

I looked over her shoulder. A young guy hollered –
Ahhh-haaa! – then ran and jumped, leapt right through the
heart of the enormous bonfire.

Twin Guitar Special

"The Dude Ranch"
MUSICIANS CLUB
THIS IS TO CERTIFY THAT THE BEARER

_____

IS A MEMBER IN GOOD STANDING FOR

THE MONTH OF_____

Signed _____

Late next morning I went for one last stroll around Turkey. RVs
and caravans and pick-ups were pouring out of town on every
road. It was a dreich morning, with a cold wind gusting in from
the west, and occasional spits of rain. Everything, including the
sun, was pulling out. It was making me feel quite melancholy.
For a second I imagined abandoning Scotland, staying on in Arch
and June's spare bedroom, being the one person *not* to pull out as
soon as Bob Wills was over. I'd stay for good, give the car back to
Hertz, find some little wooden house to rent. I'd throw myself
into life here, bring some fresh blood to the place, help out with
next year's memorial weekend . . .

No I wouldn't. That's the problem with fantasies: sooner or
later they're punctured, and you land in the dirt with a dunt.
Better to stick with reality.

Down on Main Street, the traffic was crawling along in a
convoy. I stood and watched for a while. At one point a horn

honked out 'Dixie', and the girl I'd talked to down by the bonfire stuck her head out the window of a mud-spattered car, and hooted at me.

Did you have a good time? she shouted.

Great! I called back. How about you?

I didn't go to jail, and I've got Budweiser left over: I did good this year!

I laughed, and so did she. Then the boy driving the car put his foot down and wheeched them round a corner, away.

I headed back towards the Montgomerys'.

I packed my bags, slung them in the car, then went in to say cheerio to Arch and June. Arch was in the front room, strumming away on his electric Gibson. He looked up, grinned, and waved me over.

Do you want to play a little? he said.

Sure! I replied.

We tried 'Get Along Home Cindy', me beating out the rhythm on the old Gibson acoustic, and Arch picking a nifty, jazzy lead. Despite his age and frailty, his fingers were still amazingly nimble, and I had difficulty in keeping up. We tried 'Trouble In Mind' next, then 'Sally Gooden', then a whole bunch of others: jazz standards, Thirties pop songs, fiddle breakdowns. A lot of tunes ended prematurely, with one or both of us breaking down in laughter at the other's attempts to slow down, or speed up, or remember the chords or words.

But the break downs in the breakdowns didn't matter. Sitting there in the Montgomerys' douce front room, swinging in and out of tunes half-forgotten (by him) and half-learnt (by me), tears started to well up in my eyes, and I was almost overcome by waves of powerful emotion surging up through my lungs and into my head, dizzying me.

Part of it was down to the way the Montgomerys had taken me, a complete stranger, into their home, and treated me like a long-lost son. Their hospitality and kindness were not atypical of the Texans who'd helped me out along the way, but it was given with such generosity and warmth that I'd certainly come to love them in only three days. It was very hard to be leaving them now, knowing full well that I'd probably never see them again.

Another part of it was the knowledge that I was sitting just along the settee playing western swing with a man who'd sat just along the settee from Bob Wills nearly seventy years earlier, playing exactly the same kind of music. I'd come to Texas in search of the roots of the music I loved, and here they were, withered a little maybe, but still alive and still picking: Arch was as close as anyone was ever likely to get to a personification of where western swing sprung from, and what it had sounded like in its earliest days.

Another part of it was that Arch was still a damn fine guitarist, and it was a joy to play with him. This was what my whole trip was about: the joy of good music.

But the whole trip was also about writing. I could never allow myself to just enjoy the travel, and the music, and the people; I always had to keep at the back of my mind that I was going to have to write a book about it when I got home. So eventually I laid the guitar down, and stretched.

You know Arch, I said, I reckon I'm going to have to get going. Everybody else's leaving Turkey, and . . . I don't want to. But I've got to.

Arch leant over, propped the Gibson up against the wall. Well, he said, It's over.

Yup. I nodded. Just about.

June appeared in the doorway from the kitchen. She must've been listening to us playing. Did I hear you say you were heading off? she said.

I opened my mouth to reply, but couldn't get any words out. I went over and hugged her instead. Thank you, I said, at last.

Arch had struggled to his feet. I sure am glad you came to Bob Wills, he said.

So am I!

Sometimes I go down there, he went on, But not so much anymore. I hear the music all the way up here and go down to the park, and you know what? It sounds a lot better from a distance than it does up close.

Now you tell me! I said.

Sittin' on Top of the World

Following Arch's directions, it was easy to find the Wills place. Half a mile north of the Little Red River – or its course, at least, for the river bed was completely dry, and streaked with some white, salty deposit – the verge widened out into an area of bushes and wiry grass, with a big field of red earth beyond it. I pulled up on to the verge, clambered over the gate, and started off round the field.

To me it looked like the worst soil imaginable: nothing but dry red sand. Still, maybe that was what cotton liked. For the field had been ploughed fairly recently, presumably to receive some crop or other; and here and there lay heads of raw cotton, wisps of it whisking and tumbling about in the wind. The furrows, deep and humped and maybe half a mile long, stretched away towards a low line of bushes and wind-bent trees, and my stumbling shadow went out to meet them in the low, late-afternoon sun.

Up there, where the furrows and the shadows converged, up amongst the clump of trees slightly taller than the rest, that's where I'd find the Wills place.

It was a ruin, of course. The corrugated-iron roof was still on, and the clapboard walls still standing, but all the doors and windows were gone, and the floor of the broad front porch was littered with debris: splintered timbers, shotgun cartridges, an old car seat, rusty beer cans, drifts of dead dusty leaves. Inside was the same story. The house was split down the middle into two long rooms, though it looked like there had originally been a crossways dividing wall too. Garbage lay everywhere. A door at the far end had a sheet of metal nailed over it; burlap sacks flapped at a couple of the windows.

I stepped out, and strolled round the house. The trees were broad and shady on the south side of the house, screening out the worst of the sun. Beyond them was the cotton field I'd skirted to get here, where Bob and his family had picked their cotton alongside black migrant workers back in the Twenties. Where Bob had, so he said, picked up his feeling for the blues, not to mention actual tunes. As they moved up and down the cotton rows, said Bob, They sang blues you never heard before. 'Big Beaver', his classy, glossy big-band jazz tune of 1940 was based on one of the blues he'd heard there, he said. (Bull, said his brother Luke, apparently. Bob never learned nothing from those people. That 'Big Beaver' was a fiddle tune our family used to play: 'Louisiana Blues', Daddy called it. None of us learned nothing from those people.)

Out back there was a storm cellar, a concrete water cistern, and a well. Round the next corner the ground sloped up to the north, got scrubby. A couple hundred yards away, crowning the low hill, was some sort of wooden watch-tower. Little bulb-shaped cactuses with vicious thorns grew in profusion all up the slope. I threaded through them, scrambled over a rusty bedstead and some chicken wire, and was back in front of the house again. There was a big flat grassy space here. Before the bushes invaded, and the rubbish piled up, this must have been a great place for dancing. It was very easy to imagine the Willses ranged along the porch: Bob or Uncle John fiddling, sister Ruby or Johnnie Lee on guitar, Eloise vamping on the piano. And out front the visitors and the younger children would dance on the grass of the yard. Sometimes in the winter, the dancing would be inside; on those occasions, all the furniture would be cleared out and piled on the porch, to give room for some decent squares. (Knowing how poor the Willses were in those days, moving the furniture probably wasn't too big a job.) It was such a romantic picture that I worried for a moment that I'd just seen the whole thing in a Hollywood biopic of Bob's life. But no, there'd never been such a film. And Arch had attended these get-togethers, had described them to me.

No, there was no need to distrust my imagination, on this point at least. This battered old house really was, if not *the* cradle of western swing, then certainly – along with Crystal Springs, Fort Worth, the Bluebonnet Hotel, San Antonio, and Cain's Dancing Academy, Tulsa – one of the starting points for the music I loved.

I looked around. It was a shack, no two ways about it. And the farm was a poor one. It was miles to the nearest town, and the town wasn't up to much either. From here, down between the rivers, there was only one way that Bob Wills could go: up.

Over a forty-four year studio career, Bob laid down hundreds of tracks. But a handful of tunes he kept coming back to, recording them again and again in different arrangements. A couple of these – 'Faded Love' and 'San Antonio Rose' – were big self-composed hits that it made financial sense to issue repeatedly with each new Playboy crooner. A couple others – 'Beaumont Rag', 'Silver Bells' – were old fiddle tunes, amongst the first things Bob learned; they obviously held a special place in his heart. But one of the very few numbers that Bob *sang* in the studio throughout his career – and he sang it on more records than any of the others – was an old eight-bar blues, composed by a black fiddle and guitar duo, the Mississippi Sheiks: 'Sittin' on Top of the World'.

Bob made a grand total of six recordings of it, the first at his first ever session with the Texas Playboys in 1935, when he was a young man of thirty, and the last at his penultimate session, in 1971, when he was sixty-six and already crippled by the strokes and heart attacks that would soon kill him. The changes in the Texas Playboys' approach over the years summed up Bob's whole career: starting with brassy, primitive New Orleans jazz, progressing to sparse electrified rhythm and blues in the late Forties and early Fifties, and reaching an all-time low with a tarted-up country and western version, complete with ghastly backing choir.

Bob knew where he started from: the bottom of the heap. And he knew the direction he wanted to go: up. He wanted to keep going till he reached the very top – the top of his profession, the top of the world. If success was making bestselling 78s, breaking dancehall box-office records, becoming a folk-hero for the whole South-West of the US, then Bob certainly achieved it. But if success was about being happy, content, fulfilled, he was an abject failure. He was jealous and moody, married six times, a binge alcoholic, he made a series of appalling business decisions, was depressive and insomniac – all through the years of his greatest musical triumphs.

And the song he kept coming back to, the optimistic-sounding 'Sittin' on Top of the World', was in fact a heartfelt mournful blues.

Less than eighty miles north of here, straight up Route 70, lay the town of Pampa, home to Woody Guthrie for much of his youth. He was born in Oklahoma, but moved to live with a Texan uncle after his family started to fall apart in the late Twenties. It was this uncle that taught him guitar, and started him on the long lonesome road to being America's most famous hobo, its balladeer of dust storms and strikes, dam-buildings and train-hoppings – and one of the relatively few American artists to speak from a radical left-wing point of view and survive, let alone thrive.

Bob Wills was just a few years older than Woody, and their upbringings were very similar indeed, but the routes the two musicians took through life could hardly have been more different. Whereas Woody held on to – even cultivated – his rough and ready, Okie hobo image (by preferring to sleep on bare floors than in a bed, by insisting on eating standing up for fear that using a chair would 'soften' him), Bob did all he could to appear the smart, fashionable, man-about-town music-biz pro.

Their music was different too. Woody Guthrie leaves everything *out* – his best recordings feature nothing but his own voice and basic guitar accompaniment – and Bob Wills puts everything *in* – *his* best recordings feature fifteen-piece orchestras performing elaborate, multi-layered and multi-soloed arrangements of tunes from a wide variety of sources.

Both men were known to be exceptionally generous and open-hearted, but again they showed it in different ways: Woody by giving away more or less everything that came his way, more or less immediately, to more or less the first passer-by, Bob by devising elaborate schemes for all his band-members and their families to live on his ranch, by buying a series of farms for his father to run into the ground, by (Elvis-like) giving watches and cars and jobs and cheques to anyone who looked deserving.

Their audiences were interestingly opposed. Woody was never really a big success till he made it to New York. There he became, virtually overnight, the darling of the middle-class, liberal folkniks: they loved him because he was (or seemed to be) the voice of peasant America speaking directly and authentically to them. He was America's Robert Burns, its heaven taught hobo poet. But the folk of the South-West didn't swallow that – and today in Texas it's hard to find anybody who cares about him at all. Their big hero was Bob Wills, the country boy who looked like a city slicker, the breakdown fiddler who raised himself up to play the hottest, most sophisticated dance music, who made it into the movies, who never let the slightest trace of protest, politics, or social comment slip into the lyrics of his songs.

And yet, and yet . . . In the mid-Thirties Woody was appearing on a popular Los Angeles radio show in a duo

with Maxine Crissman, aka Lefty Lou, performing western
and cowboy material in a Gene Autry vein. And in 1941 Bob
Wills recorded one of the numbers most associated with him,
'Dusty Skies', with its Guthrie-esque dustbowl imagery:

> *Sand blowing, I just can't breathe in this air*
> *Thought it would soon be clear and fair*
> *But dust storms played hell with land and folks as well*
> *Got to be moving — somewhere.*
>
> *These ain't tears in my eyes*
> *Just sand from these dusty skies*

In the late Thirties Woody allowed himself to be signed
up by the Target Tobacco Company as vocalist fronting a
fifty-piece orchestra of uniformed musicians. And some of
Bob Wills' most popular waxings were the few he was
persuaded to make at various points in his career, featuring
just his fiddle and old-timey accompaniment, performing
ancient folky breakdowns and reels.

If you look into their backgrounds, you find that Bob was
the one who grew up on ranches and in cotton fields, the
Wills family was the one who suffered from dust storms and
walked halfway across Texas in search of better farmland, a
better life. The Guthrie family had its problems, for sure, but
Woody actually grew up in a big house, supported in relative
luxury by the cash his real-estate-dealing father made during
the Oklahoma oil boom.

Who can blame Bob for wanting to raise himself up from
the bottom of the pile, for wanting to be sitting on top of
the world? And who can blame Woody for exaggerating the
lowliness of his origins out of a heartfelt solidarity with the
likes of the Wills family, out of a belief that no one should be
raised higher than anyone else, that we should *all* be allowed
to sit on top of the world?

I trudged back round the edge of the sand-field, stooping
at one point to snatch up a couple heads of matted, dusty

cotton. I rubbed them between my fingers, felt softness and grit, stuffed them in my pocket.

Directly ahead of me, the sun was setting fiercely. I squinted my eyes, kept on into it.

Song of the Wanderer
(Where Shall I Go?)

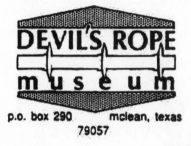

DEVIL'S ROPE
m u s e u m

p.o. box 290   mclean, texas
79057

Delbert Trew
Manager

Museum 1-806-779-2225
Home 1-806-779-3184

The first ghost town I see is Gotebo. It's ten fence posts in a row at the side of the road, a half-rotted head on top of each. From the car they look like bear-heads, though that seems unlikely so far from mountains or woods – so far from anything but prairie scrub and cotton fields.

The second ghost town is Ben Hur. I get out of the car to take a photo of the sign and the wind-blasted ruins beyond, but it's blowing so strong I can't hold the camera steady. When I drive off I find there's grit in my mouth. The radio says that Ginger Rogers has died.

The third and ghostliest ghost town is Dela Plains. Between the sign and the horizon there's nothing to be seen at all.

There's a ghost road too. It runs from Duncan, Oklahoma through Pumpkin Center, on to Lawton. Duncan is where I eat pinto beans and cornbread at noon, and the diner's about to close. It's called the Daybreak Cafe. We open at five, says the woman behind the counter. She looks tired, pours coffee like it's something she has to get through. I can see into the kitchen through the hatch beside the till. Chicken-fried steaks are cooking in a big black pan. Each has a ten-pound weight sitting on it, pressing it flat against the bottom of the pan. A man shuffles to the hob, lifts a weight, flips the steak, lowers the weight. He glances up, catches me watching. I look away. All the customers are tired-looking men, and they're all wearing overalls covered in dust and oil. Their faces are masked in dust and oil too. Duncan is proud to be an oil town; it doesn't boast about the dust.

I head off down Plato Road. Outside the Lodge is the biggest Stars and Stripes I've ever seen – big enough to wrap my car like a prize in a mall lottery. It's at half mast. I turn west, out of town.

Soon I see the ghost road: on my right, parallel to the one I'm driving. It's bright red, compacted out of the clayey soil of these plains, and it runs alongside Highway 62 for as far as I can see ahead. There's no sign of any construction going on, but it's too clear-cut and unlittered to be old and abandoned. It's just there, neither old nor new, just empty: an empty road ghosting me all the way from Duncan to Lawton.

Farm roads branch off the highway, cross over the ghost road and lead away to ranches and houses and water pumps. The farm roads are grey and rutted. They cross the ghost road, but do not connect. The ghost road carries on, unused, unusable, red, invisible. I keep watching it out of the corner of my eye. It's always there. The road not travelled. The further you drive, the more roads you see you'll never go down.

Past Lawton, I turn north, drive in a straight line for fifty miles, then turn west when Interstate 40 appears. Since leaving Duncan, there's been very little traffic, and most of that's been tractors. Now I'm in amongst semi-trucks again. Before I came here I'd read about semis and imagined them to be small lorries: half the usual size, maybe. I was four hundred per cent wrong. One passes me just outside

Clinton with an oil drilling rig on its flatbed, only slightly dismantled.

I'm surprised the town of Clinton hasn't changed its name, maybe to something like Anythingbutclinton. The President's not a popular guy in the South-West. On a local radio talk show, the host is warning about the United Nations plot to take over the US. There's a thousand tanks in stores across our great nation, he says. And whose tanks are they? They're Russian tanks! With Russian crews! And United Nations flags painted on the sides. Who ever heard of an army wearing powder-blue helmets? There's something wrong there. They're not soldiers as we know them! But be warned: when the signal comes, they'll roll out of their stores and the final battle will begin. Be warned, friends, be prepared.

A caller phones in to agree with everything the host says. The exact same thing happened in Nazi Germany, he continues. There were warnings, but no one took heed. They locked up your neighbours first, and then they came for you. They've taken our neighbours in Waco, so who's next?

Could be me, caller, says the host. Very likely to be me.

Because you speak out! says the caller. The FBI will come for you – the SS I call them. And who's giving their orders? Hitler! Bill Hitler Clinton!

And we'll be back after this important message, says the host.

I switch off the pooper scooper ad, hear myself sighing in the silence.

I'm still heading west. At the exit for Elk City there's a giant sign saying, LAST McDONALD'S FOR 150 MILES. My stomach grumbles.

Out of Oklahoma and into Texas. I've been driving past green fields, stands of trees, burns and lochans for the past half-hour. The border puts a sudden end to that. The burns dry up, the trees wither and twist in the wind, the pastures are replaced by purply grey scrub. The suddenness of the change is surprising; it seems to coincide exactly with the line of the state border. It's as if the Oklahomans were waggoning west, when they noticed the sharp deterioration in the land. Let's stop our state right here! they said, driving in their fence posts, dusty prairie on one side, lush farmland on the other.

But here's the funny thing: Texas was established long before Oklahoma. Oklahoma wasn't declared a state till 1907. It was the Texans who chose where the border would be, and they chose the rough stuff.

To compensate for the meanness of the land, Panhandle ranchers had to give their cattle vast expanses to wander over. A couple hours' drive down Interstate 40 lies the fence that marks the eastern boundary of the biggest spread of all, the XIT Ranch. In its heyday at the end of the last century, the XIT covered over three million acres, and included ten counties, several substantial towns, and thousands of people. Though not as many people as cattle: more than a hundred thousand of those. And the whole place was run from London, by a company called the Capitol Freehold Land and Investment Company. Talk about absentee landlords! Funny to think of straight-laced bowler-hatted city gents telegraphing instructions to the cowboys, ranch-hands and migrant labourers of the Texas plains.

I looked into the history of the XIT Ranch after being given a tape of old 78s by an Amarillo western swing band called Billy Briggs' XIT Boys. I switch on the radio again, hear a few seconds of rant show, and stick the tape into its slot as quickly as possible: 'Chew Tobacco Rag' bursts out. Ah, sanity!

> *If you chew tobacco*
> *Don't spit on the floor*
> *Expectorate in the cuspidor*

It's primitive electrified honky tonk, recorded about 1950, dominated by the rhythm guitarist's choppy 2/4 shuffle. There's fine jazzy fiddling from Pat Trotter, and some truly great original songs – twisted, bitter, misanthropic, but great none the less – from Briggs. These deal with such neglected subjects as the erotic attractions of uneven teeth ('Freckle-Face, Snaggle-Tooth Gal'), the trials of tipping appropriately ('Waitress Blues'), and the existential angst brought on by the fear of your favourite chickens being snatched from their coop ('The Coyote Song'.)

Best of all, though, is 'The Sissy Song', with lyrics so memorable and strange that I find myself singing along almost immediately, and feeling embarrassed about it as soon as I do. Even though I'm alone in an unmarked car, speeding along at sixty-five, windows rolled up and a hundred miles away from anyone who's even heard of political correctness.

> *When I get sissy enough to wear a moustache and a*
> *   bow-tie*
> *And wear those pretty suede shoes that a lot of those*
> *   sissies buy*
> *Smoke cigarettes and drink iced tea, and hold my little*
> *   finger up high*
> *I'll go out behind the old red barn and let a grey mule*
> *   kick my brains out*
>
> *When I get sissy enough to wear a dad-gum old wrist*
> *   watch*
> *Sleep in pyjamas and drink sweet milk, you'll know*
> *   I'm on my last notch*
> *When I get sissy enough to go with my shirt tail*
> *   hanging out*
> *I'll go out behind the old red barn and let a grey mule*
> *   kick my brains out*
>
> *When I get sissy enough to say dinner instead of*
> *   supper*
> *Eat those salads with carrots and lettuce, and toast*
> *   without any butter*
> *Drink my coffee with sugar and cream, and chase my*
> *   liquor with water*
> *I'll go out behind the old red barn and let a grey mule*
> *   kick my brains out*

When I get sissy enough to wash the dishes for my
   wife
Hang out diapers and make up beds, you'll know
   I'm ruined for life
When I get sissy enough to take a dad-gum bath
   each day
I'll go out behind the old red barn and let a grey
   mule kick my brains out

Who says Texans have no sense of irony? Why is it that it's a *grey* mule that he's going to let kick his brains out? And even that *let*! It suggests that the mule's been wanting to kick Billy's brains out for ages, but has never quite been granted permission. At last, he gets his chance, his time has come! Billy Briggs has smoked a cigarette, *and* forgotten to butter his toast! Brains must be spilled! Briggs must die!

Passing the exits to the town of Shamrock ('SEE BLARNEY STONE CHIP!') I realise another ghost road is haunting my journey: Route 66. Or rather, 'Historic Route 66'; that's what the signs say. They call it 'Main Street USA', 'America's Mother Road'. Interstate 40 replaced it on the maps thirty years ago, but it's never quite disappeared. There are historic markers every few miles, and commercial adverts every few yards, trying to borrow a little of its glamour: rock 'n' roll, cherry red T-birds, the promised land. And there are stretches of the road itself, curving away from under 40, usually when a town approaches; the two carriageways of 66 head for the town, 40 thunders on relentlessly.

When folk talk about Route 66, or sing about it, they always say it goes from Chicago to Los Angeles. That's the direction I'm driving too. But there's plenty vehicles going the opposite way. Why does nobody sing about the wonders of travelling from California to Illinois? Maybe the answer's obvious if you've been there. Maybe *LA* rhymes with three thousand miles *away*, so has to go at the end of the line. No, I'm sure it's more than that: west *is* best. Travelling west does seem to be associated here with progress, with moving forwards, into the future; going east is essentially retrograde, nostalgic.

The future always lies in the west, cause that's where the sun is heading. I watch it every day as I drive. In the mornings it's in my rear-view mirror, dazzling, like an aggressive overtaker. Most of the day it's above and to my left, so the most sun-burnt piece of me is my left elbow, crooked out the window as I cruise along. I keep up a good speed all day, trying to get ahead, to keep progressing, to get where I'm going – to find somewhere worth getting to – but round about three each afternoon I realise I've been beaten again. The sun has pulled ahead, it's shining straight in the windscreen, and even my sun-visor and raybans can't hide the blinding fact: I've been defeated, time has caught up with me, and I haven't got there. I haven't got anywhere worth getting to.

But if I keep heading west . . . if tomorrow I drive faster and straighter westwards . . . if I don't let myself get distracted by vintage diners and roadside marvels and desert vistas . . . if I leave my motel even earlier and get a head start on the sun . . . ach, forget it. That's another American dream that'll never come true.

It's nearly five, I've driven two hundred and fifty miles since Duncan, and I've just passed a thirty-foot sign saying RATTLESNAKES EXIT NOW. I pull off at the next slip road, and after a couple of hundred yards the tarmac fades out and is replaced by a road of orange bricks: now I really am driving on Route 66. This ghost is real. And the small town up ahead is real, though as soon as I pass the first buildings I see it's not as real as it used to be.

This is McLean, Pop. 849. The two carriageways of 66 run right through the middle of it. All the traffic's on 40, a mile to the south; I can hear the semis roaring and rattling. I pass half a dozen gas stations, all shut and wrecked, and one more still operating. There's a red-brick bank, a blacksmith with weird hieroglyphic sculptures out front, there's glimpses of white houses along tree-lined side streets.

Otherwise the town consists largely of facades: brick frontages of shops, hotels, offices, low-rise apartments, all with smashed windows, battened doors, sun-stripped paintwork. Out back the buildings are shells, semi-ruinous even.

I park the car in Main Street, outside the faded frontage of the Avalon Theatre. The windows are boarded, and little dunes of dust have built up against the doors. In the display case by the ticket-booth is a tattered poster advertising a Disney live action film from the Seventies. Next along is a shop with blanked-out windows, then another crammed with junk: a collapsed iron bedstead, heaps of clothes and tracts, lengths of warped picketfence, white paint ghostly in the darkness. I turn away from the cobwebbed glass and see a movement across the street: somebody watching me from inside the menswear shop.

It's a strange feeling when you think you're doing the looking, to find yourself being observed. Suddenly you become part of the scenery, part of the life in the scenery. You're involved, an event, a noteworthy event, even – *The Day The Stranger Poked About The Avalon!* And you're reminded that you're not invisible, a ghost drifting unnoticed through an almost ghost town: you're there as visibly as anyone else.

I don't let on that I've observed the observer, but casually cross the bricked street, and pause under the awning to look in. There are so few people in this place – I've seen half a dozen driving past in pick-ups, none at all walking or standing about – that it seems almost criminal to pass up this chance for a face to face encounter. I peer through the plate glass, past the outstretched arms of a row of tailor's dummies in nylon slacks and plaid shirts, wondering for a moment if it was only the dummies watching me. Then I go in.

It's murky and cool, a little musty despite the swooshing of two big wooden fans in the ceiling. The small amount of stock on display is regimented into strict piles, lines and grids on tabletops and shelves. As well as T-shirts and trousers there are plastic shoes, vinyl bowling bags, worked leather belts, tartan caps with pompoms. Many of the items are wrapped in yellow cellophane.

Well hello there!

From the back of the long narrow store comes a crackly female voice, and just behind it, a very small woman of very many years.

Hello, I reply. Okay if I look about?

Sure. She weaves through the counters and stacks of vests towards me. It's good to see a new face, she says. If you want to know, it's good to see any face!

Quiet day, is it?

Every day's quiet these days. They moved out the hospital, they moved out the factory, the interstate bypassed us, the railway went away . . .

Some folk might envy you: a bit of peace and quiet!

She raises her eyebrows. You're not from these parts, are you?

No. I'm from Scotland.

You might call it peace and quiet in Scotland. Here we call it death. It's a long slow death, but it's death all the same.

I look at her. Fluorescent light bouncing off all the yellow cellophane gives her skin a hint of jaundice. Otherwise she seems fine. You're still going strong, I say.

Do you know how old I am?

I shrug.

I'm seventy-seven. Been here fifty years. And you know something else?

What?

I'm the youngest shop owner in town.

Youngest?

Sure. John in the boot store next door is eighty-two, and the lady who runs the ladieswear, she's ninety-three. Okay, there's the gas station, the convenience store, but who owns them? Some chain! When we three go, there'll be no local businesses at all. Mind you, by that time there maybe won't be anybody living here to care. She trails off, her eyes drift away from me, and she reaches to straighten a stack of denim jackets in cellophane wrapping.

Once the crackling subsides I say, I've seen a few ghost towns. Seems like a lot of folk have left the area.

It's the young people. They all head off to the bright lights: Amarillo, Lubbock, Wichita Falls.

I suppose, if there's no work for them . . .

Not much, since they closed down the factory. Uplift City they used to call this place. Know why? Cause of the brassières. We made brassières for the whole South-West. Not any more, no sir. We've been going downhill since they closed.

I look around. Maybe I should buy a McLean brassière as a souvenir, I say. Have you any in stock?

She looks at me. Funny kind of souvenir.

It seems fitting. I grin. *Fitting.* Ha!

She sniffs. That's ladieswear.

Maybe I'll take a McLean belt-buckle then. At least that'll hold my trousers up, if not my chest!

You're not from these parts, she says. If you were you wouldn't joke so.

I walk up the Main Street of McLean, then turn on to the eastbound carriageway of The Main Street Of America and stroll there for a while. There's an old petrol tanker at the side of the road with a map of 66's route painted along it. There's a billboard of a roaring tiger and, underneath, giant white paw marks crossing the street: the route the McLean Tigers football team takes from high school changing rooms to playing fields. Then there's yet another ruined building. Some kind of garage, maybe. Taped inside the glass on the front door is a pink and black sign:

**We reserve the right to refuse
service to anyone using . . .
VILE LANGUAGE
or
INTOXICATION
when warranted**

The corrugated-iron roof is hanging off, creaking slightly in the breeze, weeds are attacking the concrete forecourt, and the brickwork is stained and starting to crumble around the windows. Junk lies everywhere. The place looks like it's been hit by a tornado, or maybe by a particularly strong blast of vile language.

I wander on. After a while I come to the Devil's Rope Museum. The Lone Star flag and the Stars and Stripes flap on each side of the door, flanked by two stone posts with enormous balls of barbed wire on top. They are undoubtedly the biggest balls of barbed wire I have ever seen in my life, and very beautiful. A ten-foot long metal plaque resting on the gravel at the foot of the posts reads, TRIBUTE TO BARBED WIRE.

I walk in and continue wandering: the place is vast. It's undoubtedly the biggest barbed wire museum I have ever seen in my life. Wall after wall is covered by eighteen-inch lengths of jaggy wire of various ages and designs, labelled and displayed on board backings: *Kelly Thorny Fence, 1868; Watkins Lazy Plate 1876; Reynolds Necktie 1878; Opham Single Snail Barb 1881; Brinkerhoff Sabre 1883*. I've heard of concrete poetry: you could make rusty-wire poetry out of these names. Billy Briggs would be the man to do it! In fact, I bet on some obscure 78's B-side there *is* an XIT Boys song on the subject; it's probably called 'You Wrapped My Heart in Plow Shear Barb'.

There are also fancy wires, with various unexpected objects twisted into the strands instead of barbs: dominoes, dice, golf balls, golf tees, pool balls, flint arrow heads. It's hard to imagine multicoloured plastic golf tees making much of an impact on the tough hides of Texas longhorns, but the fence sure must've looked pretty. As well as the wire itself, there are generous selections of posts, posthole diggers and wire cutters. Particularly impressive are the massive post mallets, arranged in delicate daisy-wheels all across one wall.

On my way out I pick up a leaflet on the Devil's Rope Museum (which, it turns out, inhabits the site of the much-missed Marie Foundation Brassière Factory) and another one on collecting barbed wire. 'Each barbed wire collector has his own reasons for pursuing this hobby,' says the leaflet. 'Among

them are: # preserving Americana # exercise in the fresh air
fellowship with other collectors # the excitement of a new
find.' The whole concept of collecting barbed wire is a new
one on me, and I'm happy to classify it as today's exciting
new find. I resolve that, when I get home, I'll start collecting
dry stone dykes.

There's a motel: the Cactus Inn. The clerk frowns as I sign
the register, then grins.

   Your name, he says, It's the same as this town.

   I know.

I go to my room, dump my bags, and spend half an hour
sorting through the stacks of leaflets, newspapers, photographs
and notes that I've collected over the past month. Then I
head out, stroll east down the middle of the westward
lane of Route 66 till I come to the town's diner, the
Cowboy Cafe.

   There I spot the day's last ghost. The six-foot high billboard
by the entrance to the place is stuck over an old faded sign,
but only half over it, so the letters OWBOY DRIVE IN
peep out. I guess that, since I–40 passed by, not too many
folk are driving in any more, hence the name change. The
new sign has a cheery cartoon cowboy shaking his spurs.
The old sign has his granded: faded, wrinkled, washed-out
and weather-beaten.

   Where do old cowboys go when they die? I walk into the
cafe, have a glass of cool water handed to me by a girl in a
pink nylon uniform.

   I'm Angel, she says. What can I get you?

Acknowledgements

Being an inexperienced traveller, I needed a lot of help before, during and after my time in Texas. Many of those who gave me encouragement, information and hospitality are mentioned in the narrative. Thanks folks.

I am also particularly indebted to: Pinckney and Laura Benedict, West Virginia; Bob Pinson, Paul Kingsbury and Ronnie Pugh at the Country Music Foundation in Nashville; Glenn White, Oklahoma City; Mr and Mrs Marvin Gearhart, Fort Worth; Andy and Nancy Lewis, Buchanan Dam; John and Tina Harrison, Clebourne; Todd McEwen, Lakeview, Arizona; Susan and Steve Morrell, Fort Worth; Nancy Brough, Midland; Sumter Bruton, Fort Worth; Tony and Beth Nalker, Washington DC. And if the Society of Authors hadn't given me a Somerset Maugham Award, the trip would have been so far beyond my financial means that I couldn't even have dreamt about it. I'd like to thank everyone concerned there for making the travel – and so the book – possible.

Many musicians gave generously of their time and memories. It was a thrill for me just to meet folk like Roy Lee Brown and Buddy Ray; to find them willing to spend hours answering my questions was marvellous. Walt Kleypas of Canyon Lake answered questions, gave me photos, *and* played the piano, and he and his lovely wife Lucille were wonderful hosts: I really appreciate their friendship.

It is with great sadness that I have to record the death, in September 1996, of Cliff Kendrick of the Skyrockets. He was one of the funniest and most open-hearted folk I've ever met. And certainly the wildest drummer. I talked to several of the Texas Playboys in Turkey; great musicians and great guys. Again I have to report a death: Glen 'Blub' Rhees passed away exactly a year after I saw him play so magnificently.

And I can't put off any longer marking the passing of John Moen of Wichita Falls. He was very sick when I met him (though he concealed it as best he could) and only lived three more months. John was an inspiration in all sorts of ways, most obviously in his love for the recordings of Bob Wills. He is survived by no family, but countless friends. Special greetings to his special friend, Pat Watson of Grandfield, Oklahoma. John was constantly in my mind as I wrote this book: he should've been around to read it. Cursed be the system which allows a man to die of a curable disease for the lack of a few hundred dollars.

There's another death. Arch Montgomery, who, with his wife June, were such models of hospitality during my stay in Turkey, passed away in December 1996 after a long illness. It was a privilege to know Arch, and to play guitar with him was a joy. It's a continuing joy to correspond with June.

Turkey was full of helpful and generous people. A few who deserve special thanks are Byron Young, Lisa Campbell, Arville Setliff, Pat Carson, Gary Johnson, Ann Coker, Dr Charles Townsend and everybody at the Bob Wills Foundation. This seems the proper place to thank Richard Downes and Tim Niel, producer and director respectively, of *Sitting*

On Top Of The World, a BBC Scotland documentary filmed partly in Turkey and partly in Orkney. I'd like to thank Tim especially, for helping me develop various ideas, and for helping me find the house down between the rivers.

Thanks to everybody who provided archive graphic material. The cover photos are from the collections of Buddy Woody, Clyde Brewer, Kevin Coffey and Mrs Ray Kennedy. The inside covers, from Tiffany Transcription promotional material, also come from Kevin Coffey. Of the business cards, posters etc. used as chapter headings, sixteen came from Buddy Woody, six from Kevin Coffey, two from Walter Kleypas, one each from Andy Brown and Doc Lewis and two from Clyde Brewer.

I've been saving my greatest debts till last. Kevin Coffey of Fort Worth, Texas, helped me so much – both during my trip, and throughout the writing of the book – that he's virtually a co-author. He has been profligate with tapes, photos, advice, information and musical criticism of infallible good taste. Many of the people and much of the music that made my trip through Texas so rewarding were introduced to me by Kevin: *Lone Star Swing* could not have been written without him. Needless to say, any errors that remain are not his fault, but mine: probably I wasn't listening to him properly. Kevin is a tireless researcher and a fine writer: I recommend unreservedly his articles in the *Country Music Journal* and elsewhere, and urge any publishers reading this to sign him up immediately to write the definitive history of western swing.

Finally, I want to thank Ingrid, for everything. As Walt and Lucille would say, Married two years, still in love!

D. McL. January '97.